CW01020387

Scallywag

**The true story of Basil,
a boy growing up in
the 1920's and 30's**

by

David Charles

Copyright © David Charles 2018

The right of David Charles to be identified as the author of this work has been asserted by him in accordance with the Copyright, Designs and patents Act 2018.

All rights reserved. No part of this publication may be reproduced, stored in or introduced into a retrieval system, or transmitted, in any form, or by any means (electronic, mechanical, photocopying, recording or otherwise) without the prior written permission of the author.

Any person who commits any unauthorised act in relation to this publication may be liable to criminal prosecution and civil claims for damages.

To, Jane
a good friend and very
special lady

David Chalke

Also by David Charles

The House of Dreams

Black Eyes and Shattered Glass

A Podenco's Tale

David Charles lives for most of the year in southern Spain, with his wife Christine, three dogs and three cats. Born in Ipswich Suffolk, he started his own window cleaning business when he was twelve in order to earn pocket money and later took on a variety of jobs to pay his way through college. After college he worked in the telecommunications business for thirty five years reaching the level of senior manager in a multi-national telecommunications company.

His literary career began when he took early retirement. His first work 'The House of Dreams' was published in October 2012 and was followed by 'Black Eyes and Shattered Glass' in 2015 and 'A Podenco's Tale' also in 2015. He has also had a selection of poetry published in two anthologies and has written and delivered a one hour lecture on the life and career of Earl Kitchener of Khartoum.

Retirement gave him the opportunity to devote more time to his other hobbies which are reading, drawing, football and studying the people and events of the two world wars.

David has two sons, and two grandchildren.

This book is dedicated to my father Basil
who enjoyed an unusual upbringing.

Also to my grandparents Charles Henry
Philip and Ellen Beatrice who both left this
world prematurely.

Double Family Tree (Principle members)

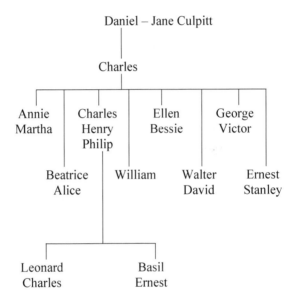

Daniel – Jane Culpitt

Charles

Annie
Martha

Charles
Henry
Philip

Ellen
Bessie

George
Victor

Beatrice
Alice

William

Walter
David

Ernest
Stanley

Leonard
Charles

Basil
Ernest

Cotton / Crane / Dumble Family Trees (Principle members)

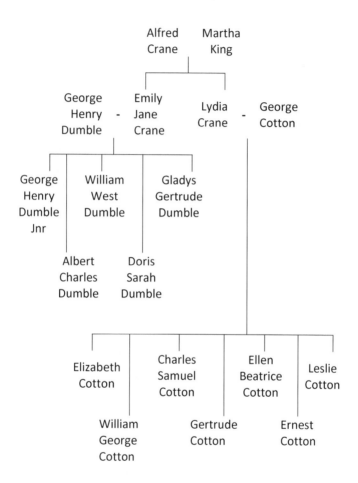

Prologue.

During my childhood my father often sat and talked to me about his early life, growing up in Ipswich in the 1920's. I was intrigued, and so, in the 1980's I gave him a cassette recorder and a bag of cassettes and asked him to place his reminiscences on record for me.

This he did and his phenomenal memory brought back events that were as clear as crystal to him even though they had taken place sixty years previously.

Following his passing in 2014 I searched for the tapes but sadly a number of them had gone missing as dementia took an increasing hold of my father's mind. Those tapes that I was able to locate, together with my memories of our conversations, formed the inspiration for this story.

This story is true, based on fact and real events enhanced, only where necessary, with my own invention and imagination.

Acknowledgements

My sincere and grateful thanks go to Joyce Pryke (nee Hurricks) for supplying a wealth of information on the Dumble family and to Sue Lucas (nee Wilding) for information on Kenny, My thanks also go to Nigel Robinson for his military research on my behalf and his advice on all matters military.

Last but by no means least, I must place on record my gratitude to my long suffering wife, Christine, who has assisted me with the research and provided much needed support and encouragement.

David Charles

Part One

Endings

and

beginnings

1920

It was a warm start to the day, the sixteenth of June 1920, a day that for one person was to be a crude ending but for another would prove to be a joyous beginning.

The rough brick walls of Ipswich prison, with their peeling green and cream paint, were cold to the touch. The hands of the clock on the wall in the governor's office clicked toward seven o'clock, the gentle chimes reinforcing the statement. The prison was eerily silent, despite holding close to one hundred inmates; they all knew what the new morning brought with it. The very prison itself seemed to be holding its breath.

There came a clatter of regular footsteps. The sound of hobnails clacking on the bare stone flags rebounded from the walls and reverberated along every passageway. Two wardens made their way purposefully down the hallway toward the condemned cell, one confidently swinging a bunch of large steel keys, the other balancing a small tray bearing a breakfast of bacon and eggs and a mug of steaming tea.

One of the keys was noisily thrust into the large keyhole and turned. There was a deep scrape and clunk as the levers of the lock responded to the pressure. The door swung open on rusty, protesting hinges to reveal Frederick Storey sitting, agitated and fidgeting, at a rough wooden table. The warden with the keys took a pace back so that his companion could enter the cell and place the tray in front of Storey, who looked up into the unsympathetic eyes of the warden. He swallowed nervously, and with good reason.

Frederick William Storey was a forty two year old Ipswich tram driver who had been having a relationship with one of the Corporation's former tram conductresses. Sarah Jane Howard was fifteen years his junior and had left the trams in September 1919 to take up work as a housekeeper to Mr William Kittle, at 133 Camden Road Ipswich, where she lived with her three year old son. In January 1920 Sarah discovered she was pregnant again, presumably by Storey, and when she informed Mr Kittle of her condition, he told her that she would have to leave his employ immediately the baby was born. Sarah was distraught. She would be homeless with two small children which meant the workhouse. She felt that Storey, through his carelessness, had taken from her employment, lodgings and probably her freedom. The terrible prospect of incarceration in a workhouse steeled her, she was determined to force him into contributing to her wellbeing and that of their unborn child and she vowed she would challenge him on the subject when she next saw him.

On Friday the sixth of February, Sarah went out for the evening without informing Mr Kittle where she was going. She was resolved to work something out with Storey, maybe to persuade him to leave his wife and live with her, although deep down she knew that would never happen.

Mr Kittle became anxious when Sarah failed to appear at breakfast on the Saturday morning and his anxiety turned to deep concern when he discovered that her bed had not been slept in. It was not like her at all. He immediately notified the police of her disappearance and began making his own enquiries, which led him in the direction of Storey. Mr Kittle confronted Storey who, while admitting to knowing Sarah, claimed he hadn't seen her for several days.

Later that day, Saturday the seventh, Sarah's body was found under a railway bridge in Halifax Lane, close to Maiden Hall allotments, one of which Storey was known to have rented. She had been battered to death.

The police were able to trace Sarah's movements on the Friday evening with the assistance of several witnesses. Albert Woodley had seen her get on a tram and then alight at the Black Bridge, Wherstead Rd, at around ten past eight that evening. Shortly afterwards he saw Storey in the same location. He claimed he had seen Storey again around an hour later walking towards the town. Constable William Snell, who knew Storey well, had also met him in Wherstead Road at about nine fifteen and they had chatted for ten minutes or so.

Rumours abounded that Storey was indeed the father of Sarah's unborn child and this gave the police sufficient cause to search his home. There they found the murder weapon, a blood stained hammer, together with items of clothing with blood spatter on them, at the back of a cupboard under the stairs. Storey claimed that the blood on the clothes was in fact his, the result of a bad nose bleed; however it didn't match his blood type. He could offer no explanation for the bloodstained hammer.

Mr Justice Darling presided over the two day trial at Ipswich Assizes on the twenty eighth and twenty ninth of May 1920. Storey's wife, Minnie, heavily pregnant with their seventh child, sat silent and stunned in the public gallery as the evidence unfolded. She was flanked by her twenty one year old daughter, Myra, and her eighteen year old son Frederick Robert.

Twelve men, straight and true, took just fifteen minutes to find Storey guilty of murder. Sentence was passed and thus Storey, destined to be the last prisoner to be hanged in Ipswich prison, now awaited his fate.

Shortly before eight o'clock, his bacon and eggs untouched, he was led to an anti-room where Robert Baxter secured his hands behind his back with a leather strap. As the hands of the governor's clock inched toward the top of the hour he was bustled into the gallows room where John Ellis awaited him. His ankles were swiftly trussed with another leather strap and a hood dragged over his frightened face. The tears began to flow and he blubbered as he felt the rope slide over his head and tighten at the side of his neck.

The minute hand moved inexorably to the twelve and the clock struck the eighth hour of the day. Storey only heard the first chime as John Ellis pulled the lever and he plummeted to oblivion.

Minnie had waited outside the prison, with Myra, Frederick and her seventeen year old daughter Annie, anxiously praying that there would be a last minute reprieve. At the first chime of the nearby church, the very moment Storey hit the bottom of his fall, she let out a heartrending scream and collapsed, weeping uncontrollably, into the arms of her son. Myra and Annie hugged each other, wracked with disbelieving grief.

Over a mile away, in the bedroom of number 19 James Street, there was another, unconnected, cry of pain, swiftly followed by the strong, rapid cry of a new born baby. As one tainted spirit had left this world it had crossed with another innocent spirit arriving. Basil Ernest Double was born at exactly eight o'clock on the sixteenth day of June 1920.

*****

Earlier Charles Double, or to give him his full name Charles Henry Philip Double, 'Chip' to his friends, perched on the side of the marital bed in the tiny front bedroom, gently holding the petite hand of his beautiful wife. He knew he had been christened Charles after his father but where the other names came from, and why he had so many, was a mystery to him. He was a short, slim man with dark hair that he kept neatly parted, even beneath his flat cap. His eyes were a soft blue set in a smooth boyish face. He was a very gentle and caring man who had fallen head over heels in love with the beautiful Ellen Beatrice Cotton, known to everybody as Beatrice, and she had fallen for him too, something that made him the envy of James Street.

Chip had joined the Territorial Volunteer Reserve Army in 1912 and had served throughout the entirety of The Great War in the Suffolk regiment of the Royal Field Artillery as a driver on a field gun and limber, he was also the company farrier. Demobbed only in April of the previous year, he had spent the majority of his war service in Egypt and Palestine, where, in 1917, an explosion had spooked the horse he was shoeing and it kicked out viciously, catching him a debilitating blow at the base of his spine. The force of the kick damaged the nerves in his back, and from that time onward he had suffered great pain, especially in cold weather. The incident hadn't affected his deep love of horses though; he always maintained that the horse was not to blame for his injury. He was more fortunate than most in that he was able to return to his pre-war employment as a blacksmith's striker in the Ransom and Rapier foundry where he once more took on the additional responsibility of looking after the horses that pulled the fire wagon, and he prided himself in their turnout.

This particular morning he had been woken extra early, two o'clock to be precise, as Beatrice went into labour. He quickly dressed and stayed with her until the dawn broke; he knew the child would not be arriving quite yet. As the first rays of sunshine rose over the slated roofs, and the hour was more sensible, he crossed the rough cobbled street to number 18 and went inside. His mother, Mary, who was to perform the duties of midwife, was preparing breakfast for his father, Charles, and his brothers William, Walter, George and Ernest.

"Beatrice has gone into labour mother, it started at two this morning."

"Alright son, you get back home and I'll be over presently." Mary flashed him a reassuring smile as she placed two bowls of steaming porridge on the table.

Back home Chip made some breakfast for his five year old son Leonard and took a glass of milk up to Beatrice before preparing his packed lunch. He stayed at home for as long as he dared, sitting with Beatrice and holding her cool, delicate hand tightly, hoping against hope that his second child might arrive before he would be forced to leave for work. He looked at his pocket watch, almost seven o'clock. Reluctantly he accepted that he would not see his new child this side of his working day. He gave Beatrice a big hug and a kiss.

"There's no time for that son," Chip turned to see Mary standing in the bedroom doorway.

'How did she always manage to arrive everywhere without making a sound?' He thought to himself.

"You get yourself off to the foundry and leave us women to get on with the important work." Mary smiled as she busied herself around the bed.

Chip grinned and winked mischievously at his mother, blew another kiss to Beatrice and scuttled down the steep, narrow staircase into the living room. Leonard was sitting at the table finishing his breakfast of bread and homemade jam, Chip gave him a big hug and ruffled his hair.

"Be a good lad for your grandma and try your hardest at school. I'll see you tonight." With that he grabbed his jacket from the hook on the back of the door and swept out into the street, pulling his flat cap out of the jacket pocket and dragging it forward to shade his eyes.

Proudly he strode down James Street and rounded the corner into Priory Street, his satisfied smile breaking into a whistle. A quick glance at his pocket watch again as he turned into Friars Road and he realised he was in danger of being late clocking on. Being late meant losing a half hours pay, which he could ill afford especially with a growing family, so he picked up the pace and ran the rest of the way to work.

His heavily studded boots spurted sparks as he slid into Harland Street and raced for the entrance to Waterside Works and the all important clocking on machine. He felt a stabbing pain in the base of his spine, that damned war injury again, but he was almost there. Just short of the gate he was able to slow to a fast walk, which eased the pain somewhat and he strode through the entrance gates and into the clock room with a minute to spare.

"Hurry up Chip or you'll lose a half." Encouraged Billy Moffat, one of Chip's best friends.

"Not like you to be late Double." Robert Griffin the ruddy faced foreman grinned as Chip joined the short queue for the machine. All the foundry men liked Griffin, he might be a stickler for the work and especially timekeeping, but he was always fair.

Chip just beamed at the rebuke. "I made it though!"

"By the skin of your teeth me boy." Griffin chuckled, his wide mouth accentuated by his bushy mutton chop sideburns. "Your new one arrived yet has it?"

"No but she's not far off boss." Chip was convinced the new baby would be a daughter.

Waterside works was the foundry for the mighty Ransome and Rapier engineering company that provided employment for hundreds of local men. Chip worked as a blacksmith's striker which was hard, hot work but the working day was made a bit easier for him because he had half an hour with the fire horses each morning and again each evening. Chip didn't have to feed or groom the two heavy shires, that was the responsibility of a young stable boy, but he checked them over, made sure the steel shoes were firmly attached and not worn before stroking and talking softly to them. Often he would give them an apple he had scrumped but not today.

As Chip began his day in the foundry proper his mind kept drifting to his beloved Beatrice, wondering how the labour was progressing. He knew she was in good hands, after all his mother had borne eight children of her own. She had also delivered Leonard, on the nineteenth of June 1915, almost five years earlier to the day, whilst Chip was serving in the army, and had delivered half a dozen of the neighbour's babies. Mary was a more than competent midwife.

Fortunately for Beatrice it turned out to be a relatively easy labour and, at eight o'clock precisely, after a labour lasting only a short six hours, she produced their second son. Mary tied and cut the umbilical cord and checked the infant before wrapping him in a shawl that had been handed down to her from her mother in law Jane; one that had previously swaddled her husband, his brothers and sisters, her own children, and now the latest addition to the family. She placed the crying child into an oak crib, itself a family heirloom, and turned her attention to Beatrice. Only when Beatrice was cleaned up and comfortable did she lift the infant gently from the crib, kiss him tenderly on the forehead, and pass him to his mother. Beatrice cradled him passionately to her bosom.

"What are you going to call him?" Mary asked inquisitively.

"We are not exactly sure yet." Beatrice replied without taking her eyes from her newborn. Chip and Beatrice had toyed with a few names but she wanted to confirm with him before she said anything to anybody, just in case.

After a hard day at the foundry Chip hurried home to be greeted by his mother in the scullery. Mary had always been very youthful in appearance, despite her advancing years and a tough life looking after her husband and their eight children. She was tall and slender with brown hair, which bore just a tinge of red in it, carefully tied in a bun. Mentally tough she was the undisputed head of the family but she always made it look as if her husband Charles was the master. Lately though she had begun to look a bit pale and drawn and she seemed to get tired more quickly, she simply put it down to her advancing years. Mary loved all of her family deeply and always wore a light girlish smile even when she was in pain and she seemed to be in pain much more often now. Again she told herself that it was just the ageing process. It was that same coquettish smile that greeted Chip as he burst through the scullery door, excitement written all over his face. He looked questioningly at his mother who nodded toward the stairs.

"Just five minutes now, don't you go tiring that wife of yours, she needs her rest." Chip made for the stairs. "And take those filthy boots off before you go tramping up there my lad, and don't touch the baby until you wash that grime off." Mary scolded him lightly but even in his own house he knew he must conform to the matriarch.

Impatiently Chip undid his bootlaces, dragged his feet from the enveloping leather and as the boots clumped to the floor he hurried up the narrow staircase. Mary picked up the dirty footwear, smiled and dropped them outside the back door ready to be polished for the next day.

Opening the bedroom door gently Chip peeped nervously in only to be greeted by a beaming face smiling back at him. He entered, closed the door, crossed to the bed and perched himself carefully beside Beatrice. She watched his face, with pride in her heart, as his smile widened until she thought it might split his head into two parts before her very eyes. He leaned forward and kissed Beatrice gently on her soft lips before carefully pulling the shawl so that he could gaze into the wrinkled face of his newborn.

"You are a clever girl and no mistake Beat, I love you so much." Chip was the only person who ever called her Beat, it was his loving pet name for her.

"I love you too, my darling, with all my heart, but I think you may have had something to do with my cleverness." She chuckled. Chip

24

stroked the tiny forehead and planted a loving kiss on the hairline.

"Mother was asking if we had a name but I wanted you to see him first before we finally decided."

"We decided on Ernest if it was a boy." Chip paused; he simply couldn't take his eyes of his new son. "Or Basil," another pause, "but I think he looks more of a Basil, don't you?"

"I must confess my dearest to not knowing what a Basil, or an Ernest for that matter, should look like." They laughed together until Chip leant forward and kissed her tenderly once more.

"Basil Ernest Double?" Chip questioned.

"Basil Ernest Double it is."

Although Chip had been confident that the baby would be a girl he was by no means disappointed to have another son and although he knew he should get cleaned up he was reluctant to leave the pair. Eventually he tore himself away.

"I'll leave you to rest for a bit while I wash up."

Back downstairs Chip gave his mother a warm hug.

"Thanks ma for looking after things today."

"Oh away with you boy, what's a mother for." She hit him playfully with the teacloth. "I'll take Leonard home with me tonight so that Beatrice can get a good night's sleep and I've put a stew in the pot that'll be ready for you both in about half an hour. I'm away to see to your father's dinner now.

I'll look in on Beatrice tomorrow morning." With a smile and a kiss Mary breezed out of the front door and hurried across the road to number 18.

The weeks passed and Basil grew stronger and stronger. Chip lavished love on both his sons and especially on his darling Beatrice. After a hard day in the foundry, even though his back ached, he would still help with the household chores. He was a very competent cook and often cooked their dinners at the weekend in order to give Beatrice a bit of a break, his meals were always delicious. On Sundays, after dinner, he would settle Basil in the big wheeled pram and proudly lead the family to the nearby dock area. With one hand pushing the pram and the other warmly enveloping Beatrice's, they would stroll along the tree lined promenade leading to the lock. Leonard would run from tree to tree and hide. Sometimes they would cross the lock gates and make the short walk up Ship Launch Road to enjoy a leisurely amble around Holywells park. Chip's favourite time of the year was autumn, he loved the rich colours of the dying leaves that fell to provide a carpet of gold, red, orange and yellow. He treasured the times when he held the hand of little Leonard as they kicked the leaves into a billowing mass of colour around their feet, laughing raucously.

Everything in his garden was rosy, everything in his life was rosy, life for Chip was perfect, or so he thought; but as Basil began to grow Beatrice hid a secret from the family. A few weeks after Basil was born she started to get a burning abdominal pain, not too sharp but annoying. She thought it must be just the aftermath of childbirth, although she had not experienced anything like it after Leonard was born. She pushed it to the back of her mind; Christmas was approaching, a time for joyous celebration and family fun. In September she made a large plum pudding to have after the main course at Christmas dinner, carefully feeding it over the weeks. She had also made a large cake, which had been regularly doused with lashings of brandy, for their Christmas tea.

A week or so before Christmas Chip iced the cake and it was placed carefully in the scullery cupboard. Icing and decorating a cake was a speciality of his, he covered the fruit laden slab in almond marzipan paste before lovingly spreading a generous layer of smooth rich icing sugar on the top. He used a pallet knife skilfully, constantly dipping it in warm water to prevent dragging, to smooth the snow white coating until it looked like polished glass. When the icing had set and hardened he added some little wooden figures he had carved himself some years before, there was Joseph, Mary, some sheep, a donkey and, of course, the baby Jesus in his manger. It looked an absolute delight.

Christmas eve, and with the boys safely wrapped up in bed, Chip and Beatrice sat at the rough dining table wrapping some wooden toys, that he had made for Leonard and Basil, in brown paper. Secretly he had also wrapped and hidden a special gift for Beatrice.

Outside Christmas morning was cold and frosty but Chip rose early, stoked up the fire in the small black leaded range and stood a full kettle on top. By the time Beatrice came down the stairs with Leonard and Basil the small house was warm and snug and there was a hot cup of tea and some buttered toast ready for their breakfast.

Leonard couldn't wait to tear the carefully applied paper from his presents to reveal a small wooden tricycle with a clown sitting on it, who pedalled as the tricycle was pulled along on the end of a length of string, the quicker he pulled the more furiously the clown pedalled, it was such fun. Next he found a wooden fort with some cut out soldiers and even some horses and a canon. Leonard was ecstatic. Beatrice unwrapped the presents for Basil, there was a wooden rattle and some blocks of wood which could be placed one on top of another to make a tower until it inevitably fell down, or more likely was pushed over by the laughing infant.

Lastly Chip handed Beatrice a package wrapped in colourful paper.

"What is this husband? I thought we were not to buy gifts for each other because we cannot afford them." Beatrice's eyes were wide with pleasure.

"That's correct my darling, but I have bought you nothing." Nor had he.

Beatrice unwrapped the parcel carefully, her jaw dropped open in amazement and tears immediately sprang to her eyes. Within the colourful paper was a beautiful sewing box with compartments inside for cottons, silk threads, needles and scissors, in fact everything a seamstress would need. But the crowning glory was the lid. Chip had made it from boxwood and had inlaid, in marquetry style, a heart bearing the letters EBD and CHPD intertwined. They embraced as Beatrice sobbed.

"Thank you my darling, it is just so beautiful."

"And you are even more beautiful." Chip smiled and kissed her full on the lips.

It was a magical Christmas, life was so wonderful.

1921

After all the hiatus of Christmas and New Year celebrations had settled down, life quickly returned to the routine slog. Beatrice was wrapped up with Basil, washing, cleaning, ironing, cooking and all the typical chores that housewives had to cope with. Additionally, as a competent seamstress, she had worked at William Pretty's corset factory until she was too heavily pregnant with Basil to continue, Beatrice undertook dressmaking in the home which boosted the family income somewhat. Chip, for his part, continued with his heavy work at the Ransome and Rapier foundry.

Increasingly Beatrice became aware that her pain was worsening, she began to feel bloated and heavy, although in reality she was losing weight, and she suffered chronic heartburn after every meal which only made her appetite disappear so that she often skipped a meal altogether. After Leonard had gone to school she would partially eat a slice of bread and jam and have nothing more for the rest of the day. In the evenings she only prepared a meal for Chip and Leonard, explaining that she had already eaten. When she retired to bed the pains came again, sometimes sharp, so sharp that she couldn't prevent a quick intake of breath, and sometimes dull and continuous. Through all the pain and discomfort she said nothing to Chip, she didn't want to worry him, it was sufficient to take some Epsom salts when the pain was too bad.

By mid February she could disguise her pain no longer, Chip feared her problem was serious but Beatrice deflected his concern by explaining she was only experiencing heartburn, she neglected to reveal to him just how long she had been suffering or how chronic was the pain. Continuously Chip attempted to persuade her to visit the doctor but Beatrice assured him it was not necessary, her condition would improve when the warmer weather arrived she told him. She convinced him it was all part of the aftermath of childbirth and Chip knew no different, after all he was in the King's army at the time Leonard had been born and women did not talk to men, even their own husbands, about childbirth, it was strictly a woman to woman thing and Beatrice said nothing, either to Mary or to Lydia her own mother.

It was mid April when the situation came to a head. Beatrice had hardly eaten anything for days, it was much too painful, and the cramps in her stomach had worsened until, one Sunday, unable to control her own body her secret took over.

She sat quietly in her chair, beside the range, head bowed, holding her stomach. She had mentioned to Chip that she was suffering a particularly severe bout of heartburn and he was in the scullery mixing a drink of Epsom salts for her. He was concerned, this seemed more than mere heartburn to him and he frowned as he entered the living room and offered her the mug. As he did so she looked up at him and he immediately recognised the fear in her eyes. He took a breath and was about to ask her what was wrong, but as she stared into his eyes her face contorted in terror and she vomited a jet of deep red blood. A trail of red trickled freely down her chin and stained the rug she had wrapped around her. For only a split second he stood spellbound, but it seemed an age, before embracing her in his strong arms. Life appeared to be running in slow motion, Beatrice choked and vomited again, the blood running over his shoulder and down his shirt, the warm sticky mass against his skin galvanised him into action, he realised immediately what he must do.

"Everything is going to be fine my darling." He hoped that he didn't sound as unconvincingly pathetic as he felt. "I'm going for help, Leonard, watch over Basil." He barked over his shoulder as he bounded out of the door and ran across the road, almost knocking a neighbour off his bicycle.

He burst through the door of number 18. Charles, his father, was sitting at the table with a mug of tea in one hand and the Sunday paper in the other, the mug arrested in mid air halfway to his mouth. Mary sat opposite and three of their sons were perched on a bench. Their youngest, Ernest, was sitting on the floor reading a comic paper. Charles and Mary froze momentarily at the sight of his bloodstained shirt before reality kicked in and they realised something serious had happened.

Initially they thought Chip had injured himself in some way but the look of horror rather than pain on his face told them differently.

"Something is seriously wrong with Beatrice." Chip blurted out breathlessly, a look of abject panic on his face, and tears began to stream down his cheeks. "I'm going for the doctor, can you help her mother, and watch the boys?"

It was more of a statement than a request and without waiting for a reply he spun on his heel and disappeared out the door. He ran as hard as he could, half blinded by his tears. Mary and Charles sprang to their feet, Charles' tea mug overturned onto the table, as he hastily discarded it, and soaked into the abandoned newspaper.

"George look after Ernest, Walter get after Chip he needs you with him, William come with us." Charles organised the family as he followed Mary who was already out of the door and half way across the road.

The front door to number 19 hung open and Mary hurried into the living room to be greeted with a horrendous sight. Beatrice was sitting, transfixed, in her chair coughing lightly. Every cough was accompanied by a gurgle of dark crimson blood which dribbled down her chin and into her blood-soaked hands. Charles and William bundled in behind her and for a split second the three of them stared at her in total disbelief.

Basil sat on the floor, one of his wooden blocks in one hand and his rag teddy bear in the other, oblivious to what was happening. Leonard sat in front of him, mouth gaping, staring at his mother with a terrified, uncomprehending look on his face. Mary was the first to react.

"William, get the boys to aunt Nellie and ask her to mind them for us, then get back here." No sooner said than William scooped up Basil and grabbed the hand of Leonard but he couldn't move, he couldn't force his eyes away from his mother. William appeared outwardly to be a picture of calmness but inside his head there was a whirlwind raging. He bent down in front of Leonard, so that his view of his mother was obscured and whispered gently.

"Your mother isn't feeling very well Lenny, best we give her some room so that Grandma and Grandpa can help her get better. Don't you worry, you come with me, you can stay with aunt Nellie, and play with little William, until your mother is feeling better. You'd like that wouldn't you?"

For the first time Leonard moved, he turned his eyes to his uncle who smiled down at him.

"C'mon, come with me sunshine."

Leonard rose and with William positioning himself so that his view of his mother remained obscured he was led out of the house and across the road to number 16. Nellie had been christened Ellen Bessie but she preferred to be called Nellie. She had been married to Benjamin Holland for just over two years and had two boys. William was now approaching his third birthday. He had been the

34

result of an over eager home leave in 1917 which precipitated a hasty if overdue marriage when he was next on leave in 1918. Douglas was the same age as Basil and quite a handful. Quickly realising there was a crisis, but ignorant to the cause or the seriousness, she readily accepted her brother's two youngsters into her home.

Fifteen minutes later doctor Benson arrived in his pristine Austin motor car which he had been proudly polishing when Chip and Walter arrived at his house. They sat, agitated, in the back seat urging him to hurry. It was the first time that either of them had ridden in a saloon motor car but they didn't enjoy the journey, Chip had big tears in his eyes and Walter had a tender arm around the shoulder of his elder brother.

The doctor strode purposefully into the living room, took one look at Beatrice and announced that, as he had suspected, she must go to the hospital immediately.

Chip gathered Beatrice in his arms and carried her gently but swiftly through the front door into the street where a crowd was beginning to gather. The commotion caused by Chip, his parents and brothers, running around the close knit community had alerted the neighbours to the fact that something was seriously amiss and when they witnessed the arrival of the doctor, accompanied by Chip in his bloodstained shirt, their suspicions had been confirmed. The majority of the women were there out of curiosity and support for their popular neighbour, the children, on the other hand, were there to admire the doctor's motor car, probably one of the first ever seen in James Street. Mothers pulled their offspring closer to them so they would not get in the way and looked on at a safe distance. Two lads standing by the gleaming mudguard and staring at their reflection in the sparkling glass of the headlamp quickly moved aside as Chip emerged from his home cradling his beloved, blood soaked, Beatrice.

Carefully Chip placed her on the back seat of the motor car before kneeling on the floor so that he could hold her hand. He also held a moist cloth in his other hand to wipe the blood from her face and to make sure not a drop fell onto the seat of the pristine motor car. Mary climbed into the front seat beside the doctor and, with a blast on the hooter to scatter the inquisitive children, the car chugged its way out of James Street and into Tanners Lane heading toward the Anglesea Road Free Hospital.

The Austin swung into the cobbled yard at the Ivry Street entrance. Doctor Benson leapt from the driver seat and, leaving the driver's door swinging freely, burst through the swing doors into the hospital. He emerged seconds later with two nurses and a porter trailing a gurney behind him. Beatrice was carefully placed on the gurney and swiftly wheeled into the hospital, her entourage following in her wake. The wheels of the gurney squeaked rhythmically as it was propelled along the corridor and through a set of double doors. As the doors slapped closed behind the doctor one of the nurses turned to Mary and Chip and raised her hand.

"This is as far as you are allowed to go I'm afraid, it's only medical staff beyond this point." She said brusquely. "You can wait here, or there is a bench in the yard." With that she turned and disappeared through the double doors.

Chip looked dazed. Mary put her arms around him and hugged him tightly. The emotion and stress of the moment flowed over him and he began to sob pitifully.

"She will be alright, won't she?" he bleated pitifully. Mary had no answer she just pulled his tearstained head onto her shoulder and kissed his forehead.

It was a full hour before Doctor Benson reappeared looking pale and tired.

"The bleeding has stopped, so that's a good thing but she has lost a lot of blood and has to make that up. We are not sure yet but it looks as if she has a burst stomach ulcer."

"Can we see her?" Chip had recovered a modicum of his composure.

"Not at the moment Mr Double, come back at visiting time tonight, by then they should have more information for you."

"She will be alright won't she doctor." Chip was visibly shaking.

"I'm sorry, I just don't know at the moment. It's early days but if it is a burst ulcer it can be very serious." Chip nodded and his head dropped.

It was a long and painful walk home, Chip and Mary hardly spoke, wrapped in their own thoughts, unaware of the looks that his bloodied shirt earned from other pedestrians.

Later, when Chip returned to the hospital, accompanied by his mother, he was directed to a side room. Beatrice was lying unconscious on the bed, there was a rubber tube coming from under the blanket and a yellowish, bloodstained fluid dripped from the end into a glass bottle that stood on the floor. Chip pulled up a couple of chairs that were standing in the corner of the room and sat as close to Beatrice as he was able. He scooped her fragile hand into his. Her eyes were closed and she gave no response to his gentle squeeze of her hand. He watched the slight rise and fall of her chest to convince himself she was still breathing. After about half an hour she slowly opened her eyes and turned them toward him, she gave an almost imperceptible smile, she was obviously very weak.

"How are my boys?" Her whisper was barely audible, and took considerable effort.

Chip gently stroked the back of her hand and reassured her that the boys were safe at home with Nellie. The hint of a smile and she closed her eyes once more. Five minutes later the nurse opened the door and told them it was time to leave. He kissed her on the forehead, told her he loved her, and reluctantly let their hands slip apart as he backed out of the room.

Over the next few days Chip struggled at work, his mind was far from the foundry, and as soon as he was able to clock off he ran all the way home, washed and changed his clothes before walking briskly to the hospital. Beatrice seemed to be improving until, on the fourth day her stomach pains returned. The doctors diagnosed septicaemia and inserted another tube into her abdomen to drain the murderous fluid. Everybody prayed that Beatrice would recover, none more fervently than Chip.

Two more days passed and Chip noticed on his daily visits that Beatrice was deteriorating, her eyes sunk deep into their dark sockets and her cheeks became taut and changed from the soft pink of her youth to take on a sallow yellowish hue. Chip was told he could visit her at any time of the day or night. He realised this meant that the woman he loved more than life itself was on the brink. He made the decision not to go to work, he could ill afford to lose the pay but he had to be with his beloved Beatrice. He sat with her constantly stroking the back of her hand, not daring to leave the room. He did not eat nor drink, save for the odd cup of luke warm tea brought to him by the nurses. He knew she was teetering on the edge and he prayed she would come back to him.

Finally, on the nineteenth of April, Beatrice's frail body could fight no more. Chip kissed her forehead and squeezed her hand as, with a gentle shudder, she slipped from his world. Clasping her hand to his heart he laid his head on her chest and wept uncontrollably. She was only twenty nine years old.

*****

The death of Beatrice had a devastating effect on the family in more ways than one. Chip was in a confused daze; he could neither believe nor accept that his beloved Beatrice had been so cruelly taken from him and that he had lost her forever. But, of course, he had to work in order to live and to feed his family. He found himself left with the massive responsibility of a five year old schoolboy and a ten month old baby. In the depths of his grief he felt he was all alone in the world, he would have to face the future alone. He knew he had to find a solution to his dilemma with his sons, and quickly, so he turned toward the only people that he knew for sure would help him, the extended family, and they closed around him like a protective glove.

His main concern was how to care for his children, Leonard was a strapping young lad that would need precious little special care but with Basil it was a different situation. He had no idea how to look after a ten month old infant and anyway it needed a woman's tender touch. Firstly he considered his parents, Charles and Mary, conveniently living opposite, but Charles at fifty nine was still working as a carter, with his own pony and cart. It was gruelling work. Most of his trade came from the nearby docks but there was plenty of competition which meant he had to ensure that he was in the right place at the right time. Fortunately he had a small group of regular customers, that helped, but it was by no means sufficient. Even when he was successful at finding additional work he had to load the goods onto his cart single handed, transport them to their destination and then unload. With three to four loads a day to move he was exhausted when he finally arrived home, usually around dusk, and was not really in the right frame of mind for a young family. Mary, at 54, was still relatively young but noticeably unwell. Their house was identical to Chip's, a small two up two down in a long terrace, and they still had four of their eight children living with them. William was the eldest at twenty four and working as a stitcher in a boot factory. Then there was Walter who, at eighteen, was working as a labourer on the docks along with his sixteen year old brother George. The youngest was Ernest, known to all as midget although nobody quite knew why as he was a strapping ten year old schoolboy. The house was bursting at the seams and it was painfully obvious to everybody, especially to Chip, that for Leonard and Basil to live there was not a viable option.

Sister Nellie was near and handy but she had precious little room in her house either, and with a three year old son and a ten month old baby to care for, in addition to the sewing work she took in, Chip knew it would be unfair to ask her to take on another two. He didn't ask.

Then there were Beatrice's parents, George and Lydia Cotton. They lived in a reasonably sized, three bedroom semi detached house a mile or so away in Cavendish Street, along with two of their children, twenty seven year old Ernest, who worked at Fisk the grocer on the corner of Gladstone Road and Foxhall Road, and Gertrude who worked at Cranfields milling company as an office clerk. George had started out as a coal heaver at the nearby Derby Road railway station, shovelling coal from the railway trucks into sacks, weighing them and loading them onto delivery carts. It was back breaking work, more suited to a young man and inevitably it had eventually taken its toll on his back, prompting him to make the change to being a bargee. Again the work was hard but he was fortunate enough to find a barge he could afford to rent, he secured some lucrative contracts and managed to build up a reasonably profitable business.

After ten years on the barges he had enough put by to enable him to invest in his own coal shop, supplying coal to homes and businesses throughout Ipswich. It was a reasonably strong business that generated a meagre income but increasingly it had been his wife Lydia who had undertaken the running of the shop, in addition to the house, whilst George organised the deliveries and did his best to drink away the profits. To help with family finances, or more likely to finance his nightly binges, they had taken in a lodger, Walter Vincent, a widower who worked as a cellar man in the 'Blooming Fuchsia' beer house.

Although George and Lydia undoubtedly had the room to take in both of Chip's boys it was too much to expect Lydia to run the business, run the home, cook, clean and look after a ten month old baby. It was just not possible. However, as Leonard was a schoolboy and needed very little personal attention, George and Lydia readily agreed to take him in. That just left Chip with little Basil.

Gertrude Cotton was Basil's maiden aunt, the elder sister of his mother by three years; she had taken the death of Beatrice very badly. Her other siblings were all male and as a result she had always been extremely close to, and very protective of, her little sister. Gertrude was a short, slightly built woman who always wore dark clothes and had her long auburn hair permanently tied up on the back of her head in a bun. Her chiselled features and harsh, pained eyes hid her true feelings from the world. Born in 1888 she had always found it difficult to mix with other people, especially men. That was until, as a coy twenty four year old office clerk in the office of the William Pretty corset factory in Tower Ramparts, she encountered Albert

Frost. Albert worked as a maintenance man, keeping the banks of sewing machines in working order. Every time she had cause to cross the factory floor, whether taking a message to the foreman or seeking an answer to a question posed by her supervisor, Albert would pause in his work to watch her as she floated past him. She held the front of her dress slightly above the wooden floor, smoothed and polished by thousands of footsteps over the years, as she appeared to glide across the workshop. She knew he was watching her, she could feel the friendly warmth of his gaze burning into her. She surprised herself one day when she realised that she had deliberately slowed her progress as she neared him.

"Morning Mistress Cotton." A wide smile blossomed on his handsome rounded face.

"Master Frost." She turned her head toward him and returned the smile. She detected a faint flutter in her heart, a sensation she was definitely not accustomed to. If she had realised that she had generated exactly the same sensation deep in his chest she would, no doubt, have been even more surprised and probably extremely embarrassed. It wasn't long before she realised that she was actually inventing reasons to cross the factory floor just to see him and slowly the two became good friends. Albert thought that Gertrude was very pretty, and indeed she was, she had a glowing complexion, especially for a clerk working in the confines of an office all week. Some of her colleagues began to taunt her gently, knowing that she was naturally shy, by telling her that Albert had a crush on her and that he wanted to ask her to walk out with him, but that he, like her, was too shy.

It was Phyllis Evans who took on the mantle of matchmaker, she was a bit of a flirt and knew that her two friends were attracted to each other but if left to their own devices they would never get any further than smiling and exchanging pleasantries. She told Albert that Gertrude was keen on him and was hoping that he would ask her to walk out. She then told Gertrude that Albert dearly wanted to court her but that he was concerned about receiving a rejection. The ploy worked. They started walking out together during the summer of 1912 and their relationship blossomed.

Gertrude fell in love with him and privately fantasised about being married to him. She took him home to meet her mother and father, who were suitably impressed, and it looked to everybody as if their marriage would only be a matter of time.

However, their romance was destined to be interrupted by the Great War when Albert joined up to serve with the eighth battalion, Suffolk Regiment. He vowed he would not marry until the war was over because he was fearful of leaving Gertrude as a young widow. Tragically their romance was cut cruelly short when Albert died from wounds sustained in a gas attack at Bellewaarde on twenty fourth of May 1915 during the second battle of Ypres. Gertrude was utterly devastated. She became introverted and, despite the best efforts of the family, refused to leave the house other than to go to work. Unable to face the building without the smiling face of Albert, she resigned from her job at the corset factory and found new employment with 'Cranfields' flour millers as an office clerk. There she was viewed by the other office employees as being a miserable, incommunicative woman, which of course she was, but with good reason. The only people who could reach her were her sister Ellen Beatrice and her elder brother Samuel. Beatrice had understood exactly how Gertrude was feeling and together with Samuel, who was home on shore leave from the Royal Navy, was successful, up to a point, in trying to help her come to terms with her loss. Together they began to nurture the green shoots of recovery. A recovery that was shattered following Samuel's death in April 1916, when the minesweeper 'Lena Melling', on which he was serving, hit a mine and sank in the Thames estuary. Totally distraught, she was never seen to smile from that time onward. She did, however, manage a flicker when her little nephew Basil came on the scene. She took to the little man straight away.

And now her little nephew was without a mother and she was without the sister she loved so dearly. Everybody she ever loved was destined to be taken from her, or so it seemed to her. Gertrude had spent as much time as she could with Beatrice and Basil and came to regard him, in her mind if not openly, almost as her own son. She desperately wanted Basil to come and live with her and tried extremely hard, and sadly in vain, to get her parents to change their mind and take Basil in along with Leonard. She promised that she would undertake looking after him all the time when she was not at work and that she would not allow it to put more pressure on her mother.

George was adamant, however, although Gertrude had the impression that her mother, Lydia, was gradually weakening her resolve.

"I have made my decision, the answer is no." He boomed. "We will take in Leonard but not the baby. There's an end to the matter." George, stone faced, stomped out the front door and made a beeline for the White Elm Inn.

Further up Cavendish Street, on the opposite side to George and Lydia lived Lydia's sister, Emily Jane Dumble. Two years younger than her sister, Emily Jane also had a three bedroom semi detached house which she shared with her twenty four year old son Albert, known to everybody as 'Sonny', and her two daughters Doris aged twenty, and Gladys nineteen, who were both seamstresses at Ridleys clothing factory in Kemball Street. She also had two other sons but they were both in the Navy, George Henry was serving on submarines whilst William West was serving with the marines.

Emily Jane was a cheerful woman with long, greying hair that was always tied in a bun. Her square set face with its sharp features gave the impression of a very stern character but in fact beneath that firm exterior beat a heart of liquid gold. She had always been a hard working woman who never shied away from taking on more, possibly in an effort to hide her emotions, especially following the great hardships she had experienced over the past eight years. She had raised her five children alone following the death of her fifty six year old husband, George Henry Dumble, in 1913. Two years ago she had taken in the then eight year old Leslie Bushen. Leslie's mother had remarried, following the death of his father and, tragically, didn't want to take him with her into her new life. His aunts and uncles had likewise refused to take him, probably because as a schoolboy he would be a financial liability. Now aged ten he was doing well at school and taking a strong interest in English literature and journalism, he was always to be found with his head in a newspaper or a book. The small allowance that his step father paid Emily Jane just about covered his keep although the primary reason for her taking him in was based purely on compassion and love.

Emily Jane was not an outwardly emotional woman, there were precious few hugs and kisses for the children, but she was exceptionally kind and caring, happily going to any lengths for her family. She always wore a long plain black skirt with a white frilled blouse, and an immaculate white apron. Despite everything finances were such that, although Sonny and her two girls contributed to the household accounts Emily Jane took in washing each week, along with a bit of dressmaking and sewing, in order to balance the books. Four years earlier she had even taken in a lodger, the kindly Mr Belsey, to enable her to provide her children with the odd luxury or two.

Emily Jane always had a soft spot in her heart for Chip and recognised that his options for Basil were both restricted and diminishing by the hour. She also felt that, as she was always home working at the washing and ironing she took in, she would be able to cope with raising an infant. Inwardly she rather relished the change that a young child would bring, and thought that perhaps getting her girls involved might just stimulate some maternal instincts within them. When Chip approached her she readily and happily agreed to take her niece's baby into her home.

Relieved, Chip was now able to concentrate on pulling together the threads of his own life. He was able to work at the foundry for five and a half days and spend most Sundays visiting his two boys separately. His family was well catered for but he felt desperately sad and empty inside and, as he lay alone in bed at night, he longed for the day to come when he could restore his family. Hoping against hope that day was not too far in the future, he refused to relinquish the tenancy on 19 James Street, instead he sub let the property to a young childless couple, Mr and Mrs Stannard whilst he moved in with his sister Nellie at number 16.

Part Two

The Cavendish
Street Years
(The first time around)

1921 (Continued)

The young Basil thrived with Emily Jane and her family. Whilst the girls fussed over feeding, washing and dressing him, Sonny would play with him at every opportunity. Belsey too had a soft spot for the chubby little lad and would often sit with him on his lap telling him stories or singing nursery rhymes. Gertrude Cotton was also a very frequent visitor, not wishing to sever the relationship between herself and her nephew, the only remaining link between herself and her dear sister. Emily Jane could see that there was almost a sense of desperation in her love for the boy and she made it as easy as she could for Gertrude to spend time with him.

When Basil reached the grand age of one year Sonny decided that it was high time the 'crawling monster', as he lovingly called him, mastered the art of walking. He stood Basil up against the wall of the living room and, with his arms outstretched, held the little man's hands, all the time encouraging him to move toward him. Basil toppled forward, keeping his legs firmly planted on the floor, until he realised that if he moved his legs he could, with assistance, move toward Sonny, although for some reason he never seemed to get any closer, he didn't realise that Sonny was constantly backing away. With each traverse of the living room Sonny lessened his grip and before long Basil was shuffling, unaided, across the polished floorboards. This exercise continued over the next couple of weeks. If the weather were warm Sonny continued Basil's walking lessons at the back of the house, standing him with his back against the wall, between the French window and the garden gate. Basil turned his head upwards to see the grey galvanised bath hanging on the wall above him, think of bath night, which was not one of his favourite nights, and shuffle away. In no time at all he was walking unaided and soon after, in the way of toddlers, he learned to run, and ran everywhere.

Sadly the close bond that developed between Albert and Basil was not to last however. Albert was becoming restless and disillusioned. He had served in the Great War in the Medical Corps and, in common with thousands of servicemen, had experienced at first hand the trauma and horror of modern warfare. Like so many others he expected that there would be a brave new world waiting when hostilities ceased, but this new world never materialised. Ex servicemen were not looked after in the manner Albert felt they should be. Jobs were hard to come by, men who had received a promise from their employers that their jobs would await them when they returned from the front, as they joyously volunteered, found the jobs were no longer there for them. Sonny had had enough.

As autumn turned toward winter, 1921 revealed that it had one more tragedy to lie on the shoulders of the still grieving Chip. November swept in with a wintry coldness that laid his mother, Mary, low with an infection of the chest. Only then did the family discover that her continued loss of weight and drawn, sallow appearance had, in fact, been the harbinger of lung cancer. Mary's infection turned to pneumonia and she was confined to bed. Charles made up a bed in the living room so that Mary could get maximum benefit from the ever burning range and be close to her family. Her deterioration continued until gradually her vital organs began to fail. As most families enjoyed the build up to the Christmas festivities Mary slowly slipped into unconsciousness, one from which she was never to awaken. Mary passed over on Christmas Eve at the age of only fifty four. 1921 was certainly a year that the Double family and the Cotton family were pleased to see the back of.

1922 - 1924

1922 started poorly for Emily Jane. She had known for some time the discontentment that her eldest son was harbouring, but had not fully appreciated how deep that discontentment was. His resolve cracked with the New Year, he was completely disinterested in the festivities and spent the evening in his bedroom, deep in thought. By the seventh of January his mind was made up, he no longer wanted to remain in England and, having considered his options most carefully and thoroughly, decided that he would seek a new life in another country. The following day, being a Sunday, he walked his fiancée Marjorie Stevens through the town to Christchurch Park and up through the Arboretum. Sitting on a bench in a sheltered corner, collar turned up against the cold breeze, he explained to her the decision he had reached. She listened carefully, watching the vapour clouds swirl about his head as his warm breath met the cold air, she loved him dearly and dreaded the thought of losing him. As he expanded on his idea she became frightened and an emptiness grew inside her, was he telling her their relationship was at an end?

"I have a great desire within my heart to start a new life, my love." Marjorie saw the beginnings of a tear in the corner of his eye. "But, my heart's greatest desire is to start that new life with you."

The dam burst, she flung her arms around his neck and bursting into floods of tears, pressed her head deep into his shoulder.

"Oh my darling," she sobbed, "I thought you were going to leave me behind."

"Never my sweetheart, never."

They sat making plans for a while before the cold began to seep into their overcoats and they were forced to continue their planning as they strolled around the upper arboretum, generating a bit of welcome body warmth. By the time they reached Marjorie's home their future was set.

Later that evening he returned to Cavendish Street, walked confidently into the living room and proclaimed to his gathered family the direction he and Marjorie were to steer their future. The announcement was greeted initially with a stunned silence, followed eventually by a gaggle of sound as his sisters talked animatedly over each other, desperately attempting to change his mind. All the time they were entreating him Emily Jane sat silently in her chair, waiting for them to exhaust their onslaught, until, thrusting her hand into the air, she signalled for silence.

"You have obviously given this much thought Sonny," she whispered, "and if that is what you want to do," she eyed her daughters sternly over her reading glasses, "nobody will attempt to stand in your way."

Doris and Gladys opened their mouths to protest but were cut short when Emily Jane once more raised her hand.

"Enough!" Was all she needed to say. The girls, silenced, retired to their bedroom.

The next few weeks were very hectic for Sonny and Marjorie. Amid much discussion they packed their essential belongings into two large wooden trunks he purchased in a local pawnbroker's shop, he quit his job as an office clerk at Ransome and Rapier, and bought two tickets for a steamer bound for New Zealand at the end of the month. Despite outwardly supporting him, deep inside Emily Jane was heartbroken, she could see her family, the family she had worked so hard to keep together, in danger of becoming totally splintered, with two sons serving in the Navy and now her eldest departing for heaven knew what.

Marjorie arrived at 251 Cavendish Street promptly at eight in the morning of twenty third of January. As she opened the front door Emily Jane could see, over Marjorie's shoulder, the taxi idling at the kerbside and she felt a shiver of emotion as she realised there was to be no going back for Sonny now. Their trunks loaded into the taxi, along with two suitcases containing essentials for the journey, he hugged his mother and swayed her to and fro as the tears began to run down her pale cheek, he kissed them away.

"When we are settled Ma you can come and visit us." It was an empty statement for they both knew beyond any doubt that Emily Jane would never make the journey and they would never see each other again. He gave each of his sisters a hug and a kiss on the forehead before making for the taxi. Emily Jane stood outwardly emotionless on the top step, the gaping front door behind her. The girls stood sullenly at the kerb, waving forlornly, as the motor made its way down the hill toward Fore Hamlet and disappeared round the curve, taking their dear brother out of their lives forever. The road became uncannily silent.

Little Basil was standing between the sisters, oblivious and unconcerned, at only seventeen months it did not register that things around him were changing. So long as he had his teddy bear, made for him by young Doris with scraps of cloth she had picked up at her work, he was most happy. Doris looked down at the little boy, took his eager hand in hers, and turned back towards the house. He grinned up at the feminine tears.

******

On a warm Saturday evening in July 1922 Doris and Gladys attended a dance at the Social Settlement, a large building at the junction of Fore Street and Duke Street, which housed the Empire cinema, a room where men played billiards and cards and a grand hall which was used for Sunday evening services, lantern slide shows and dances.

This particular evening there were a number of servicemen present and one in particular caught Doris's eye. Samuel Perkins a twenty five year old who had been raised by his grandparents was tall and slim with a head of thick wavy hair, pale blue eyes set in a lightly tanned face and a small but ever smiling mouth, he cut a very striking figure, attracting the girls had never been a problem for him. He enlisted into the Oxford and Bucks Light Infantry in 1915 at the age of eighteen, later transferring into the Royal Flying Corps and was currently serving in the fledgling Royal Air Force at Martlesham Heath Aerodrome, to the north of the town. He had decided to go to the dance, with half a dozen of his fellow servicemen, intent on enjoying a little bit of female company and to sink a few beers.

From the corner of his eye he noticed that Doris was eyeing him, and eager to make an impression, he propped himself on the bar and made sweeping motions with his beer glass in a pretence of explaining something interesting to his colleagues. Doris thought he looked extremely suave in his light blue uniform and peak cap and found it difficult to divert her gaze from him, a fact not missed by Samuel who had the same problem with the slim, attractive, dark haired young girl. Full of confidence he made his excuses to his comrades and sauntered across the dance floor to ask Doris if she would grant him the pleasure of a dance. Trying not to appear over enthusiastic she agreed with a pert smile.

After just one dance he bought both the girls a drink and motioned them to sit with him at a table to one side of the dance floor. They talked, or more accurately Samuel talked, mainly to Doris who held his full attention and was avidly hanging on his every word. Gladys listened spellbound too but was most definitely just an observer. He captivated them with his smooth ways and with his tales of daring feats in ungainly aircraft during the latter stages of the Great War. Both sisters were mesmerised by his charm but he only had eyes for Doris. When the dance was over he offered to walk the girls home, an offer that was accepted in almost indecent haste. As they stepped out the door, he casually took Doris' hand in his and she immediately felt a tingle of excitement. It was only a relatively short journey to their home but Doris did not want the spell to be broken and ensured that she walked very slowly in order to prolong her pleasure. Hand in hand they walked and talked with Gladys trailing silently and disappointedly in their wake.

Their romance blossomed. Doris was completely smitten with the smooth talking, gallant airman and quickly fell head over heels in love. Samuel too was beguiled by the attractive, intelligent seamstress but most importantly of all Emily Jane liked the polite, jovial airman. She gave her unspoken approval by agreeing to him staying at the house whenever he had a weekend pass. As a result he spent most of his free time at number 251, taking Doris out for walks, dancing at the Lyceum, to the picture palace to see Charlie Chaplin and Harold Lloyd or to a variety show at the Hippodrome. It was a marvellous summer.

In December of 1922 George, Emily Jane's eldest son, came home on leave from HMS Dolphin, the submarine shore base in Gosport, to marry his long standing fiancé Emily Miller. They both knew he intended to remain in the Royal Navy, and not wanting Emily to be alone for long periods, they decided not to set up home at this point and so he remained in single quarters in Gosport while Emily moved into number 251. Space being at rather a premium the only solution was for Basil to be taken from Emily Jane's room, the front parlour, and moved into the small bedroom at the back of the house to share with Leslie. This would allow for a blanket to be strung across Emily Jane's bedroom, so that she could share with George's wife and both could retain a modicum of privacy.

Basil enjoyed the change, he now had a small bed of his own, beside young Leslie's, in the tiny bedroom above the outhouse. It was a cramped but cosy room, if a little damp, with only just sufficient room to squeeze between the beds. Leslie didn't mind having to share with his little 'orphan brother', in fact, despite the ten year age gap, they got on famously together. At night, by the light of a flickering candle, Leslie would read to Basil from one of his many books, stories of adventure and derring do which both excited and frightened young Basil and ignited in him a fascination for the written word which would last him a lifetime. Leslie made a point of teaching Basil about words and letters, and he did such a good job that, by the age of four Basil could both read and write to the standard of a seven year old.

******

The courtship of Doris and Samuel blossomed and nature took its inevitable course. In July 1923 Doris discovered that she was three months pregnant by the man with whom she was in love. Samuel, similarly devoted, did the decent thing and proposed marriage, a proposal that was eagerly accepted by Doris, partly to protect her reputation but mostly because she wanted to spend the rest of her life with him. They were hurriedly married in August 1923 and Samuel moved into what was by now becoming a heavily overcrowded house, it was literally bursting at the seams. The only person fortunate enough to enjoy a room of their own was Belsey, and as he was a paying guest there was no way he could or should be asked to share. The options were limited so, in order for the newly married couple to have a room to themselves, Gladys had to move out of the bedroom she shared with Doris and into Emily Jane's half room and share the bed.

This arrangement was destined to be short lived, however, as fate was on hand to step in and ease the problem slightly.

It was a cold Sunday afternoon in mid February 1924, an icy wind blew down Cavendish Street swirling the light snowfall. A coal fire burned in the grate of the living room, Emily Jane was preparing the evening meal in the scullery, Leslie and Basil had their collective heads in a new adventure comic, Gladys sat busily sewing her new dress while Doris and Samuel sat near the fire with Marjorie their six week old daughter cuddled in Doris' arms. George's Emily had wrapped up warm and gone for a walk around Alexandra Park and Belsey was at work collecting and washing pots in the White Elm. To all appearances it was a normal winter's afternoon.

The scene was rudely disturbed by a loud thumping on the front door.

'I'll go.' Volunteered Leslie, dropping the comic into Basil's lap.

The front door was heard to open, causing a cold draught that slid under the living room door and up the chimney, making the coals flame. There came the muffled sound of deep, official sounding voices.

The door to the living room opened and Leslie entered followed by two men in blue Royal Air Force uniform, the collars of their greatcoats pulled high against the cold and their peaked caps, with red bands around them, tucked under their arms. The shock showed on everybody's face, transfixed they studied the new arrivals. The taller of the two cast his eyes around the room, taking in the whole scene; his gaze came to rest on Samuel. Samuel swallowed nervously.

"Samuel Perkins?" Not so much a question more a statement.

"Yes." There was a tremble in his voice, almost as if he knew exactly why the two military policemen were there.

"You're under arrest; you're to come with us."

"What is going on?" Doris was visibly shaken. "You can't just walk in here and take my husband."

"Oh believe me we can Miss, and we will."

"What on earth has he done?" Doris was standing protectively now, squarely between the policeman and her husband. "Surely this can wait until he reports for duty tomorrow morning."

"I'm afraid not Miss." He moved Doris aside with a strong arm on her shoulder. "Come along Perkins."

Doris was about to object but Samuel calmed her and explained to everybody that there was obviously some misunderstanding somewhere, he would sort it out and be back in time for dinner.

However, Samuel didn't sort it out and he was not back in time for dinner. It transpired that he had married a Sarah Thompson Bell in Scotland in 1921 and they even had a child together. His marriage to Doris was bigamous, and therefore invalid. To add insult to injury Doris was informed that, far from being an intrepid pilot, as he had professed, Samuel was, in fact, a lowly airman second class with a penchant for exaggeration.

Doris was desolate, left unmarried, with a small child and an unfair stigma while Samuel received six months hard labour for his crime. Following his release he was dishonourably discharged from the Royal Air Force and the family never saw him again. Gladys happily moved back into her sister's bedroom to comfort her and help her with the baby Marjorie whenever she could.

******

With Basil growing older and able to enter into a bit of rough and tumble Leslie, who Basil, unable to pronounce his name correctly, always called 'Seshy', spent hours playing with him. One particular favourite game of Leslie's was to have a play fight. Rolling around on the floor he always ensured that they ended up under the heavy wooden dining table. Once there Leslie would let Basil get the upper hand and be on top, whereupon he would lift Basil up sharply until his head banged against the underside of the table, never with enough force to hurt his playmate, but sufficient to make him cry out.

Another romp was for Leslie to hold an old kitbag, which had originally belonged to Sonny, and for Basil to punch it like a boxer in training. One day Leslie swung the bag when Basil punched it to make out that Basil had given it a real belter. Unfortunately it did a full three hundred and sixty degrees and hit Basil heavily on the back of the head. Basil let out a loud scream and burst into tears. Emily Jane, who was carving meat at the table at the time, took the top off her finger with the razor sharp carving knife. Leslie never did that again.

All the romping was simply good clean fun and totally without malice, Leslie would never have deliberately hurt anyone, especially his little 'brother' and most definitely not Emily Jane.

All good things must end, however, and when Leslie turned fourteen, at the end of 1924, his uncle and aunt suddenly realised they could now take him in, after all they were his blood family were they not? The fact that Leslie had secured an apprenticeship with the East Anglian Daily Times newspaper and was about to embark on his career in journalism, bringing in a very reasonable wage for one so young, had no bearing on their decision of course. Leslie left 251 very reluctantly but vowed that he would always stay in touch with Emily Jane, who loved him as if he were her own son and treated him so well at a time when nobody else was interested, also with Doris and Gladys who had always spoiled him and teased him unashamedly. Most of all he regretted having to part from little Basil who had stolen his teenage heart. True to his promise he was to return frequently to visit what he referred to as his 'real' family.

Basil was now four years old and regularly played outside in the street, kicking stones and chasing the odd delivery cart up the hill. It was when he was sauntering back down the hill one day, having followed the bread van to the top, he bumped into Douglas Marsh. Douglas was a year older than Basil and he lived at number 262 Cavendish Street, an end of terrace that bordered onto Mr Goss's orchard.

"What's your name?" Douglas always went straight to the point.

"Basil, what's yours?"

"Douglas, but you can call me Doug, everybody else does." There was a silence that Doug was eager to break. "Do you like apples Basil?"

"Dunno!"

"Haven't you ever eaten an apple then?"

"Dunno!"

"Don't say much do ya?" Doug smiled and Basil relaxed a bit. "Do ya wanna try one now?"

"Yeah OK!"

"Come on then, follow me." With that Doug took Basil to the bottom of his garden where there were some loose boards in the fence. He swung two of the boards apart to make an opening big enough for them to scramble through and they emerged into a large area full of trees. Basil looked round in wonder, there were many different kinds of trees including apples, pears, plums and greengages.

"We better be quick 'cos Gossy don't like people nickin' his apples." Doug reached up, plucked two large green apples and the duo quickly disappeared back through the fence and into his garden. Leaning up against the fence they took a bite. The apples were very sour and Basil's face screwed up.

"They're cookers. Taste good don't they." Said Doug, his face screwed.

"Yeah!" Basil felt his teeth go on edge, he wasn't too sure.

From that day onward they became the very best of friends and were always together getting up to innocent mischief.

Doug also introduced Basil into the gang of youngsters that regularly played up and down Cavendish Street and pretty soon he had a wide circle of friends but Doug was always his 'besty'.

Number 262 just happened to be almost opposite number 251 so neither of them had far to go to see each other and they regularly played in each other's gardens and even in the cellar of Doug's house where his three sisters kept their dolls house. One day the intrepid duo found some thin wire in the cellar and spent a whole afternoon wiring the entire dolls house for electric lights. They took the wires to the chimney first, just like with their own houses, and then ran it round every room. Fortunately they never thought to plug the wires into the mains.

******

In the late summer of 1924 the resourceful pair were rummaging about in Doug's father's shed, something they did on a regular basis, there they found the chassis of an old pram and a couple of lengths of wood. Imagination in full flow they rescued the items and fixed the boards in place across the axles.

"Got our own car Bass." Doug had found a way to shorten his mate's name. "Let's go and try it out."

So they pushed the 'vehicle' to the top of Cavendish Street hill, jumped on board, and pushed themselves off without considering how they might stop. The cart quickly gained momentum and was soon hurtling down the hill at breakneck speed. The wheels went into the gutter and scraped the kerb, just as well or they might never have stopped, and as the road levelled out so the cart slowed until it finally came to a stop. They both sat for a minute, hearts racing, but with great big smiles stuck across their faces.

"That was wizard." Exclaimed Doug finally, "let's do it again." They did it again: and again, until they were both totally exhausted from pushing it back up the hill. Carefully they garaged their cart in Doug's back garden until another day.

When that other day came they grew much more adventurous and pushed the cart to the top of Devonshire Road hill. This hill was a shorter run, but an incredibly steep one, with the added hazard of ending in a 'T' junction with Cavendish Street. There was, however, a passageway that led beside Goss' orchard and they were both confident they could steer up there safely, but they would have to build some sort of cushion at the end to stop the run. Undeterred they built a ramp up against the kerb and put anything soft that they could find at the bottom of the passage, they were sure that would be sufficient. They heaved their cart to the top of the hill and pushed off. By some minor miracle they managed to fly up the ramp and steer up the alley finally crashing, cheering, into their improvised safety barrier.

Two days later, whilst making the same dangerous run, Basil got his bearings slightly wrong and their flying chariot failed to make the entrance to the passageway and crashed into the wooden fence. The cart stopped dead but not so the pilots who were propelled unceremoniously off the front, to land in a crumpled heap. One of the springs from the pram chassis penetrated Basil's leg just below the kneecap and a trickle of blood snaked slowly down his leg. Crestfallen they headed for home and while the uninjured Doug returned their chariot to its shed Basil limped into the kitchen and presented himself to Emily Jane for running repairs.

"What have you been up to, you scallywag?" she tutted as she cleaned the wound and bandaged it tightly.

"I fell over Nan." He flexed his knee; it worked fine, so he jumped down from the chair and raced into the street to play once more.

******

One autumn day the boys were sitting on the edge of the kerb talking when Doug happened to mention his mother.

"You know she is not your *real* mother don't you." Basil said.

"What you talkin' about 'corse she is." Doug was more than a little indignant.

"No she isn't, honestly. Nobody has their real mother because when they are born their real mother dies." Basil continued confidently.

"I don't believe you." Doug wasn't sure now and there was a note of concern in his voice.

"It's true, I know."

Doug didn't know what to say. He jumped up and with tears rolling down his cheeks he went running indoors to confront his mother. A few minutes later his mother came out and lowered herself to sit on the kerb beside Basil.

"Would you like to come in and have some lemonade Basil? I've got some currant buns that I have just cooked too."

"Cor, yes please." Basil jumped up and she took his hand gently and led him into her scullery, sat him down with some lemonade and a bun, and pulled up a chair for herself. Carefully and sympathetically she explained to him that all mothers didn't die when their children were born and that he was one of the unlucky ones. His mother had been ill with something that was nothing to do with having a baby and that was why she had unfortunately died. From that moment on Mrs Marsh always looked upon Basil with tender eyes and he often looked to her to explain the unexplainable.

All the other children in the gang were about the same age as Doug, who was about nine months older than Basil, this meant they would all be a year ahead of him in school, which came as a bit of a shock. It was early September, Basil went into the street after breakfast, ready for a bit of play, only to see all the other members of his gang going off to school. Doug waved as he skipped down the road. Basil went to the steps in front of his home and sat, alone, Billy no mates.

For the remainder of that week he was sullen and brooding, life was not as enjoyable without his playmates, and this did not escape the attention of Gertrude who, in an effort to cheer him up, decided to treat him to a film show at the Empire cinema, which was housed within the Social Settlement building in Fore Street. It was his first visit to the cinema and 'Our Hospitality' starring Buster Keaton was showing. Basil loved it, he also loved the way the accompanying piano music changed his mood in line with the developing storyline. That was the time that Basil became infatuated with the cinema, an infatuation that would stay with him for all of his life.

A few weeks later they made their second outing to the Empire, this time to see a Roscoe 'Fatty' Arbuckle film, 'The Fast Freight'. Basil and Gertrude thoroughly enjoyed the movie and laughed all the way through, they were still laughing as they emerged into the grey overcast afternoon. A tram stood motionless at the top of Duke Street with an interested crowd gathered around it. Gertrude held Basil's little hand tightly as they crossed over the road to see what all the interest was about. Peeping between two workmen, who had just finished work for the day, she noticed the tram driver and the conductor on their knees in the road. They were wielding a long cane pole, the one that they used to move the arm on top of the tram to different electric cables, and were poking it repeatedly under the tram.

"Whatever are they doing?" Gertrude asked the two workers.

"They're tryin' to get 'er out missus."

"What do you mean, trying to get her out?"

"Young girl. Seems she was runnin' alongside of the tram when she fell and went underneath."

"Oh the poor little mite, is she badly hurt?"

"She's a gonner for sure missus, nasty mess and no mistake."

Turning her head Gertrude noticed, for the first time, the thin stream of blood that was creeping out from under the tram and snaking down the joins in the cobblestones towards Duke Street.

"What is it? What are they doing?" Basil's inquisitive mind knew there was something of interest going on and he wanted to know what it was.

"Never you mind," said Gertrude as she spun him away from the scene of the carnage "come along it is high time we went home for dinner." She cast a parting glance over her shoulder to see a policeman arriving on his bicycle and heard the shrill ringing of a bell in the distance heralding the imminent arrival of an ambulance. She gave a light tug on Basil's hand to encourage the reluctant boy before turning and hurrying away in the direction of home.

"What were they doing?" Basil was inquisitive and persistent.

"Oh the conductor's cap went under the tram and they were trying to get it out."

"Is that all." Basil's curiosity was assuaged and his interest faded instantly.

'It's a good thing he hadn't noticed that the conductor had been wearing his cap all the time' Gertrude thought to herself.

1925

With all his friends at school during the weekdays Basil had need of somebody else to befriend and spend his time with, and that somebody turned out to be the affable lodger, Belsey. Basil always referred to him affectionately as 'Big Belham' because to a four year old he seemed very tall, he also had a rather rotund physique where the muscular frame of youth had given way to middle aged spread, but he possessed a very gentle nature. His years on the barges had given him a barrel chest which had now fallen into his stomach and his broad shoulders held a large head with a mop of tightly curled grey hair and long whiskery sideburns. His eyes were rather small for his face, a bit pig like, and when he smiled they almost seemed to close above the round, ruddy cheeks. His voice boomed but he was a real gentle giant who could not have loved little Basil more if he had actually been his grandson.

Belsey worked as a cellar man in the 'White Elm Inn', a public house at the bottom of Cavendish Street, which meant, of course, that he worked mainly evenings and was free for most of the daytime. This fitted well and the two of them began to spend a considerable amount of time together, cutting a strange figure of opposites as they walked hand in hand. Belsey loved the way little Basil chatted to him all the time and happily ran little errands for him. One of those errands was a weekly visit to George Huddleston's' butcher shop on Fore Hamlet, between Albion Street and Wykes Bishop Street, almost opposite the bottom of Cavendish Street.

As part of his rent, Belsey used to look after the gardens both in front of, and to the rear of, Emily Jane's house. He didn't regard it as a chore because he had never had a garden before so planting flower and vegetable seeds in the springtime and seeing them poke their delicate shoots through the dark sandy soil gave him a feeling of immense satisfaction. To his surprise he discovered that he was rather good at gardening and consequently he really loved pottering around with plants, it came as a welcome break from the stuffy smoke laden atmosphere that enveloped him each night.

In the front garden he wanted to present a colourful display so he raised many species of bright, sweet scented flowers, which made the house look attractive, in fact people often used to complement him as they walked by. The rear garden was totally different, in order to help make ends meet he planted different kinds of fruit and vegetables destined for the table. He laid the plants out in neat rows and constructed a rough path running up the centre of the plot using stones, unearthed whilst digging the ground over, in order to reduce the mud on wet days. This is where Basil's errand came in. The path needed an edging and it had to be free, so Belsey had negotiated with George Huddleston to have all the empty corned beef tins.

To Basil it was one of the highlights of the week and he would go skipping off down Cavendish Street to the butcher. There were always rabbits hanging outside the shop, sometimes alongside a few scrawny looking chickens or even pheasants, when Huddleston could get his hands on them. Basil stood a while and gazed up at their bloodstained snouts and pulled faces at them, sometimes he pretended he had a shotgun and lined them up in his imaginary sights before blasting them. George Huddleston was one of the true old fashioned shop owners, standing behind the glass fronted counter resplendent in a starched white coat with a blue and white striped apron that came down to just above his ankles, a black bowler hat and white shirt with a neat bow tie. His face was permanently flushed and his rounded red cheeks perched on top of a neatly trimmed moustache reminded Basil of two balloons. Always cheerful and with a broad smile eternally on his face he loved children and young Basil, being a regular visitor to the shop, was well known and liked. Huddleston knew as soon as Basil walked into the shop that he was either there for some small item for Emily Jane but more often than not he was after the empty corned beef tins and his trademark smile was there to greet the young man.

"I'll get your tins presently young master Basil." He said as he wrapped some pork sausages in brown greased paper for a customer.

"That's all right sir, I don't mind waiting." Emily Jane had always impressed on Basil to be polite at all times.

The statement that he didn't mind waiting was no exaggeration either, Basil loved to watch as Huddleston cut joints of meat or sliced bacon and ham. He was awe struck by the big meat cleavers, as they were wheeled in the air to come slamming down through the carcasses on the thick wooden table, and he was mesmerised by the slicing machine. He watched excitedly as the butcher put the side of bacon or ham on the machine, pushed down the bar with the big teeth to hold the meat steady and turned the big red wheel with the circular cutting blade. The tray holding the meat moved backwards and forwards, each time it went forward a thin slice of bacon or ham peeled off and flopped onto a piece of greased paper that the butcher held just below the spinning blade. It all seemed like magic. Basil liked it best of all when the butcher was busy making his sausages. The pieces of pork were put into a hopper on top of the sausage making machine, the handle was turned and sausage meat squirted into a tube, which was actually the pig's intestine, which was held on the end of the machine, to make a long tube of sausage. The butcher's hands regularly nipped the tube and spun it around revealing, as if by magic, a string of sausages which he proceeded to hang on a hook at the back of the shop.

Eventually, when Huddleston had finished serving any customers that had preceded Basil, he disappeared out the back and returned with half a dozen empty corned beef tins. The corned beef was delivered to the shop in tapered tins, each of which contained seven pounds of meat. Huddleston removed the larger of the two ends and shook the meat out into his display cabinet. When a customer requested sliced corned beef he took the lump and placed it onto the slicing machine and cut the required number of slices, in the same way he did for the bacon or ham. It was quite normal for him to use six or seven tins in a week because it was a relatively economical meat at only four pence for a pound.

With his gathered hoard of empty tins Basil hopped and skipped back to number 251 and watched as Belsey removed the small end and washed the tins before assembling them, small end inserted into big end, into a length of metal edging which he then placed in the earth to form the side of the path.

Besides gardening Belsey enjoyed walking and loved nothing better than to take young Basil with him. The feel of Basil's small, innocent hand clasped in his made him feel as if he were a granddad proudly taking his grandson out for some exercise, in fact, to him, that was just what it was.

In his younger days, Belsey had worked on the sail barges which regularly plied their way between Ipswich, Harwich and the port of London and, although he entered into a few light relationships, he had never succumbed to the urge to settle down and marry. There had been one girl who had stolen his heart, many years ago. Amy Gooderham was her name, a sweet young girl with sparkling eyes, a flashing smile, unbounded energy and big plans for her future. She worked in an alehouse in London, one that Belsey used to frequent when he was staying in the city between unloading the hay, straw or timber they had brought in on the heavily laden barge and loading the return cargo the following morning. Belsey and Amy were very attracted to each other, although perhaps, as it turned out, the attraction was more in his eyes than in Amy's. Each occasion that he arrived in London they would meet, if she was working it would be over the bar counter, while on the rare occasions that she was not working they would either go for long walks or spend the evening talking over a beer or two in another local tavern.

Belsey eventually broached the subject of marriage but that seemed to frighten Amy, she had big plans for her future, plans that didn't include settling down and certainly precluded marriage. He was, it seemed, just a convenient distraction to her. The next time he sailed into the port of London Amy had disappeared and he never saw her again. His big tender heart was shattered. He vowed he would never allow himself to be drawn into another relationship, he would walk away rather than risk another deep involvement. Now in his sixties he was alone, without a family, except for Emily Jane, her girls and his adopted grandson Basil, he regarded them as his family but the feeling was not reciprocated, to them, with the exception of Basil, he was simply the friendly lodger.

******

In Ipswich every Tuesday was livestock market day, held at the Spurling and Hempson sale yard situated at the junction of Princes Street and Cecilia Street, just round the corner from Basil's family home in James Street. Belsey loved to see the animals and explained to young Basil how busy and exciting market day was. Basil was enthusiastic to join him and so Belsey asked Emily Jane if he could take the young man to experience it all at first hand, she readily agreed, and the two of them made it a regular excursion. Together they watched as the cattle, pigs and sheep were unloaded from horse drawn carts, or the very occasional motor lorry, and herded into the waiting pens. When the auction was about to start Belsey hurried Basil into the saleroom, making for the benches high up at the back, away from the bidders, and there Basil sat and stared in awe as the animals were led into the small steel fenced ring and paraded in circles to show off their condition for the buyers to scrutinise.

The auctioneer gabbled away in what seemed to Basil to be a foreign language until, with a start, he heard the sharp crack of the gavel and the purchase was concluded. Once sold the animals were ushered out toward the holding pens via a special gate that trapped their neck and held them secure while one of the stockmen punched a hole in their ear with a big, vicious looking machine. An identity tag was clipped into the hole, to register the purchaser's identity, before the animal was released to be herded to the relevant holding pen. Each time the stockman cleared the punch Basil eyed the small round pieces of ear as they fell to the ground, with desire in his heart, and when the time came for the two of them to leave Basil rushed down the steps to where the stockman stood and collected as many ear pieces as he could find, stuffed them in his trouser pockets and walked off grinning from ear to ear.

After the sale was completed they spent half an hour watching as the purchasers loaded their newly acquired livestock into carts and transported them away, Basil all the time fiddling excitedly with the ear plugs in his pocket. Most of the young animals went to farms where they could be fattened up ready to return to the market at a later date but almost all of the older livestock was carted away by butchers, one or two local butchers herded their purchases up Princes street bound for their premises, ready to slaughter them behind their shops and have them on the slab, ready for sale, or in cold storage before the next morning.

Arriving back at number 251, after a tiring but exciting and rewarding day, Basil thrust his hand into his trouser pocket and produced a handful of his trophies which he proudly displayed to Emily Jane.

"My goodness, what are those?" questioned Emily Jane.

"Them is the bits they punch out of the ears of the pigs and cows Nan."

"What!" Emily was horrified. "Take them away you nasty scallywag." She scolded.

Basil ran up to his bedroom and placed the fleshy disks carefully in his little cardboard box of treasures.

******

One such excursion to the livestock market turned into a rather uncomfortable and potentially dangerous visit. While the animals were being unloaded Basil felt a pain in his tummy but said nothing to Belsey, he didn't want to miss the spectacle. The pain grew steadily worse until finally Basil knew he had to go to the toilet, but there were no toilets so still he said nothing, hoping the pains would go away. Eventually nature took its course and Basil evacuated his bowels into his trousers. Sheepishly he looked up at Belsey as the thick brown mass slid slowly down his legs to mingle with the mess that the animals had deposited. Belsey soon noticed the problem and smiled down.

"Don't you worry little man," he whispered reassuringly, "we can sort you out. You come with me."

With that he took Basil's little hand in his and together they walked across Princes Street into Market Road, Friars Bridge Road and Portman's Walk until they reached Alderman Road recreation ground, at the northern end of which was a canal that fed off the river Gipping. Belsey made straight for the canal, and when they got there he gently pulled off Basil's short trousers and underpants together with his shoes and socks and stood him in the water at the edge of the canal. He then proceeded to wash his trousers, along with his legs and bottom, using handfuls of grass that he ripped from the bank and doused into the canal.

"Hey! What are you doing with that child?" It was an elderly man in a long black coat, wearing a bowler hat and brandishing a walking cane. "Stop him, stop him, he is trying to drown that small boy!" the elderly man hurried over and struck Belsey a hefty whack across the back with his cane. Fortunately for Belsey, being a strong man, the strike didn't hurt him unduly and fortunately for the old man Belsey's placid nature prevented him retaliating.

The furore was fuelled by two or three people who had been strolling in the sunshine and who now rushed to encircle the hapless Belsey. He protested his innocence but the gathering group would not listen. Two men held him down while a middle aged woman in a flowing cream and brown dress swept Basil into her arms. Belsey thought about fighting the crowd off but realised that there were too many of them and to do so would make him look even more guilty.

"The poor lad is so frightened he has messed himself." Announced the woman who held Basil, seemingly oblivious to the fact that the mess was rubbing off onto the sleeve of her cream bodice.

"Don't worry, just hold him, somebody has already gone for a constable." Put in another.

Belsey tried in vain to get the throng to listen to him but eventually gave up not wishing to antagonise the crowd for fear that things might turn even more nasty and knowing that he could easily explain to the constable what had happened. Then out of the group holding him came a clenched fist that smashed into his nose, luckily not hard enough to make it bleed.

"Take that you fiend." Snarled the face at the other end of the fist. Belsey railed against him.

"Stop that. There is no need for violence." It was the elderly man who had started the ruckus. Basil was crying loudly in the woman's arms, everybody assumed that he was crying because of the fate that had almost befallen him whereas in truth he was crying because of the way his big friend was being treated. Turning, the elderly man spied a constable striding, with an air of authority, across the grass.

"Here comes the constable now, he will take over."

And take over he did. He told the crowd to disperse; he would deal with the situation now. He glanced at Basil's brown smeared legs, thought about his smart uniform, and asked the middle aged lady to keep hold of the boy. The crowd dispersed still muttering about how disgusting it was that somebody should try to drown a little boy in broad daylight. Belsey and Basil, still crying in the woman's arms, were marched to the police station under the Town Hall where a statement was taken from Belsey while Basil was being cleaned up in the toilets by the middle aged woman and one of the female clerks. For Belsey it was a traumatic and worrying episode but to Basil, once he had stopped crying, it was all a very exciting adventure. He had been the centre of attraction at the recreation ground, he had been cradled to the police station where he was pampered by two women and to top it all he was taken home in a police motor car because he was exhausted, and a policeman wanted to confirm with Emily Jane that Belsey was indeed permitted to be out with him. Basil slept like a log that night.

******

Basil saw very little of his grandparents while he was living at 251 Cavendish Street. Charles was struggling to look after his family without Mary, although he did have the help of his youngest daughter Nellie, and despite the fact they lived almost opposite each other, Basil saw precious little of George and Lydia Cotton. Lydia was hard at work looking after the house and the business affairs in addition to caring for nine year old Leonard, while George spent his days shovelling coal and his evenings shovelling beer. If he happened to meet Basil on his way home he would, as often as not, produce an apple for the boy, pat him on the head and continue on his way. When he did speak to Basil he always called him 'Beaver' although Basil had absolutely no idea why.

Likewise Basil very rarely saw his brother Leonard.

There were two people that he did see regularly though, one was his aunt Gertrude and the other was his father Chip who endeavoured to see his boys at least every other weekend. His first call was to Leonard to see how he was getting along at school; he spent the morning with him and stayed to dinner with George and Lydia, making suitable excuses as to why he couldn't accompany George to the White Elm. Chip always offered money to Lydia for Leonard's keep, although not until George had departed for the hostelry for fear that it would only sponsor another pint or two of beer.

Lydia refused every time. He then made the short walk to number 251 to see his youngest son.

Basil was always overjoyed to see his father and he told him in great detail everything he had done since the last visit. Chip invariably stayed until Basil's bedtime, he carried him up the stairs and tucked him in for the night, gave him a kiss and retreated sadly downstairs to say his farewells to Emily Jane and the family. The trudge home back to James Street was the saddest walk of Chip's week, his gait was laboured and slow, he found leaving his boys behind very difficult. He really loved seeing them but parting was so painful for him and he always had the embryo of a tear as he left Basil, he longed for the day to dawn when he could reunite his family, he would do anything to make it happen.

Sunday dinner was something for Basil to look forward to because it was the day aunt Sarah came to dinner. Sarah was the elder sister to both Lydia and Emily Jane and she lived alone in nearby Duke Street. Her small and dark Victorian house reflected her lifestyle, its furnishings were very spartan, the scullery sported simply an old gas cooker, a deep earthenware sink and a single cupboard which clung to the damp, flaking wall. A small pantry was tucked under the stairs, its bare shelves testament to her hermit like existence whilst the living room contained a small wooden table with two wooden chairs that squeaked and creaked when sat on, tucked neatly underneath. In front of the fire was her only concession to comfort, her chair, a rocker with two soft cushions. Upstairs her bedroom was similarly furnished with only the basic necessities. It contained a feather bed, a half empty wardrobe and a scratched dressing table in front of the window, with a water set and the obligatory under watered aspidistra that prevented the daylight from brightening the dark paintwork.

Basil had only visited her house on one occasion and he disliked its dark, damp and dismal feel. He did, however, like aunt Sarah very much, she always had a mildly cheerful air that never quite broke into happiness but she always made a great fuss of her 'little soldier' and usually brought him some sweets, tucked deep inside the large black handbag that was permanently welded to her arm.

As dinnertime approached and the expected time of her arrival drew near Basil went to the front door and stood on the top step staring down the hill waiting to catch the first glimpse of her. She was easy for him to identify because she always dressed in the same clothes, a long black skirt that almost touched the ground, a spotlessly white blouse heavy with frilly lace, a black bolero top and an enormous black hat held on with a big hatpin that had a large glass sphere on the end. She always told him it was her diamond. In cooler weather her ensemble was complemented with a heavy serge coat.

The moment he spied her he ran indoors to tell Emily Jane she was coming before running down the road to meet her. As they walked back to the house he looked in fascination at the hem of her skirt, mesmerised by the way her highly polished shoes poked out with each step before disappearing beneath the curtain again.

Once they had completed their greetings Emily Jane usually gave Basil some money and dispatched him to Murrill's shop, further down Cavendish Street, for two bottles of stout, one for her and one for Sarah to have with their dinner. It was the only time Basil could ever remember seeing either of them drink alcohol.

Most weeks they had a joint of beef which Belsey carved at the table. The vegetables, yorkshire puddings, roast potatoes and gravy were brought to the table by Doris and Gladys and everybody settled down to eat. The table was a bit cramped for space, after all there were usually eight of them, and there was the odd elbow clash, but Basil and Leslie enjoyed listening to the ladies banter whilst Belsey ate in stoic silence.

******

September 1925 changed Basil's life again, but this time it brought him into line with all his friends. He started his school career. Fortunately he didn't have far to go because the school was only at the bottom end of Cavendish Street. As he walked through the entrance gate he was awed by the imposing red brick building that he had passed by so often on his way to Huddleston's butcher shop. He had never really noticed it before but now its high gables and pointed windows gave it a church like presence. Outside there was a small tar macadam play area and in one corner a rather smelly toilet consisting of just one small cubicle, shared by all the pupils, boys and girls alike. It boasted a rough wooden door that stopped a full twelve inches from the floor, a wooden seat and high above the pan was a cistern with a length of chain to pull the flush. Beside the cubicle was a trough, just long enough for two boys to stand side by side as they peed, it was formed using a half drainpipe set into the floor and was, bordered by a brick wall, rendered in black painted cement for half its height. Basil was not impressed.

On his very first morning Emily Jane walked him to the school and made sure that his name was on the register before telling him to be good, work hard and learn. As she turned and left the teacher directed him to an empty seat in the second row and Basil slid in beside a rather scruffy boy of the same age.

That first day was a bit unfamiliar and daunting for all of the new standard one pupils, as they attempted to come to terms with their new routine. The teacher, Miss Edwards, opened a big register and looked over her half glasses at the motley group of urchins in front of her. Scanning their faces she addressed nobody in particular.

"When I call out your name from the register," she paused for effect and scanned the class, "I want you to say 'Present Miss', that means that you are here." Straightening up she allowed time for her instruction to sink in. She drew in a breath preparing to announce the first name on the list when William Carter butted in.

"What do we say if we are not here missus?" he smiled smugly, his elder brother had told him to say that to impress the other pupils and to cement his place as the class clown.

"Firstly, when you wish to speak you will put your hand in the air and wait for me to give you permission." Miss Edwards spoke slowly and clearly, obviously not impressed by Carter's outburst. Again she slowly scanned the array of scruffy youthful faces as reinforcement. "Secondly you will always address me as Ma'am. And thirdly you will refrain from silly comments. Is that understood?" The last three words were expressed with emphasis. William smiled and nodded slowly. "All of you; is that understood." A resounding chorus of 'Yes Ma'am' reassured her.

Turning back to the register she called out all the names in alphabetical order. First was Frederick Abbott who lifted his head from the rough worn desk, where he had been studying the initials carved into the top, and stared back with a confused smile on his face.

"Present ma'am." He whispered, eliciting a smile of satisfaction from Miss Edwards.

After registration was completed the classes filed into the assembly hall, youngest to the front, seniors behind with the teachers lining the sides of the hall to keep the pupils in check. Basil anxiously looked around him searching for a familiar face. He didn't have to look far before he saw the smiling face of Doug Marsh peeping between a pair of shoulders a few rows behind him.

"Hello Doug." Doug put his finger to his lips in a sign to be silent.

"No talking in assembly Basil Double." Miss Edwards chided. Basil turned to the front just as the head teacher strode onto the low stage. Quickly he guided the gathered assembly through two hymns, a reading from the bible and two or three instantly forgettable notices before turning on his heel. As he left the stage he called 'dismiss' over his shoulder and was gone.

Seated back in their classroom the youngsters were immediately plunged into reading lessons. That was not quite so daunting for Basil as it was for most of the others thanks to his grounding with Leslie Bushen which had put him far in advance.

At morning play time Basil and Doug searched for each other and soon renewed their friendship. Now that Basil was old enough to go to school Doug didn't mind being seen with him, he explained, but it was bad form for a schoolboy to be seen playing with a baby. Basil said he quite understood, but he didn't really.

Within two weeks Basil was home again for a long spell as first chicken pox and then an abscess on his ankle restricted him to bed for six weeks. During that time he kept up his reading. Two weeks school followed by six weeks off, 'if this is how it's going to be,' he thought, 'I'm really going to enjoy school'.

******

Christmas Day 1925 was a very happy day for Basil, partly because his father came to spend the whole day with the family at number 251, but what made him even happier was the present that Chip had made for him. A sledge. Basil ran eagerly to the window but was disappointed to see that there was no snow outside.

"There's bound to be some soon son," said Chip, "and when it comes you will have the newest and best sledge in the street."

Basil smiled, stood the sledge in the corner of the room and turned to the wooden model car. He lay on the floor and played happily.

Around two o'clock in the afternoon Emily Jane announced that the Christmas dinner was almost ready and everybody jumped up eager to help, Chip brought a large baking tin that held two well browned chickens, he turned back toward the kitchen.

"You get on with carving Charles," Emily Jane never used his nick name, "the girls and I will bring the rest through."

Belsey, feeling a little put out that his prestigious position of meat carver had been usurped, carried in a large, willow patterned bowl overflowing with steaming roast potatoes. Other bowls containing sprouts, carrots, parsnips and peas followed, with Doris bringing up the rear carrying a large jug of thick juicy gravy. They were eleven for dinner that Christmas: Emily Jane, Chip, Belsey, Doris, Gladys, Emily, aunt Sarah, Leonard, Basil, Leslie and two year old Marjorie. Belsey and Chip had previously made a temporary table for the youngsters using a couple of planks of wood and a trestle seat from another plank because there was not enough room for them at the table, in fact even with just the adults it was somewhat of a squeeze. This only added to the excitement for the youngsters. Basil and Leonard sat one each end with Marjorie in the middle so they could help by cutting up her food for her so she could eat it easily with a spoon, even so, quite a bit of her lunch found its way down her smock dress.

Emily Jane proudly announced that all of the vegetables had been grown in their own back garden by Belsey, ably assisted by Basil of course, and that the two chickens were from her own flock, they had stopped laying so it was a case of 'waste not'. Everybody tucked in heartily and when they had finished Belsey leant back in his chair and patted his stomach, with an air of satisfaction and a thinly disguised belch.

"That was a grand meal Mrs Dumble." He pronounced, he never used Emily Jane's christian name and she always addressed him as Belsey.

"You're not done yet Belsey," she said with a gratified smile, "we still have the pudding to come." With that Emily Jane rose from the table, smoothed her long white apron, which protected her full length black skirt, and headed for the scullery.

"Girls!" she called as she passed through the doorway.

Doris and Gladys jumped up immediately and collected the dishes while Basil and Leonard rose to follow behind with the empty vegetable bowls and everything was stacked beside the sink in the scullery. Basil watched, full of interest, as Emily Jane took a pot out of a saucepan of boiling water. Curiously it was covered with a piece of cloth held on with string. Emily Jane cut the string and removed the cloth to reveal a steaming Christmas pudding. Quickly she turned it upside down on a plate, stuck a sprig of holly in the top and paraded it into the parlour to the accompaniment of applause from the children and expectant smiles from the adults.

That evening the adults played charades, which Basil found rather boring, instead he looked out of the window, still no snow. He was allowed to stay up until nine o'clock that night and, although he protested, secretly he was pleased to finally crawl into his nice soft bed, feeling the coldness of the cotton sheets welcoming him to dreamland. He fell asleep instantly.

1926

Basil didn't have to wait too long for the arrival of the snow; it came with a vengeance on the first of January and heralded the coldest winter for many years, much to his delight. Unable to contain himself he donned his scarf and woollen gloves, both knitted for him by Gladys as a Christmas present, and made a beeline for Doug's house trailing his new sledge behind him on a length of rope.

The two of them were the envy of the street because, while the other kids had to make do with a sheet of wood, or in some cases a piece of scrap metal, as a make shift sledge, Basil and Doug were able to fly down the street in style on his new wooden sledge with metal runners. Some of the other boys thought the hill too steep for them and as their bravado disappeared they melted away. Finally there were only two brave souls besides Basil and Doug.

Albert Copping was the same age as Doug, a happy go lucky boy with a thick mop of jet black hair and chicken pox scars on his face. His father was a very hard man who was out of work most of the time, only managing to pick up a day here and a day there doing manual work on the docks. He believed in total obedience and reinforced this doctrine by taking his belt to his offspring, most often when he came home drunk from the local public house having spent his meagre pickings for the day on beer and incurring the wrath of his wife. For her part, she took in washing in order to scrape together a few shillings to feed the family, but her hard work did not prevent her from feeling the sharp end of the belt too. Being the youngest of eight boys all of Albert's clothes were hand me downs, with more patches on them than there was original material, but despite the mended clothes and the boots with the toes kicked out he remained cheerful and it was this quality that made him immensely popular with the other boys.

William Barwell made up the gang of four. Slight and underfed he was a sickly child, always unwell, but always determined to prove himself equal to the others. His clothes were only fractionally better than Albert's but, perhaps because of his delicate health, he was the apple of his parent's eye.

After an hour spent careering down one hundred yards of fast, sweeping snow, using the kerb to help steer, they became rather bored and the intrepid quartet found themselves looking for something more challenging, something more exciting.

"I know, why don't we go down Devonshire Hill?" suggested Doug. He looked at Basil who returned a wide grin.

"Yeah! That sounds great." said Albert gesturing enthusiastically for William to follow them. William was none too sure but didn't dare say anything negative so he nodded in agreement and they all ran off toward the steepest hill in the area. They stopped at the bottom and looked up the daunting slope.

"It doesn't half look steep." Said William, who was feeling somewhat nervous at the prospect of riding this incline.

"Nonsense," piped in Doug, "we come down on our carts don't we? This is no different. We just need to make sure we steer up the alley, that's all."

Irrespective of the safety angle, which did not enter the head of any one of them, the ride certainly was in need of a bit of modification to make it work, that was obvious, even to this intrepid, fearless band. Leaving their sledges they banked up the snow on the far side of the street so that as they shot out from the bottom of Devonshire Road they would be channelled up the alleyway opposite, the one that ran beside Goss's orchard.

"Perfect." Said Albert as he made for the hill. He had to use the safety rail which edged the pavement, to haul himself to the top, dragging his makeshift sledge slowly behind him by the string that he had wound round his waist. Proudly he stood atop the hill and looked down the icy slope.

"Here I come." He shouted, and was just about to launch himself down the piste when Basil noticed that a horse drawn cart laden with coal sacks was coming gingerly down Cavendish Street.

"Not yet," he shouted back, "there's a cart coming." Albert just stopped himself in time. The cart passed, the coal man casting a grimy grin to the boys.

"OK, all clear." Yelled Basil and Albert dug the heels of his boots into the soft snow and pushed. He gathered speed really quickly and careered down the hill, across Cavendish Street and disappeared up the alleyway in the blink of an eye. All the other three heard was a loud crash as he reached the end of the alleyway, followed by a painful groan.

The three spectators charged up the alleyway in the direction of Albert's groans and found him in a heap up against the end fence.

"I think we need something to stop us," observed Doug, "let's build a snow barrier."

A chorus of 'yeah's' convinced him to run off to search for his father's shovel from the shed and in no time at all there was a large, soft snow barrier at the end of the alley to arrest their speed and cushion their arrival.

Doug was determined to be the first to try out the snow cushion, grabbing the rope attached to Basil's new sledge and climbing the hill. Pushing off from the top he hurtled down the hill, shot across Cavendish Street, careered up the alleyway and ploughed feet first into the snow bank. He picked himself up, laughing loudly, and made his way to the bottom of the hill to act as flag boy for Albert, who was to be the next rider. When Albert was ready to go Doug waved his arms vigorously to signal that all was clear and Albert pushed off, whizzed down the slope and crunched into the snow wall. Retrieving his sheet of wood he took up the flag boy post as Basil and William made the exhausting trek to the summit, Basil with his sledge and William with his length of timber. Basil jumped eagerly onto the sledge and looked down the daunting piste. Albert waved furiously, shouting for Basil to hurry up and get going, while William was a reluctant last to shoot the hill but he surprised himself by enjoying it enormously.

The job of flag boy was not an arduous task as, during the whole afternoon that they were shooting the hill, the total traffic movement was only one horse and cart, four bicycles and three handcarts.

Time raced by and all too soon it was time for the exhausted boys to go home for their tea. Basil was shattered and happily allowed Doug to drag his sledge up the street for him. It was only when Albert asked William if he had enjoyed himself, despite his fear, and there was no answer that the boys realised William was no longer with them. They scanned every direction but he was nowhere to be seen.

"Where's William? Where's he gone?" Basil and Doug looked at each other and shrugged. The three stood looking back towards the bottom of the hill, William was nowhere to be seen, in fact all they could see was Prices bread cart struggling up

Cavendish Street. The plodding horse was tired from a long day struggling in the snow and the driver, head down against the cold wind that had sprung up, trudged beside the cart.

Just as the cart was crossing the bottom of Devonshire hill an anguished scream hit the air and William, astride his makeshift sledge, emerged and careened into Cavendish Street. Too late the driver saw the helpless boy, but in truth there was nothing he could have done had he seen him earlier, William shot underneath the cart narrowly missing the hind legs of the startled horse, hit the inside of the front wheel which spun him around beneath the cart, and the large rear wheel ran over both legs, shattering them.

William's screams filled the air. The boys were paralysed with disbelief and watched, open mouthed, as the shocked driver dragged him from beneath the vehicle. Basil, regaining his composure, ran to number 251 and shouted for Emily Jane to help. The tone of Basil's voice alerted her to the fact something was seriously wrong and in moments she came hurrying into the road. The driver lifted William carefully from the wet, crimson stained snow and was ushered into the parlour where he laid the crumpled boy on the floor in front of the fire to keep him warm. As William lay crying and moaning at the same time Emily Jane administered to him as best she could until the ambulance and a police constable arrived and he was transported to the hospital.

Sadly William's legs were so badly broken that it was impossible for them to heal correctly and he had to spend a lengthy time in hospital before learning to walk again. He carried a pronounced limp for the rest of his life, as his reminder of a moment of recklessness. He wanted to prove that he was as brave as the others and had made one last run, without the flag boy.

The episode failed to daunt the bravery of the other three, however, and they were all out with sledges the next day and almost every day until the snow finally turned into wet brown slush and eventually disappeared completely.

******

It was the week after Easter when Basil was told that he was to go to see his elder brother and the Cotton family at 120 Cavendish Street after dinner on Sunday, what's more he was going to stay for tea. This took him somewhat by surprise because it would be the first time he could recollect even having been inside the house, although he supposed he must have been there when he was a baby. Emily Jane saw the question on his face.

"Your brother Leonard has a surprise for you. You'll enjoy it."

A nervous smile cut across Basil's face, his grandfather George was a big muscular man with a deep, loud voice which always made him appear rather frightening, but Grandma Lydia was a very gentle person. He was excited at the thought of seeing his brother again, the last time was Christmas, and he had a surprise, Basil liked surprises and wondered what on earth it could be. It was with a mixture of anticipation, eagerness and trepidation that he walked down to number 120 on that bright, sunny but cool Sunday, and knocked on the door. Nobody came, there was no answer, he knocked louder and heard footsteps within, heavy footsteps, 'it must be grandpa' he thought to himself. Sure enough the door swung open to reveal George. He looked a bit intimidating in his striped shirt with no collar, baggy grey trousers held up with a broad leather belt, the end of which hung down after the brass buckle. George looked down menacingly, he looked none too happy.

"Why on earth are you banging on the door Beaver? Next time come right round the back and walk straight in." His face broke into a smile as he bent down to usher the youngster in and Basil felt a little less alarmed, although he did catch a hefty whiff of alcohol on his grandfather's breath as he passed him. Leonard poked his face round the door to the back room, a big smile burst out at the sight of his little brother.

"Bass, you're here! C'mon in. Look what I've got."

Basil walked into the parlour to find many other family members present. There was grandma Lydia, aunt Gertrude, uncle Ernest with his fiancée Harriet and William with his wife Susannah. 'It must be a special occasion for a gathering like this' thought Basil.

"Well: what do you think?" Leonard was pointing toward the dining table and trying hard to hide his excitement.

Basil looked at the strange object that sat atop a box on the table. It was a square wooden box with a large tube sticking out the front and an even bigger tube pointing out the top. There were one or two brass attachments on the box but Basil didn't have the faintest idea what it could be.

"What is it?" Basil was beginning to lose interest.

"It's a magic lantern." Basil's interest was immediately rekindled. "We are going to have a magic lantern picture show."

Now that really did excite Basil, he moved to have a closer look at the strange object. The two boys put their heads together as Leonard explained the workings of his new contraption. The box held a mentholated spirit burner to provide the light and the large tube sticking out of the top was in fact a funnel to take the fumes away. The large tube sticking out of the front was the lens made up of a pair of glass prisms which could be adjusted by rotating the brass ferrule on the front to focus and make the image sharp.

Leonard couldn't wait to get things working so, while granddad George hung a white sheet from the picture rail, Leonard filled the little container with mentholated spirit and fixed the wick in place.

Everything was ready to go. William drew together the thick heavy brocade curtains and the room was instantly thrown into darkness. Leonard struck a match and lit the wick of the lamp which burned with a bright blue flame. Carefully he slid the lighted lamp into the box and immediately there was a white circle projected onto the sheet.

Leonard produced a brown cardboard box and, removing the lid, revealed a row of glass slides. Cautiously he removed the first one and slid it into the holder of the box. The white circle became a smudgy grey circle.

"I don't think much of that." Exclaimed Basil, everybody chuckled.

"I've got to focus it first." Leonard smiled, slowly rotating the brass ferrule on the front of the box until, as if by magic, the blur gained shape and form and transformed itself into a picture of a ship on the sea. Leonard moved a pair of small tags that were attached to the slide and amazed everybody as the ship appeared to rise and fall on the moving waves of the sea.

"It's just like the movies aunt Gerty takes me to!" exclaimed Basil, his eyes almost popping out of his head. Everybody laughed.

One by one Leonard went through the collection of slides, there were exotic animals such as elephants, tigers and giraffe that appeared to walk across plains or creep through jungles, there were also pictures of aeroplanes, trains and cars that flew, puffed and raced on the make shift screen.

The coup de grace was a painted picture of a warship that went into the machine together with a painting of another warship. Everybody was surprised when Leonard manipulated the slides so that one fired a shell at the other, there was an explosion and the target ship sank to leave only one warship on the water.

"Cor! How did you do that Lenny?" Basil enthused.

"Look, I'll show you how it's done." Leonard demonstrated to Basil how he had controlled three slides to give the desired effect.

All the slides having been shown Leonard began packing the magic lantern into its wooden case, leaving the burner out to cool, and placing it on the sideboard. Grandma Lydia and Gertrude brought sandwiches and cake through from the scullery and placed them on the table while George brought through a large pot of steaming tea. He poured a cup for everybody except himself and then retrieved a bottle of stout from the scullery, twisted the top off and took a swig. Grabbing himself a couple of sandwiches, he slumped into his favourite chair.

******

Each morning around eight thirty the milkman came along the street and, when he was not at school, Basil listened for the tell tale clip clop of the horse as it slowly worked its way up the street pulling a small wooden cart.

"Milko!" the milkman called loudly and the housewives emerged from their houses in response and formed a queue at the side of the cart, jug or pail in hand, taking the chance to exchange gossip as they waited their turn. The milkman's cart was a two wheeled wooden affair, similar to a trap. It had a single bench seat on the front and two steel churns full of milk held by two broad leather strops on the back. As each housewife approached in turn the milkman lifted the top off one of the churns and dipped a steel ladle into the rich, creamy white milk which he carefully poured into their container. Basil liked to go out with Emily Jane to get the milk, although his interest was more with the horse something he no doubt inherited from Chip. He stroked the snout of the blinkered nag and, feeling in his pocket for one of Belsey's carrots, which he had purloined from the scullery, he fed it to the horse as a treat. He then continued to pet the horse until it was Emily Jane's turn to be served. To keep the milk cool and preserve it for as long as possible she always decanted it into a large brown earthenware jug with thick sides and a wooden lid, which she stored on a large stone in her pantry.

Basil was always keen to be near horses. Aside from the milkman there were a number of other tradesmen who regularly appeared in Cavendish Street with horse drawn carts, namely the coalman, the animal feed man and most children's favourite the 'Hokey Pokey Man'. The 'Hokey Pokey man' was the children's name for the ice cream seller a bright and cheerful man who came up the street every Sunday afternoon with his gaily painted cart drawn by a beautiful brown and white pony. It was a four wheeled cart that had twisted wooden posts at each corner supporting a scallop edged canopy. Painted mainly yellow it sported red and gold motifs of leaves, flowers, scrolls and shells over all of the surfaces. At the forward end, just ahead of two churns of ice cream that stood in a bed of ice to keep them cool, there was a small glass cabinet holding the wafers, boats and cornets. Basil's favourite was a half penny boat. He would hold it flat on his hand and lick the cool flavoured ice cream until it had all gone before munching the wafer.

******

Emily Jane kept chickens in a run at the top of the garden predominantly for the eggs but once a hen stopped laying it was destined for the pot. They were fed on a boiled up concoction of all the kitchen scraps, potato peel and the like, together with some of the waste from Belsey's vegetable garden, all mixed with discarded egg shells and a couple of handfuls of some proper corn feed. Emily Jane bought her feed in bulk from Barnard Brothers, who had a shop on the corner of Grimwade Street and Church Street, and it was delivered in two large heavy sacks. This gave Basil another opportunity to befriend a horse, an opportunity that he was not slow to take advantage of. The driver arrived outside and dropped the reins before jumping down and pulling one of the half hundredweight bags onto his shoulder. The horse remained stationary and swung his heavy head to and fro, he never once tried to wander off. Basil was ready by the gate and opened it for the driver before running to the horse and stroking his snout. The horse pushed against Basil's hand in a gesture of satisfaction and it was impossible to tell who was enjoying the contact most, Basil or the horse. The driver returned to heave the second sack off the wagon and carry it into the back garden where he deposited it in the small storage shed alongside the first sack. Returning to his wagon he turned to Basil and flashed a broad smile at him. Basil was expectant for what had recently become a regular treat.

"Wanna ride son?"

"Yes please sir." A wide smile lighting up the young face.

"You can drive him this time if you like."

"Wow, really!"

Eagerly Basil climbed up the front wheel and deposited himself beside the driver. The driver passed over the reins and showed Basil the correct way to hold them.

"Now all you have to do is shake the reins so that they touch his hind quarters and tell him

'Hup' and we are away." The driver knew that the horse was so familiar with the route that he could have completed the round without any interference or guidance from anybody so, despite what he thought, Basil was not really driving the horse at all.

Holding the reins tightly he shook them and encouraged the horse forward with a couple of 'Hup's' thrown in for good measure. Slowly the horse plodded up the hill until they reached Alan Road and the driver told Basil to pull on the reins and call 'Stop'. Reluctantly Basil handed the reins back and, with a broad grin stretching from ear to ear, he jumped down to the pavement and watched as the wagon moved off along Upper Cavendish Street. It was only when they were out of sight that he turned and walked proudly and contentedly back home. He was the only boy who ever got to ride on that wagon and it made him the envy of all the kids in the street.

******

On school holidays Basil often returned to James Street, to spend a bit of time with the Double side of his family. He stayed with his father at aunt Nellie's and during the daytime amused himself playing with her three sons, William who was now eight, Douglas six and the youngest Cyril aged four, always known as 'shrimp' because of his small stature. During the day the boys frequently visited the tram sheds in Constantine Road and played on the trams that were not in use, nobody seemed to mind. They took turns standing in the driver's area and pretended to be the driver for a while, ringing the bell and making all of the appropriate noises they associated with the trams. They also took turns at being the conductor, giving out imaginary tickets to imaginary passengers and ringing the bell to tell the driver he needed to stop because somebody wanted to get off or that everybody was on board and it was safe to proceed.

Far from being concerned, the engineers seemed to welcome the boys company, they answered all of the questions that were fired at them, talked about what jobs they were doing, even showed them how the trams worked and let them watch as they worked on them. At that time engineering was experiencing an explosion with exciting and rapid progress being made in so many fields and the boys soaked up as much information as they could. One thing Basil loved to do, before they made their way home, was to collect as many used tickets as possible from the on board bins and join them together to form a concertina which he would take home to show to his father.

It was always a sad time when the school holidays came to an end and Basil could no longer play with William, Douglas and Cyril, he returned to the familiar friends in Cavendish Street and his 'other life'.

******

It wasn't far from Cavendish Street to the Empire cinema, located in the Social Settlement building at the junction of Fore Street and Duke Street, and now that Basil was growing up he was sometimes allowed to go there without an adult accompanying him. The Social Settlement was split into two halves, one of which was used by the local men who were either too old to work or couldn't find work. Very often, on a Saturday evening, there would be magic lantern shows, similar to the show Leonard had put on for them earlier in the year, or talks by local dignitaries and scholars. Every Sunday there would be morning and evening religious services. Other times the men of the area congregated to play billiards, sit at rough tables playing cards or just sit and talk to each other. Basil and his best friend Doug liked to climb the stairs to the balcony and count how many bald heads they could see.

The other half of the building was used as the Empire cinema. Every Saturday afternoon there was a show specifically for children that became known as the 'tuppenny rush'. As the name suggests it cost two pence, or 'tuppence', entry if you sat downstairs and four pence if you wanted to sit upstairs. The programme always comprised a news section, one or two short films and a serial. The serial was always shown last and was used as an encouragement for the kids to return the following week to see what happened next in the story. Most times the serial ended with the hero in, what appeared to be, a situation that would be impossible to escape from, but mysteriously the following week, when the serial started, the situation would be far less serious and the hero escaped easily. The makers obviously used the suspense to lure the youngsters back for the following week and relied on their memories not being too sharp.

Basil and Doug went along each week, accompanied by half a dozen of their Cavendish Street pals, including the intrepid sledging pair Albert and William. They took it in turns to purchase a four penny ticket while everybody else bought a tuppeny one. In a huddle they would put the four penny ticket on the top of the pile and all troop upstairs, handing the stack of tickets to trick the attendant into believing they were all four penny ones. Most of the time they got away with the rouse and all sat together watching the programme from the balcony and throwing the odd screwed up paper ball down into the plebs below. On the rare occasions that they were rumbled one of their number was forced to watch the programme from the balcony on his own while his comrades were ushered downstairs where they belonged.

As the kids filed into the auditorium they would rush to the front hell bent on grabbing a seat as near to the screen as possible because it was common knowledge the nearer you sat to the screen the better your view of the programme. When the show was about to start the lights gradually dimmed and all the audience cheered excitedly but the operator raised the lights again and the audience booed for all they were worth. Usually the operator lowered and raised the lights three or four times in order to build up the excitement for the audience before the programme started.

After the show there was always an excited babble as the kids left the cinema, each saying what he or she thought would be the next twist to the serial.

1927

It was in early March when Gertrude decided to take Basil to the Hippodrome to see the world famous 'Willy Pantzer's Midgets' perform. Holding her hand firmly and turning his head to smile up at her, a smile that instantly made her think of her dear Albert, they made their way through Salthouse Street, Star Lane, Turret Lane and Rose Lane to St Peters Street and the impressive, ornate building. Basil looked up at the gilded sign in awe as Gertrude guided him to the stalls entrance to the left of the main doors.

They both enjoyed the show immensely, laughing at the comic movements and actions of the little people as they performed acrobatics and stunts and they were still chuckling as they made their way home. Gertrude felt a warmth deep inside every time she was with Basil, she had always vowed to herself that she would provide him with some of the motherly love that had been denied him following the untimely death of her sister.

Their next outing was to the Empire to see a Buster Keaton film. This was at the time when Ipswich was making the change from trams to trolley busses and it was something of an event to see these new vehicles that did not require tracks. There was a bus stop almost opposite the Empire and as they emerged from the cinema they noticed two policemen with a tape measure, measuring up points on the road, next to them stood a bright new trolley bus. A crowd of people were looking on and so, her curiosity getting the better of her, Gertrude took Basil across the road to see for herself what was going on. Two policemen appeared to be measuring something in the road. She moved closer with Basil at her side, they were both trying to see what the policemen were doing, however, they soon wished they hadn't because what they saw made a lasting impression on them both and caused Basil to have nightmares for the next few weeks.

The body of the trolley bus conductor, Eddie Morphey, lay on the ground in a pool of blood. His head was shattered, its contents spilled onto the pavement like offal on a butchers slab. Gertrude quickly covered Basil's eyes and ushered him away, too late to prevent the horrific sight registering in his juvenile memory. Later reports in the newspaper described what had happened. Apparently, as the trolley bus approached the bus stop at the top of Duke Street, Eddie had leaned out to see how many passengers were waiting to board and his head had smashed onto one of the steel poles, that supported the overhead wires, shattering like an over ripe melon. He died instantly.

Although he didn't witness either the accident or the aftermath the event had a profound effect on Chip also because Eddie was a friend of his who was not simply a near neighbour, he lived at the end of James Street, but he had been a long term colleague within the Territorial Army. They

119

had both joined the reserve in 1912, had trained together, were posted to France together and had only been separated when Chip, serving in the Royal Field Artillery, had been posted on to Palestine while Eddie, as an infantryman, had departed to Etaples in France, and the trenches.

Two weeks after the accident Eddie, as a serving member of the Territorial Reserve, was honoured with a funeral with full military honours, before being laid to rest in Ipswich cemetery.

******

Chip missed his boys dearly and thought it would be good for all three of them to spend some quality time together so he resolved to take them for a weekend holiday to the seaside, staying overnight in a bed and breakfast. He chose early summer when there would be vacancies in many of the bed and breakfast houses, the crowds would not be too overpowering and, importantly, the prices would not be too high. He also decided to take sister Nellie and her boys as a gesture of thanks for her looking after him. This was an exciting adventure for Basil, Leonard and their cousins so on the Friday afternoon, directly he arrived home from school, Leonard packed a few clothes into one of Chip's old army bags and walked to number 251 to collect his little brother. Emily Jane had gathered together some clothes for Basil and Leonard stuffed them in the army bag with his. Grabbing Basil's hand and calling a hasty goodbye to Emily Jane they walked quickly down to aunt Nellie's house in James Street.

It was a bit of a crush that night but the boys were happy to sleep on the floor of the parlour although anticipation and excitement prevented them from getting much sleep and they were up bright and early next morning. Nellie had packed a bag for her and her boys and it was placed by the front door with Leonard's. They all trouped up Princes Street toward the railway station, Chip leading the way, Nellie at his side holding the excited hand of little Cyril while William, Douglas, Leonard and Basil trouped behind, carrying the bags.

The road bridge that joined Princes Street to Burrell Road and Ranelagh Road had recently been demolished and was being replaced with a new one which was now nearing completion. In order to maintain the river crossing for vehicles and pedestrians alike a temporary wooden bridge had been constructed adjacent to the new bridge. It was a two tier construction which allowed vehicles to cross at normal road level whilst providing a pedestrian footbridge underneath, accessed by a wooden staircase at each end. The boys were intrigued by the new structure and, as they emerged at the side of the Station Hotel, they studied the exposed steelwork, soon to be encased in concrete.

It was the first time any of the boys had been on a steam train and they jumped excitedly into the second class carriage and moved quickly along the corridor looking for a free compartment.

"Here's an empty one." Called out Basil, as he pulled the door open and launched himself into the window seat. Chip hoisted the bags onto the net racks above the seats and flopped into the seat by the door, opposite Nellie, just as the train began to pull slowly away from the platform. Leonard looked puzzled.

"Have we got on the right train dad because we seem to be going the wrong way, we're heading inland, away from the sea." Concern was written all over his face.

"Don't worry Lenny," Chip smiled across the carriage to Nellie, "the train loops around the town because there is no rail bridge across the river. We will soon be heading straight for Felixstowe."

The train stopped at Westerfield to pick up more passengers before passing back into town, over the impressive Spring Road viaduct and steaming into Derby Road station. As the engine hissed Chip looked out to the coal yard on the other side of the tracks.

"That's where your grandfather used to work as a heaver." Chip pointed to the heaps of shiny coal. "Now he sells it from his shop."

Eventually the train steamed into Felixstowe town station and the boys jumped up ready to leave, as they reached for the bags Chip put a hand on Leonards arm.

"Not yet, we still have one more station to go."

The boys sat down again and looked apprehensive as the train pulled out of the station seemingly heading back toward Ipswich. There was a swaying and squealing of the wheels as they rode a set of points that took the train in a different direction.

"It's the beach station we want," said Nellie," not long now."

Once the train pulled into the beach station and ground to a halt, with a loud gush and a cloud of steam, Leonard and William dragged the bags from their perch and the whole troupe bundled out of the carriage and onto the small platform. Chip and Nellie led the party down Beach Station Road, past the Dolphin public house and turned left into Langer Road. It was quite a walk but eventually they turned right into Beach Road West.

"We are looking for a lighthouse." Chip announced, chuckling to himself.

The boys looked up and down the road but could see nothing that even resembled a lighthouse.

"I can't see one." Said William.

"Nor me." Said Leonard.

"Let's walk down the road, we might see one then." Chip was amused.

After a short walk Chip stopped outside number 9 and announced to the group.

"Here we are I've found it."

"But it's just an ordinary house uncle, not a lighthouse." Observed William. Leonard looked up and laughed, now he realised why his father had been so amused.

"Look Billy," Leonard chuckled as he pointed to number nine, a three storey Victorian house that sported a 'No Vacancies' sign, and above that a large sign that read 'The Lighthouse Bed and Breakfast.

Once inside it didn't take long for them to unpack their bags and soon they were heading for the promenade and the beach.

Everybody agreed the weekend was a great success. The boys spent much of their time playing on the paddle boats in the boating lake behind the promenade, or on the rowing boats in Butlin's where they went as close as they dared to monkey island. They had a stone hopping competition where they skimmed stones into the sea to see who could make the most skips. Leonard won easily with a nine hop stone. They searched for lucky stones with a hole through the middle and, when the tide receded to reveal a strip of golden sand, they built sand castles with towers and a moat. Chip and Nellie left them to play in the stewardship of Leonard while they walked the length of the promenade from the 'Fludyers' in the east to the Manor end in the west. Chip particularly liked sitting in the promenade shelter near the convalescent home. The 'Herman de Stern' home had been opened in 1902 with money provided by

Baroness de Stern in memory of her husband, Baron Herman de Stern, who was a German banker and brewing magnate and whose title had been bestowed upon him by the King of Portugal no less. The home was used for the recuperation of men from London following hospital treatments, where it was thought the sea air would accelerate their recovery. To Chip it provided a source of ex servicemen who, like him, had served in the Great War and although many were reluctant to talk of their experiences to 'outsiders' they felt a comradeship with a fellow soldier and were able to readily discuss their experiences.

Basil enjoyed an ice cream cornet each day and walked the entire length of the pier to inspect the paddle steamers as they arrived, spilling their cargo of passengers and taking on new ones before departing for Yarmouth and London.

It was an exhausted family that piled into Nellie's house late on Sunday evening. Tossing their bags on the floor the boys crashed out beside them while Nellie headed for the scullery.

"I think a nice cup of tea is the order of the day, don't you Chip?"

"I certainly do. What say you boys?"

He was greeted with a smile and a nod from Leonard and William accompanied by gentle snores from the other three boys. Worn out from their weekend adventure they had quickly fallen into a deep, satisfied sleep.

******

A couple of weeks after their brief holiday break Basil lost another playmate and special person in his life. This time it was not as a result of a tragedy or accident but rather a coming together of two forces.

Belsey was growing discontented with his situation in the household of number 251 and he approached Emily Jane with his concerns. He told her his room was suffering from damp, citing the fact that there was black mould forming on the outside wall above the window. Emily Jane opined that it was not damp as such, it was a little bit of condensation and she would clean it up for him. Later that week she washed the wall with soda and the black mark was gone.

Two weeks later Belsey complained again, saying that the mould was returning and it was definitely caused by damp. He suggested his rent should be reduced as a result, something which incensed Emily Jane, already struggling to make ends meet for her household, and she retaliated by informing him that he had been living in the house, without having to share his personal space, for a preferential rent and that in her opinion it should be raised rather than lowered.

A heated argument broke out, something that was very rare for both of them with their normally placid natures. Both parties said things that perhaps they should not have said, and indeed would not have said if they had remained calm. The result was that Emily Jane gave Belsey one week to find alternative accommodation and vacate his room. The following weekend he left, heading for a rented room in the run down Rope Walk, never to return to Cavendish Street. Basil stood on the front step and cried as he watched Big Belham hoist his two carpet bags, containing all of his worldly possessions, onto his shoulders and lumber off down the hill and out of his life.

Unbeknown to Basil there were further life changes in the offing. He was enjoying regular Saturday evening treats when his father took him, almost every week, to the Lyceum in Carr Street to see the latest films, which were enormously popular, there were always long queues waiting to get in. In Basil's eyes these outings were simply that, treats to the cinema for him. They did not go alone, however, Chip invited Doris Dumble to accompany them every week and, although Basil did not mind that at all, he noticed there was always something for them to discuss, quietly, with their heads close together, although he could never quite make out what it was they were talking about.

Had he been privy to their conversations he would no doubt have been excited in part but also disappointed in part. Chip had made no secret of the fact that he was desperate to reunite his family but he could not look after two boys of school age and hold down a full time job. He had never looked at another woman since the traumatic loss of his beloved Beatrice and he had no intention of starting now, but if he was to succeed in drawing together his boys under the same roof as himself that is just what he would need to do. It was Emily Jane who had initially put forward a potential solution that would kill two birds with one stone, and so it was that Chip and Doris began to see each other away from the confines of the family.

The huddled conversations that Basil had missed were in fact the preparations for combining two families. It seemed a perfect solution because, while Chip needed a mother for his boys to give him the opportunity to reconstruct his family, Doris needed a father for her growing daughter, Marjorie, who was now three and a half years old. Doris had no greater inclination to seek out another lover than had Chip, both had been so besotted with their former partners in life that the mere thought of another taking their place was untenable. On the other hand, a union of convenience would enable the new family unit to take their place in society with nobody being any the wiser, and if love should follow, well that would be an unseen bonus.

Both Chip and Doris wanted a quiet wedding with as little fuss as possible and there were, therefore, not many arrangements to be made and the knot was finally tied in December. Only close family members were in attendance, Lydia was the sole representative of the Cotton family, and the reception, consisting of a few sandwiches and homemade cakes, was held at number 251.

Their wedding night was also spent at 251 and the following day Chip went back to stay at his sister Nellie's house. Unfortunately it was not possible to complete the cementing of the family under one roof because Chip had negotiated with Mr and Mrs Stannard, who were subletting his home in James Street, that they would not have to vacate until after Christmas. They would have three weeks to find alternative accommodation.

Part Three

Return to
James Street

1928

It was over a weekend in early January that the exciting event took place, it entailed a whole load of work for the entire family but it was well worth it. The Stannards had vacated 19 James Street on the Friday so that Doris, ably assisted by Gertrude and Gladys, could spend the Saturday morning cleaning, polishing and airing. Chip and his boys went to Cavendish Street to gather together their meagre possessions and carried them down to James Street. Meanwhile Nellie had collected together Chip's belongings, such as they were, and taken them across the road so that when he arrived they were waiting for him. This only left the cutlery, the linen, the crockery and Doris's personal things which were all stored at number 251. This was where Chip's father, Charles, stepped in. He still had his pony and trap so he happily trotted up to Cavendish Street, loaded the remainder of their household belongings and brought them to the newlyweds. It was a long day but by six o'clock everything was in the house, albeit strewn over the floor of the small living room. Nellie had cooked a welcome meal for the family which they all devoured with gusto before finally crawling off to bed, exhausted but happy. Chip was probably the happiest, he had his boys back and they were a family once more, closely followed by Leonard and Basil, who were delighted to be permanently reunited with their father. Doris and Marjorie were simply contented to be part of a complete family at last.

It had been seven years and nine months since Chip, Leonard and Basil had last occupied 19 James Street together. Basil of course had been too young to remember so for him it was the first time he had experienced living with a brother, and he found it very strange. It was not quite as strange to have a sister though, because he had lived under the same roof as Marjorie since the day she was born, also Doris had always been in his life and lately had looked after him as a son, so he had already bonded with her. Now they were all together in their own home; Chip, Doris, Leonard, Basil and Marjorie.

However, there was one important person missing from Basil's life, aunt Gertrude. Actually it was the reverse, Basil had a new family and the separation didn't really register in his juvenile mind, it was more that there was one person missing from Gertrude's life. She was happy for the family, but for herself she was heartbroken, she felt that yet another person she loved so dearly had been taken away from her. Doris and Chip had told her she was welcome in their home anytime, she was welcome to take Basil out if she wished, but to her it was not the same. It would never be the same again. The last firm link between her and her beloved sister was to become more and more tenuous. Basil would be living over a mile away so she wouldn't see him every day. Her excursions with him would require the sanction of another, her cousin Doris. The day the new complete family moved into James Street they were smiling, happy and contented, Gertrude cried herself to sleep that night, everybody oblivious to her pain.

******

If there was one thing Basil loved doing above almost anything else it was going to the cinema. It had become a regular excursion for him, usually to the Empire, most often he was accompanied Gertrude but there were some occasions when he was in the company of Gladys and more recently he had escorted Chip and Doris on their regular weekly visits to the Lyceum in Carr Street. Now, living in James Street, he was close to all of the main cinemas in the town. Leonard, currently enjoying his last summer school holiday, favoured cowboy films, so it was very convenient that Pools Picture Palace in Tower Street showed mainly westerns. They had two films showing from Monday to Wednesday before changing the programme and showing a different pairing from Thursday to Saturday. Sunday of course they were closed. Leonard began taking his younger brother with him and they both thoroughly enjoyed both the entertainment and being together.

Basil preferred comedy films, well to be honest he liked all films but especially comedy, so he was always overjoyed when Leonard announced they were going to the Central Cinema in Princes Street because, more often than not, it meant they were going to see either a Charlie Chaplin or a Buster Keaton movie.

Another favourite entertainment for Basil was the circus. Every year the circus rolled into town and set up their ring in the Hippodrome, most times the animals were stabled at the Rose public house in Rose Lane. It was only a stone throw from the Hippodrome so it was convenient all round. Basil and his two cousins William and Douglas decided one day that while the circus was in town they would try and have a personal up close look at the animals. They were certainly not disappointed. When they arrived at the Rose they saw the big cages on wheels that the animals were transported in parked in a tight group at the side of the road. The lions and tigers were prowling up and down inside their cages, giving the odd roar at passing pedestrians, but the trick riding horses and the elephants were tethered in the open yard to the rear of the public house.

"Hello boys." A voice came from behind them. They turned to find a scruffy man in tattered trousers.

"We weren't doin' anything mister, honest." William exclaimed, but then he was always rather a nervous sort.

"That's alright. Come to see the animals have we?"

"Yeah!" Douglas was always a bit more brash and forthright.

"Come on then, I've got to feed some of them now. D'ya wanna help."

"Wow! Yes please!"

Basil did something that morning he had never dreamed he would do. He fed an elephant, and he adored it. The boys helped to feed the horses and watched at a safe distance as the lions and tigers were fed great lumps of meat. Making their way home for dinner they chatted excitedly, unable to believe their luck, the scruffy man was in fact the owner of the circus and as a parting gift he had given them two tickets each to the show the following evening. Basil chose to give his second ticket to Leonard as a thank you for all the cinema visits they had made together, William gave his to his mother Nellie while Douglas thought it would be ideal to give his to his little brother Cyril.

The next night they made the short walk to the Hippodrome and took their seats on the front row where they had an uninterrupted view of all the acts. There were the lions, tigers, horses and elephants of course, but additionally there were sea lions, acrobats, trapeze artists and everybody's favourite, the clowns. It was a brilliant evening out and they all enjoyed it enormously.

******

It seemed to Basil that the summer holidays were over almost before they had begun and as September rolled around thoughts turned to school. For Basil it was not simply a case of returning to school, for him it was starting at a completely new one. When he moved from Cavendish Street he had continued attending the school at the bottom of the hill until the summer break when he had reluctantly left behind all his pals, especially Doug Marsh, Albert Copping and the crippled William Barwell. Now he had the daunting task of dovetailing into an already established group at the Stoke School although, thankfully, cousin Douglas would be in the same class which definitely made him feel somewhat more relaxed about the situation. His new school was situated at the bottom of Stoke Street near its junction with Vernon Street, which meant it was not a great distance for him to walk and the route had the added attraction of crossing Stoke bridge, at the very end of the new cut docks, with all the exciting activities associated with a dock.

His first day was quite cold for the time of year, and the rain, falling from the leaden sky, dribbled uncomfortably down the back of his shirt collar. He arrived in front of the main building, with its forbidding dark red brick facade, feeling decidedly sorry for himself wishing that he could have stayed at home tucked up in a warm bed.

'Oh well,' he sighed to himself, 'here goes nothing.'

The first activity on the agenda was assembly where the headmaster, Mr Charles Finch, strode onto the raised dais in the main hall, clasped his hands behind his back and ran his gaze across the gathered multitude over the top of his half glasses. First appearances were that he was a very hard man, a fact that proved to be correct time and time again over the ensuing months. His manner was stern and he had a habit of twitching his voluminous moustache which ran into his bushy sideburns and stopped short at his bald pate.

For the benefit of all newcomers Finch introduced himself and went on to point out some of the rules of the school.

"Those of you who flaunt these rules," he boomed, "will experience the undoubted pleasure of a one to one meeting with me," he paused for effect and his gaze swept the room once more, "and my associate Mr Cane." Another pause. "Is that crystal clear?"

A suppressed ripple of understanding flowed round the hall.

"I said, is – that – crystal – clear?" there was a chorus of agreement. "Good."

Standard one, had all of the youngest pupils and was assigned to Miss Trott and at her command they followed her toward their classroom, no doubt dazed by their reception but totally in fear of headmaster Finch.

Standard two was the level Basil was currently at and he was assigned to Miss Thrower's class. Sarah Thrower was young, pretty and inexperienced, attributes that convinced Finch would never make an effective teacher. She also possessed a gentle nature which tempted some of the more crafty boys to take advantage of her. Despite all of this she was actually quite an effective teacher although Basil didn't stay in her class for very long, it was soon recognised that he was more advanced than the other pupils and he was raised to standard three which meant that he was one year ahead of his age group.

Standard three was a different kettle of fish. That was the class of Mr Craggs. He was a rough customer who believed that learning improved with the application of pain, and his ambition was to improve every scholar's ability to learn as much as he could. He had a glass eye which was a bit more prominent than his natural one, scruffy unkempt hair that was reminiscent of Albert Einstein and a made to measure suit, that had obviously been measured and made for someone half as big again as him, and it had certainly seen better days. His favourite pastime was to amble around the room while the pupils were working and smack them across the back of the head if they were not doing it correctly.

One day as morning playtime ended and the whistle was blown, Basil inadvertently took an extra step forward and was rewarded with a hard slap across the back of his head from Craggs. It really hurt and he could still feel the effects at lunchtime.

The rest of the teaching staff comprised Mr 'Stud' Baker who took standard four. He was a very popular teacher both with the pupils and the other teachers. Resplendent in his high starched collar and tie and his three quarter coat he had a habit while writing on the blackboard of turning quickly and hurling a lump of chalk at a boy who had been either talking or misbehaving. He always hit the right boy and everybody was mystified as to how he knew who the culprit was, some boys even suggested that perhaps he had eyes in the back of his head. The truth of the matter was in fact far simpler and involved no mystic powers whatsoever. The headmaster's study was opposite and, in order to preserve his privacy, the headmaster had put brown paper on the inside of the glass. This effectively made his door into a mirror. All Baker had to do was glance into the 'mirror' and he could easily identify exactly who the recipient of the chalk missile should be.

Standard five was in the capable hands of Mr 'Jew Boy' Thomas while standards six and seven belonged to Mr Overfield.

******

There was no electricity in James Street, very few houses had electricity at this time and those that did were the bigger houses belonging to the well off and newly built houses. The only concession to modernity in James Street was a piped supply of town gas which fed a small cooker in the scullery and provided light in both the living room and the scullery. This light was achieved by igniting a jet of gas that came out of a small pipe hanging from the ceiling in the middle of the room. There was a tap on the pipe so the gas supply could be turned off to extinguish the light source. The light that the flaming jet emitted was not particularly bright and it flickered and popped rendering reading, needlework or any close work, requiring concentration, extremely difficult.

Lighting for the rest of the house was provided by wax candles that left a greasy residue as they burned. This residue would accumulate in the base of the candle holder which meant that every week they had to be cleaned out, this was Chip's job every Sunday morning. He secured the candleholder between his knees, scraped the grease out with a blunt knife and tossed it onto a small ledge sitting at the back of the range, behind the hot coals.

He was merrily carrying out this chore one Sunday in November, humming his favourite song softly to himself, whilst prising a particularly large lump of grease from a holder. Nonchalantly he tossed it onto the ledge and returned his attention to the candleholder. Almost immediately there was a loud roar accompanied by a sheet of orange flame which shot up the chimney; he glanced at the range briefly before returning his attention to the job in hand, thinking no more of it. A few minutes later there was a thumping on the front door and the sound of people shouting.

"What in heaven's name...." Chip crossed to the front door. Billy Prentice from number 17 stood on the pavement with his hands on his hips.

"Are you de-sooting your chimney Chip?" He asked.

"Of course not. Why?"

"Just you come and have a look."

Chip stepped into the road with Basil trailing in his wake, and looked up to where Billy Prentice was pointing.

"Oh my good god." Chip was taken completely by surprise to see flames shooting five to six feet out of the chimney pot. It was common practice for people who could ill afford to employ the services of a chimney sweep to deliberately set fire to their chimney in order to burn off the soot; this was known as soot burning. However, this was certainly not the case on this occasion because Chip had recently borrowed a set of brushes from a friend and swept the chimney himself. He was at a loss to know why his chimney was on fire, but there was no doubt that it certainly was well alight. Basil thought it was a great show with all the flames, the smoke and the interest that everybody was showing. He thought it all the more exciting when he heard the clanging of a bell in the distance, somebody had called the fire brigade.

The fire appliance came swinging into James Street with four brass helmeted firemen hanging on to the sides of the vehicle for dear life and two more riding in the front seats. One was struggling with the heavy steering wheel while the other was ringing the bell furiously. As the fire engine came to a stop the fireman in the seat beside the driver released the rope attached to the bell and jumped down to the road, barking orders at the four on the back as he did so. It was obvious that he was the senior man because he had more gold braid on his tunic than all the others as well as a more ornate brass helmet and an unmistakably authoritative air. The ladder was unhitched, extended until it reached the now volcanic chimney pot and, while two firemen steadied it, a third ran nimbly to the top dragging a canvas hose behind him. On his shouted command the remaining fireman turned on the pump, sending ripples up the hose until water gushed from the open end, hissing as it met the flames, and it was stuffed unceremoniously into the top of the chimney. When the flames were completely extinguished, leaving only a soft hissing sound and gentle wisps of steam rising into the cool air, the order was given to turn off the water supply and the firemen began the task of stowing their gear back into the vehicle.

The fireman with the braid stepped inside the house, accompanied by one fireman, Chip, little Basil and a very large police sergeant who had arrived on the scene unnoticed. As they all fed into the tiny living room they were greeted by an extremely irate Doris, and no wonder for the stone flag floor was swimming two inches deep in wet soot and muck. The mess extended half way up the walls too, thrown there by the force of the water hitting the range and cascading in all directions. The fireman turned out to be no less than a Deputy Superintendant and he sloshed his way to the range, hitting his brass helmet on the gas light in the centre of the room as he did so, and stuck his head into the dripping hole of the chimney.

"Yes, that seems to be extinguished alright sir. Now, were you soot burning?"

"No I was not." Chip was indignant. "In fact it was swept not long ago. I was just cleaning out the candleholders and the next thing I knew, up it went."

The Deputy Superintendant swished his boot in the sludge, lifted and studied it.

"I'm inclined to accept that sir, seeing as the residue is not very thick."

"Not to you maybe but you haven't got to clear the mess up, it's quite thick enough thank you very much." It was the first time Doris had spoken since the debacle began and she was fairly bristling.

The Deputy Superintendant moved across the room, his brass helmet hitting the gas lamp again.

"Mmm I don't think there will be any need to pursue it any further then, do you agree sergeant?" The police sergeant was still standing near the door, looking down at his once shiny boots, as the waves of sludge, caused by the fireman's movements, lapped gently at the lace holes.

"I think that will be in order Walter," the two obviously knew each other well but a glare from the fireman made him stutter a correction, "I mean, Deputy Superintendant Double."

Everybody looked up in astonishment forcing a quizzical expression to grow on the sergeant's face, wondering what he had said that had caused this reaction.

"Dad, dad." It was Basil's turn to speak excitedly. "He's got our name dad." Chip smiled.

"That's right, I'm Charles Double and this is my house."

"Well I'll be buggered, I mean blowed." The sergeant corrected himself on seeing Basil's eyes light up at the swearword. "I'm Sergeant Harold Double."

They all forgot about the sludge swimming around their feet as they roared with laughter. Deputy Superintendant Walter Double and Police Sergeant Harold Double had both been called to a chimney fire at the residence of Mr Charles Double, and none of them was related to the other two, at least as far as they were aware. While the laughter continued Doris sloshed her way into the scullery in search of a bucket. She returned and held it out to Chip.

"Here, you had better get clearing this mess up hadn't you." The laughter died and the sergeant beat a hasty retreat. The Deputy Superintendant tripped over the soggy floating rag rug in his haste, helmet clanging against the gas light one final time.

"OK boys, back to the firehouse."

Chip heard no more from official sources but he heard a lot more domestically. Basil chuckled as he got a broom to help his father, what an adventure to relate to his pals at school.

1929

January and February were exceptionally cold months, the worst for many years, so much so that the river Gipping froze over almost as far downstream as the new Princes Street bridge. Leonard asked Basil if he would like to go for a skate on the river, he readily agreed, he had never been skating before and wasn't sure what it was but it sounded like fun. They wrapped up warm, each with a new scarf that Doris had knitted for them as an annual Christmas present, and headed for Alderman Road recreation ground and the canal that ran along its north side. At every opportunity they slid on the footpath or kicked plumes of snow into the air as they followed the massed footprints crossing the park until they reached the canal itself. Basil began to untie his ankle boots.

"What are you doing?" questioned Leonard.

"I'm taking my boots off so I can put my skates on."

"We haven't got any skates." That small fact had obviously escaped Basil in his haste to try something new.

"Well how do we skate if we haven't got any skates?"

"We pretend. Like this."

With that Leonard ran onto the ice and slid to a halt. He then placed his hands behind his back and pretended to skate.

"See. You don't really need skates." He called over his shoulder.

Basil retied his boot and joined his brother on the ice. When they reached the end of the canal they went onto the river Gipping itself and headed off toward Needham Market, but of course they did not go very far, after all it was very tiring skating without skates, so after a couple of hours Leonard suggested they make a move for home. Walking back across the recreation ground Basil realised just how cold his legs had become, he couldn't wait to be old enough to wear long trousers like his brother. He pulled his soggy knitted socks as high as they would go and, grabbing his brother's hand, together they headed for home.

******

Things were going rather well for Basil at school, he had made many new friends and had also progressed well in his lessons. He had a penchant for Arithmetic and enjoyed anything that involved numbers earning praise from Craggs along the way, unfortunately though it didn't prevent him from getting the odd hand, or even book, wrapped round the back of his head from time to time.

Shortly before Lent the school was informed, at assembly, that there would be a church service that would require full attendance. Nobody would be exempt. Sure enough, on the Friday before Lent all the classes were lined up in the hall and marched, in a two by two crocodile, with their respective teachers at the head, out of the front door and up to Stoke church. There was a fair bit of commotion as the pupils filed into the church, punctuated every now and then by a hymn book delivered to the back of the head by Craggs, accompanied by a consequent cry of pain.

To begin with all of the pupils were just pleased to be getting out of lessons for a while but their enthusiasm was short lived and soon turned to frustrated boredom. A couple of hymns were sung, with Miss Flower the school music teacher providing the organ accompaniment, followed by a couple of prayers and a bible reading. Headmaster Finch then rose to the pulpit and delivered his words to a huge wave of indifference. Basil found himself looking around the church, at the plaques on the wall, seeing how tightly he could squint his eyes and still read them. He counted the windows, studied the stained glass until, at last Finch was done. The whole service lasted for an agonising and bottom numbing one and a half hours. Why were the pews in churches always so uncomfortable, Basil mused.

Finally, and not a moment too soon, the congregation was told to stand, a final hymn was sung and they all filed out and trudged down the road to resume their studies.

******

Spring soon began to lighten the world, trees in the parks began to sprout leaf buds and Basil turned his thoughts to nature. He had heard other kids talking about the towpath beside the river Gipping and how it was quite possible to walk it as far as Stowmarket, so one Saturday, accompanied by cousin Douglas, he thought it would be exciting to walk the whole length of the towpath. It was fairly easy going to start with and before they realised it they were near the Co-operative dairy in Sproughton Road, about two miles away from home and it was here they discovered a pond. It looked rather deep so they thought perhaps it was inadvisable to strip off and have a swim, the water would be far too cold in any case, but they did notice that there was an abundance of frogs spawn. Unfortunately they had nothing with them that they could put it in and a search of the surrounding area revealed nothing suitable. Nothing else for it, they would have to return the following Saturday and hope the spawn was still there.

The following week they equipped themselves fully for their safari and set off once more down the towpath. Fortunately for them the spawn was still there, and if anything there was even more of it. Basil had made a rudimentary fishing net, using a scrap of muslin cloth he had found amongst Doris's sewing scraps, attached to a piece of bent wire that was tied to the end of a bamboo stick. Douglas had managed to get hold of three old jam jars and had made a handle for each of them with a length of string. They amused themselves for a couple of hours, first collecting a jar full of spawn and then filling the other two jars with a couple of dozen tadpoles. Proudly they marched home carefully carrying their gains. Douglas had nowhere to keep the spawn or the tadpoles but Basil had managed to find an old steel drum near the livestock market and had installed it in the back yard and filled it with water in anticipation of a good haul. The contents of the three jars were emptied carefully into the drum. The boys checked on the tadpoles each day and studied them as they turned into small green frogs. Once the frogs became large enough they began, one by one, to escape from the drum and hop around the yard which did not please Doris, especially when she was attempting to hang the washing out, so Basil took them, a few at a time, and released them into the river Gipping where they belonged. In any case the frogs had quickly lost their play appeal, after all what can you do with them? Well the odd one or two found their way to school and down the necks of the girls, until the headmaster put a stop to that bit of fun.

******

One bright sunny morning Basil heard the letter box rattle and the flutter of post hitting the rough stone floor. Rushing to collect the letters he was disappointed to find there were only two, one each for his father and Doris, but as he picked them up, intending to carry them to Doris in the scullery, his attention was drawn to an advertisement card lying underneath. The card excited him no end. It was a circular from the Old Public Hall in Westgate Street, yet another cinema, and of course he was fanatical in his love of the cinema. These cards were somewhat different to the normal advertisements or fliers that were posted through letterboxes in that they made an offer which Basil especially found difficult to resist. If one person paid for their admission they could use the card to admit a second person absolutely free of charge. Fortunately for Basil his brother Leonard was now only days away from his fourteenth birthday and was shortly to leave school. He had managed to secure himself the promise of a job in the Co-op shop in Fore Hamlet where he was already employed as a Saturday boy. This meant he could earn himself a bit of pocket money, enough for a cinema ticket perhaps?

That evening Basil broached the subject of the card and to his great delight Leonard didn't need any persuasion because he too enjoyed the cinema and he readily agreed to take his little brother as the free seat.

Summertime came rolling around, and with it the annual Co-operative and Labour Party Fete which was held on Alexandra Park. This year it was held on July the first and as a special treat Basil was going for the very first time. Doris was a staunch

Labour Party member and as such she was heavily involved in the Labour party tent, which would be very boring for Basil, and so Gertrude had eagerly stepped forward to be his guardian for the day, and what a fun day it turned out to be, Basil had not witnessed anything like it before. There were dozens of tents housing all manner of people showing off their businesses as well as displays of arts, crafts and pastimes. Gertrude hovered over demonstrations of needlework and sewing, which didn't interest Basil at all and quickly passed by the examples of home winemaking with tastings, which did not interest her and, of course, Basil was too young to sample alcohol in any case.

There were, however, dozens of activities and competitions for him to watch and enjoy. First up was a competition called 'eating an apple with no hands', and he thought it hilarious to see grown men wearing blindfolds, trying to take a bite out of an apple that was hanging in front of them on a length of string. Each time a competitor went to take a bite the apple swung away from them only to swing back and strike them on the face. There was also a competition for the women, 'who can skip for the longest'. Despite his enthusiastic encouragement, Gertrude flatly refused to enter saying that she was much too old for such silliness. Basil watched as each woman or girl was given a skipping rope and on the command they all commenced to skip. If they stopped or if they got the rope caught around their ankle they were eliminated from the competition. The numbers gradually diminished as one by one the women succumbed to fatigue or poor rope control, until finally there was just one young lady remaining. She beamed as she was presented with a small silver cup for her efforts.

More amusing to Basil was the ladies balloon race, although all of the entrants seemed to be of school age. The object of the competition was to hit a balloon with a stick along a one hundred yard running track to see who could reach the finishing line first. Basil soon realised that they were not ordinary balloons because they stayed low on the ground and seemed to have a mind of their own.

"The balloons have some water in them to make it more difficult." Chuckled Gertrude. The competition was eventually won by a young schoolgirl who had come third in the skipping contest.

The next competition was the men's tug o' war, and there were a number of teams representing different companies in the town. Basil recognised two of the men in the Ransome and Rapier team as being work colleagues of his father and he was overjoyed when they became the overall winners.

By now Gertrude was feeling a bit thirsty so they made their way over in the direction of the beer tent, veering off as they approached to arrive at another bigger tent beside it. This tent was more of an afternoon tea affair than a beer hall, and was naturally better suited for a lady as the beer tent appeared to be solely for the use of men. Gertrude purchased a cup of tea for herself and a glass of lemonade for Basil, who was looking longingly at the array of cakes on the table alongside sandwiches which were already beginning to turn their corners up in the afternoon heat. Gertrude saw the expectant look on the face of her favourite little man and asked for two cream scones with strawberry jam. Basil's eyes almost popped out of his head as the plate with the scones was passed to him and he followed his aunt to an available table. Gertrude took the programme sheet out of her bag and studied it as Basil gnawed energetically at his scone leaving a moustache of cream under his nose.

"When we have finished our refreshment we should just be in time to see the judging of the fancy dress competition and then we can find somewhere to sit and watch the athletic races."

The answer she received was a wide grin beneath the cream smudge. Lovingly she took her handkerchief from her bag and wiped the little face clean.

The fancy dress competition was, as expected, very amusing. There were pilots, vicars, cowboys, pirates, clowns, soldiers and even somebody dressed up as a parcel. Basil pointed and laughed out loud at the people wearing big papier mache heads and everybody clapped as the Mayor, with his chain of office sparkling around his neck, stepped forward with his wife the mayoress to judge the entries. All the competitors walked round them in a big circle as the mayor and mayoress discussed points quietly between themselves, although why they whispered was a mystery because with all the laughing from the spectators and the music from the fairground, nobody would have heard anything they said anyway. Finally they made their decision and the circle of competitors came to an expectant halt.

"I hope the cowboy with the black hat wins." Said Basil, just as the mayor announced that the winner was in fact a lady dressed as a nurse with a big red cross on her white apron. The mayoress presented a little silver cup to the winner and was duly rewarded when a young schoolgirl emerged from the crowd carrying a bouquet of summer flowers which she presented with a curtsey. Basil thought it unfair that the winner received a small tin cup for all their efforts whereas the mayoress received a big bouquet for doing precious little.

Gertrude and Basil left the chattering crowd and made their way to an area that was cordoned off with a rope on wooden stakes. It delineated the athletics field. They found a space and sat on the firm grass to watch the races, which ranged from a one hundred yard dash to a mile and there was even a one mile steeplechase. Suddenly Basil jumped up in excitement as the athletes in the eight hundred yard race came into view because he realised his brother Leonard was leading the field home. He

157

jumped up and down, cheering and shouting, and as Leonard crossed the finishing line Basil gave a big whoop of pride and clapped until his hands were sore.

The athletics continued into the evening and the light was fading by the time the races were all completed, and they wandered off to an area where there was a raised boxing ring. The boxing competition was well under way but Gertrude was not interested in the slightest, she knew that this was the best vantage point from which to watch the firework display which was the grand finale, programmed to start about thirty minutes after the boxing stopped.

Part way through the boxing however, as dusk fell, people began to turn away and look across town, it was easy to see what had grabbed their attention. There were huge flames leaping into the air and clouds of billowing smoke moving as a thick dirty smudge across the sky. Gertrude was curious and suggested they go and investigate but Basil was adamant, he wanted to see the fireworks first.

Immediately the last sparkle died from the last firework Gertrude grabbed Basil's hand and led him out the gate into Back Hamlet. Hurrying toward home through the dark streets Gertrude became more inquisitive and decided to take a short cut along the docks, so eager was she to discover where all the smoke and flames were coming from. As they neared home Gertrude realised that it would be quicker, and judging from the direction of the smoke and flames they would get a better view, if they diverted along Cardinal Street and came out of Metz Street. Emerging onto Princes Street they became immediately aware of the full extent of the blaze. Where, only this morning, the furniture factory of E H Wrinch had stood there was a blazing hulk. The roof had completely disappeared and the shimmering heat that the walls gave off was almost unbearable, even where they stood and stared, almost one hundred yards distant.

Douglas Holland spied Basil in the crimson glow and pushed his way through the crowd until he stood alongside.

"Wow!" Exclaimed Basil, transfixed by the sight of this large building in its death throes. "That is a really big fire."

"That's nuthin'," Douglas scoffed, "you should have seen it a couple of hours ago. The flames went right up to the clouds they were so big."

The building was still a blazing inferno as Gertrude led Basil home. Doris and Chip hadn't arrived home yet so she let herself in and made a sandwich which Basil polished off in no time at all. He climbed the stair to his bed a very exhausted boy and as soon as his head touched the pillow he was dead to the world. Marjorie was staying the night over the road with Aunt Nellie, so Gertrude sat in one of the two comfortable chairs in front of the range and drank a welcome cup of cocoa as she waited for Chip, Doris and Leonard to return.

A full hour later, as the trio trouped through the door they were confronted by a totally worn out aunt, fast asleep with her mug still in her hand. Gently Chip took the mug and passed it to Doris before taking a blanket from the cupboard under the stair and laying it carefully over his sister in law.

******

Leonard was an extremely talented athlete who not only competed every summer at the Labour Party Co-op fete, where he regularly won cups and prizes, he also entered in the athletics tournaments at the annual British Legion fete and in Ransome and Rapier championships at the waterside Works sports ground. His prowess on the sports field also landed him the position of captain of Red House at the Ipswich secondary school in Smart Street in this his final year. It was in recognition of the fact that every year since he first attended the school Red House had acquitted themselves well on the sports field. In this, his final and special year Leonard made a clean sweep of every event he was entered for and won the individual Athletics Cup for the third year in succession. He had hoped achieving the triple would mean that he could keep the cup, but his hopes were dashed when the head master reminded him that as he was leaving school the following week the cup must remain on school premises. Basil was justifiably proud of his big brother and he looked up to him with plain and open admiration.

Every August Ipswich held a boys week, for Boys Brigade, Scouts and Cubs which culminated in a big sports day held on Portman Road football pitch. Chip took Basil to cheer on his big brother in what would be Leonard's final appearance, for once he left school he would, even as only a fourteen year old, be considered an adult and no longer qualify to compete. There was a mound of grass that ran the full length of the pitch facing the long wooden spectator stand, where the important people were seated in relative comfort, and Chip found them a suitable vantage point where they could sit and watch the competition. Every field event imaginable was being contested so Chip knew that it would be a long day and to get them through it all he had packed some sandwiches and a bottle of his home made ginger beer, which Basil could not wait to open.

Leonard was competing in all of the running races from the one hundred yard dash to the one mile steeplechase but he only entered for the javelin and long jump in the field event categories. Every time Basil saw his hero he jumped up and shouted at the top of his voice, it didn't take Leonard long to work out where his family were seated and each time he took to the field he waved back to Basil. More than once Basil turned to the other spectators sat around them and announced proudly that was his big brother, much to their amusement.

It was an exceptional display and Leonard won every event he entered except the javelin, which he lost by ten inches, and the four hundred and forty yard hurdle race, where he clipped a hurdle on the finishing straight and stumbled before recovering and finishing second.

His victories were sufficient for him to win the cup for 'Best Boy' which he received from the mayor on a special podium that had been constructed in front of the prestigious wooden stand. Basil clapped and clapped with a beaming smile that stretched almost from one ear to the other. This was one cup that Leonard was allowed to retain.

******

The summer school term finished and Leonard went off to work at the Co-op instead of enjoying the sunny weather whilst Basil prepared himself for another year at Stoke School. The next school year could be a decisive one for him because he would be in standard four, still one year ahead of his age group, and he would have the chance to sit exams to see if he could be eligible for the secondary or the municipal school.

"You will have to work very hard Basil, to see if you can do as well as Leonard did."

Encouraged Doris. Basil returned his cheekiest smile.

When, on September the second he arrived for the first day of term, the pupils were greeted with the news that Charles Finch had been replaced as headmaster by Mr Edward Thorpe. He introduced himself to the whole school at assembly, standing on the dais in his three quarter jacket with his thumbs tucked into the belt of his trousers so that his waistcoat, with the bright silver watch chain linking the pockets, showed off his portly belly. He sported a carefully manicured beard that neatly linked to his short sideburns and as with all headmasters he appeared to be very strict but Basil detected softness in his voice, time would tell.

On the Monday of the second week of the autumn term Basil and Douglas were walking to school, minding their own business, reliving the capers they had got up to over the past weekend and planning more for the next weekend. Suddenly Basil felt something sting his neck, he spun around but there was nothing and nobody to be seen, they resumed their walk. A few seconds later there was another sting on his neck, again he spun round, just in time to catch sight of somebody ducking behind the corner of Cardinal Street. Basil dragged Douglas into a shop doorway and waited. They did not have to wait long, slowly and guiltily two boys crept round the corner, it was William Gardiner and Percy Lightfoot both wearing broad smiles and carrying a handful of stones.

"There they are." Shouted Percy as he spied Douglas in the doorway.

"Get 'em Perce."

A hail of stones rained down on the hapless two and rattled off the walls and onto the cobbles.

"This way." Shouted Basil as he dashed into Cutler Street.

"This aint the way to school." Douglas pointed down Greyfriars road with a mystified look on his face.

"There are more people this way, they won't stone us with people about."

Skidding into St Peters Street, Basil felt more secure so he stopped running and Douglas fell into line beside him. Basil flashed a smile at Douglas.

"Told you."

Hardly had the words escaped his lips than there came another very painful sting, this time on the back of his leg. Basil looked down as a thin line of blood emerged from his calf just above his half mast socks.

"That's it, enough is enough." He shouted, as he stooped and swept up the large stone that had caught his leg.

Percy and William were in fits of laughter so they failed to notice as Basil took careful aim and launched the stone towards Percy's head. Percy saw it late but managed to duck under its path and the stone flew over his right shoulder and disappeared from view. Despite the fact they could no longer see the stone there was certainly no doubt where it ended up as they heard a loud crash followed by a tinkling sound as the frosted window in the door to the barber shop disintegrated behind them.

A startled look towards Douglas was followed by Basil's entreatment to run for their lives but much to Basil's astonishment nobody came running after them and nothing stirred. They arrived at school and nonchalantly hung their caps on their pegs and entered the classroom. Assembly passed without incident and the boys returned to their classroom where Basil made for his seat and, with a sigh of relief, sat and waited for the lesson to begin. 'Stud' Baker swept into the room with a flourish.

"Double." Baker's voice boomed as it only did when he was irritated.

"Sir." Replied Basil, sounding as innocent as he could.

"Headmaster's office at the double Double."

The rest of the class chuckled at the joke and were rewarded with a glare from Baker, but it was a glare with a slight grin. Basil rose slowly from his seat and made his way to the headmaster's office, which meant going through two other classrooms, attracting stares as he went.

Headmaster Thorpe gave him a sharp telling off, explaining that it was wrong to throw stones and, despite pleas that it was only in retaliation for his leg injury, there could be no justification. Basil received six strokes with the cane as a reward for his actions, along with a letter to pass to his father asking that the window be replaced at his cost.

Basil expected severe retribution from his father but Chip was not that kind of man, he knew that Basil had learned his lesson and that further chastisement would serve no purpose.

"You are a right scallywag and no mistake." Was Basil's only admonishment, but it was sufficient.

There was, however, to be a financial penalty for his recklessness, Chip paid for the window to be replaced and halved Basil's meagre pocket money but only until half of the bill was paid, Chip absorbed the remainder of the cost. The event was never mentioned again but Basil for one would never forget it.

******

The following week Gertrude came to visit Chip. There was to be a showing of a new film at the Picture House in Tavern Street, entitled 'Broadway', it was a landmark movie because it was the first talking film to be shown in Ipswich. It was billed as being '*all talking, all dancing, all singing*' and starred Glen Tryon, Evelyn Brent and Merna Kennedy. Gertrude desperately wanted to see it but did not wish to go alone and she asked if she might be able to take her little man to see it.

"Well, that sounds like something special to me, what do you think Dolly?" Chip called into the scullery. Doris thought it sounded exciting too.

"In that case why don't we all go." Said Chip.

Everybody agreed it was a good idea and so the following Saturday they queued outside the cinema, Chip and Doris were at the head of the party with Gertrude holding Basil's hand behind them and Leonard holding Marjorie's hand bringing up the rear. There was a chill wind blowing but nobody minded. The doors opened and they made their way to the ticket office.

"Three adults and three children please." Chip spoke into the glass, he glanced at Leonard who returned an expression that clearly protested that he was not a child any more. Chip winked at his son playfully and Leonard smiled back.

They all thoroughly enjoyed the movie and agreed that hearing the music and the voices made the whole experience so much more enjoyable, so much so that cinema going was to become an even bigger part of their lives in the future if that were possible.

The development of talking movies heralded a golden age for the cinema and like so many others Basil, who had been a keen cinema goer in the silent era, became even more enthusiastic and was totally hooked on this new innovation. When the news was released that a new cinema, The Regent on Majors Corner, would be opening soon he was very eager to go along, but at only nine years old he knew that he wouldn't be allowed to go alone. He was very disappointed to discover that brother Leonard was not able to take him, and his disappointment grew when he also discovered that his father and Doris would not be able to go either.

Full of anticipation he felt sure that Gertrude would save the day and take him to the first film but as the opening drew closer there was still no contact. He had been told that the grand opening would be on Monday the fourth of November, a date that was looming large and still he had no means of attending. His spirits lifted considerably on the Friday before the grand opening when Gertrude came to visit. 'This is it,' he thought, 'she has come to tell me we are going to the opening night.' Basil sat quietly in the living room as Gertrude talked with Doris for what seemed an age but there was no mention of the outing, he was getting anxious. The two women had a cup of tea together, dunking biscuits laconically, until at last Basil could wait no longer, if he had he was sure he would have wet himself.

"Are we going to the opening of the Regent on Monday aunt Gerty?" his enthusiasm had finally got the better of him.

"Basil, don't be so rude, we are talking." Doris chided.

"Sorry mother." But he wasn't sorry at all, he was burning up with impatience.

"Oh, the Regent. What's that?" Gertrude wrinkled her forehead and managed to hold a confused look on her face. It was all she could do to stop herself from laughing out loud.

"It's the new cinema that is opening, you must have heard about it. Everybody's talking about it."

"No Basil, I'm afraid I've heard nothing about it, and in any case I have somewhere else that I have to be on Monday evening. Sorry." It was said with a smile but Gertrude couldn't help but recognise the deep feeling of disappointment that swept over her little man's face. She felt a little twinge of guilt.

"Oh, I see; I understand." Said Basil, but he didn't understand, what could be more important than this. His head dipped as he tried, unsuccessfully, to conceal his desolation as the realisation hit him that he was not going to be at the opening. In doing so he missed the quick knowing smile that flashed between Doris and Gertrude. Unable to resist any longer the two women burst out into guilty laughter, laughter that rapidly developed into a coughing fit for Gertrude who was still recovering from a rather heavy cold.

Basil looked from one to the other with a confused expression on his face, he just couldn't comprehend what the big joke was.

"Your face is a picture." Gertrude spluttered between coughs, pointing directly at Basil. When she had recovered her composure she explained the trick that had been played on him.

"So you do know about the Regent!" Exclaimed Basil.

"Yes, I know all about it."

"And you are going to take me!"

"No, I'm sorry. That part was true, I have somewhere else that I must be on Monday and I can't take you." Basil's face drooped again. "But," she paused; his face lifted, there was a 'but'. Doris took over.

"Your aunt Gladys is going to take you."

"Yes, yes, yes!" Basil jumped up and down and whooped at the prospect.

All weekend there was a great big smile on his face that almost stretched from ear to ear, he couldn't wait for Monday evening to come. He told all his friends at school and anybody else that would listen.

Despite the fact that they arrived well in advance of the show, there was a very long queue of people waiting to gain entry, Basil was concerned that there would not be enough seats for everybody and that he might miss out after all. Approaching the main door they were greeted by a heavy set man with a bushy moustache and beard that melded into his mutton chop sideburns. He was wearing black trousers with a shiny stripe down the outside seam, a heavy maroon coat and peaked cap that were both festooned with gold braid. With a broad smile he ushered them through the open door

170

into the ticket hall, stopping the queue immediately after them.

"Who's he?" questioned Basil.

"He's called a commissionaire," explained Gladys, "he makes sure that not too many people come in all at once."

"Oh!"

Basil waited as Gladys took her turn at the ticket office purchasing two seats in the stalls and taking his hand she guided him toward another bank of glazed doors. He glanced back over his shoulder to discover that the commissionaire had allowed another group of people to enter. Basil was amazed at the luxurious softness of the deep pile carpet beneath his feet as they passed through the doors into a vast carpeted lobby where there were soft sofas, armchairs and drinks tables. Elegantly dressed ladies lounged across the sofas, some brandishing long cigarette holders that they wielded to accompany their conversation whilst intermittently blowing clouds of bluish cigarette smoke toward the ceiling. Their gentlemen companions stood casually by with one hand in their trouser pocket, talking animatedly they wheeled their glasses, looking for all the world as if they were joined in a ballet with the cigarette holders. Basil was awestruck, he hadn't been exposed to the middle class before, and their behaviour was alien to him.

Gladys steered him toward one of the many open doorways leading to the main auditorium, stopping only briefly at the entrance to have their tickets inspected and torn in half. Walking down the dimly lit aisle Basil was surprised to see there were small rooms at the back of the stalls with individual chairs in. Slowly these chairs were being occupied by the drink laden middle classes he had witnessed in the lobby.

"Wow aunt, some people have got private rooms." He exclaimed.

Gladys spied two free seats near the centre of row W and, gripping Basil's hand firmly, she shuffled her way along the row as seated patrons pulled their knees to one side. Basil was amazed that the seats actually tipped up when you weren't sitting on them and he got up and down four times before he convinced himself that they were supposed to do that. He marvelled at the size of the auditorium, the rotunda in the ceiling seemed so high, and turning he realised that there was a large balcony above them. The lighting was low which accentuated the impression of size, he just looked around with his mouth wide open in awe until the lighting dimmed and the massive curtains swung open to reveal a huge screen.

A hush crept through the auditorium as the audience waited for the programme to commence. The film was 'The last of Mrs Chaney' starring Norma Shearer and Basil Rathbone which, having a relatively unexciting plot for a nine year old, failed to grip the attention of Basil who spent almost the whole film looking around at the impressive surroundings.

Two or three weeks later he returned, again with Gladys, but this time the film was more successful in grabbing his interest as he watched a new Disney cartoon featuring Mickey Mouse as 'Steamboat Willie'. The film only lasted seven and a half minutes but it was supported by Buster Keaton in 'Battling Butler', which had Basil holding his stomach as he laughed loudly, and a couple of other short films. Gladys even bought a cup of tea for them both during the interval.

The Regent became one of Basil's favourite cinemas.

1930

January and February combined to provide one of the coldest winters on record and it was certainly not a comfortable time to be in school. Before he left home Doris made sure that Basil was well wrapped up in a warm woollen coat, she had purchased from the pawn shop in Princes Street. It was far too big but she gave him the time honoured assurances that mothers use to placate undersized children in oversized clothing that he would soon grow into it. A thick scarf she had knitted for him for a Christmas present hung round his neck in swathes and his ensemble was completed with a pair of woollen mittens knitted lovingly by Gladys. So, from the waist up Basil was as warm as toast as he hurried to school, however, his short trousers, a hand me down from brother Leonard, stopped well above his long woollen socks which left him with red and freezing knees. When he first inherited the trousers they had engulfed his knees leaving a sliver of bare skin above his socks, but that was over a year ago and he had grown into them, just as Doris told him he would, unfortunately she had neglected to tell him that he would also grow out of them. Thankfully he had a stout pair of boots, also passed on by Leonard, which he kept tightly laced to keep his feet warm and dry.

On the way to school he joined with the other boys making snowballs and throwing them at each other, with the odd one accidentally on purpose flying in the direction of the odd motor car that might pass, or even at a cyclist if they could get away with it. The snowballing continued into the playground but as soon as the whistle was blown the missiles were hastily released to break apart as they hit the frozen tarmac. Any pupil who was too slow discarding their ammunition could expect a smack on the back of the head from the duty teacher. If by any chance that teacher happened to be Craggs it proved to be a very painful smack.

The classrooms were only slightly warmer than the playground. The teacher had a desk sitting upon a raised dais in front of the blackboard and to the side of this dais there was a small fire grate. The caretaker had seen to it that all the fires were lit in the classrooms, the headmaster's office and the teacher's common room and there was a small bucket of fresh coal sitting beside each hearth. The fire did not emit much heat and most of what it did manage to release was swallowed up by the teacher's rear end as they sat on the metal fireguard in front of the flickering coals.

The first thing that Basil and his fellow classmates noticed when they sat at their desk was that the ink in the inkwells was frozen solid and they were unable to dip their nibs. They were permitted to bring their inkwells, one at a time, and place them in front of the fire before returning to their seat. The pupils were never permitted to linger near the fire so they gained no extra warmth at all, they had to sit at their desk wearing overcoat and gloves which restricted their studies somewhat. Those pupils who were unfortunate enough to be seated at the back of the room and therefore furthest from the heat source, were frozen through and spent the day shivering. Basil was one of these unfortunates but, being a resourceful lad, it didn't take him long to formulate a way of warming himself up just a little bit.

He kept a watchful eye on the coal bucket and as soon as Baker emptied the last of the coals onto the fire he would jump up and volunteer to refill the bucket. This meant that he had to knock on the door of the adjacent classroom in order to get permission to walk through, there were no corridors in the school. This was also the procedure when wanting to use the toilet, which was situated outside in the yard. The other teachers were most irritated by the constant interruptions but in this case, of course, they recognised that Basil was running an errand of mercy for a fellow teacher and they were, therefore, quite acquiescent. The coal stock was stored in a pile at the back of the playground and the walk gave Basil the chance to stamp his feet and run quickly round the yard before scooping a bucketful of coal and running back. Sometimes as he passed through another classroom the teacher would cast an eye to their own coal bucket and, if it was getting a bit low, they would ask Basil to fill theirs too. This he did, never carrying more than one bucket at a time, and it enabled him to generate enough warmth to get him comfortably to the end of the lesson.

Playtime provided another opportunity to generate some warmth into cold and stiff limbs as the boys and girls ran around playing their games. Most days one of the male teachers poured a few bucketful's of water onto the playground so that by the time the bell went for playtime there was a long, smooth slide. Everybody stood in line and when their turn came they would run as fast as they could and try to slide from one end of the ice slick to the other. There were the usual accidents as some kids failed to keep their balance and ended up in a heap, much to the amusement of the waiting queue. As February turned into March the cold spell eased and the pupils began to feel warmer and happier as they undertook their studies, although they were sorry to see the ice slides melt into wet tarmac again.

******

The spring term proved to be an important time in Basil's educational journey. He had already been moved up a grade, when his teachers considered him to be too advanced for his age group, which was fine for lessons but being in standard four with the eleven year old scholars meant that he was eligible to sit the examinations that had the potential to shape his future. If he was successful he could qualify for either the Secondary school which was known as Tower Ramparts, in the town centre, or even for the Municipal school, known as the Northgate. Unfortunately he was unsuccessful in his efforts and was informed that, as a result, he would be held back in standard four at the end of the school year. Thus he was destined to rejoin the boys that he had started with in 1928.

The summer term was Basil's favourite term for two reasons. Firstly it meant that the school year was coming to an end and the six week summer school holiday was just around the corner, secondly it also heralded a change to the school playtime. The male teachers would patrol the playground and join in with the boy's games by chalking a cricket wicket on the wall of the toilets, something the boys were forbidden to do, and providing a bat and ball. All the boys would queue up for a turn in bat, with the queue extending round half of the playground, while the older boys and the teachers took a turn at bowling. When someone had the bat he could stay at the wicket until he was either bowled out or the ball was caught when he hit it. Originally there had been many arguments over whether the ball had hit the wicket or not but the teachers announced that they would be the umpires and their decision was final, the arguments stopped immediately. Once 'out' a boy would run to join the back of the queue and wait for another turn.

Being relegated to the standard that matched his age had one big plus for Basil, he was now in the same class as Kenneth Wilding, known to his friends as Kenny, a boy with a similar penchant for excitement and innocent devilment, in other words another scallywag, always ready for an adventure and a bit of innocent rule breaking they quickly became the best of friends. Kenny lived in Vaughan Street, over Stoke, with his parents Frank and Ethel. Kenny's father was something of a character in the area, being well known for his over indulgence in beer. Working at the Tollymache and Cobbold brewery in Cliff Road didn't particularly help his situation because the intoxicating smell of the hops and the vats only served to stimulate his thirst, and as soon as he finished work for the day he could not resist the temptation to visit every public house on his way home for a 'swift half', which was usually a not so swift pint. By the time he rolled out of his last port of call, 'The Old Bell', he was very much the worse for wear and upon arriving home he cautiously opened the front door and threw his flat cap into the parlour and waited. If his cap came flying back out of the door like a boomerang he knew he was not welcome and staggered up the passage that ran along the back yards until he found his gate. Settling down in the coal shed for the night he slept off the alcoholic excess. On the odd occasion Ethel softened slightly and took him his cold dinner but he was still not allowed into the house.

After school Basil and Kenny were loathe to make their way home directly without getting up to some caper or other and it usually began at the new Stoke bridge. The bridge was only completed in

1925, but its design had a built in excitement for adventurous little boys and girls. Both sides of the bridge were constructed with a concrete arch, twelve feet high in the centre, and not content with walking on the footpath like everybody else, the intrepid pair found the temptation too great and they clambered over the curved arches to stand proudly on the top where they had a perfect view of the water, thirty feet below. It became a daily ritual for them.

Having clambered down the other side of the bridge they looked for their next exploit and, if it were low tide, they jumped down onto the foreshore that ran beneath the bridge and walked through the thick black mud to the other side. The dock wall beneath the bridge consisted of large stone blocks with mortar joints that were beginning to crack and crumble. Using a stick they eased small crabs from these cracks and popped them into their pockets. Having collected about a dozen crabs each they retraced their steps and pushed the crabs through the slot in the post box that stood on the corner of Commercial Rd.

"Do you think there will be a piece in the 'Star' one day, saying about the mystery of the crabs in the post box?" said Kenny.

"Yeah! How do they keep getting in there?" Chuckled Basil.

The pair fully expected to see an article in the 'Evening Star' newspaper one day telling of the strange phenomenon of crabs taking up residence in a post box, but, although it must have made a mess of the letters, there never was a mention in the paper, which they found disappointing, they never achieved the fame they sought.

Doris was none too happy, however, whenever Basil returned home with boots that were caked in the thick glutinous mud and he was regularly banned from the house until he had thoroughly cleaned his footwear. It took him a good half hour to scrape, wash and polish his boots ready for school the next day, but he considered it well worth the trouble. It never prevented him from doing it again either. Kenny, however, was a bit craftier, washing the mud off his boots under the standpipe before he went home and leaving them in the scullery out of sight of Elsie.

******

June proved to be a joyous time in the Dumble household as Gladys prepared for her wedding day. Emily Jane busied herself making arrangements for the reception and baked a beautiful fruit wedding cake which Chip iced and decorated as only he could. Emily Jane's wedding dress was altered by Doris who also made a page boy outfit for Basil and a bridesmaid dress for Marjorie.

The lucky man was Ernest Hurricks, a journeyman painter who pedalled his bicycle around Ipswich looking for painting work. His father Thomas ensured that there would be sufficient beer by buying a barrel of mild through a friend who worked at the Tollymache and Cobbold brewery.

It was a warm sunny day as Gladys walked down the aisle of St Peters church on the arm of her brother George Henry junior, her train held by Marjorie, and Basil walking solemnly behind.

Following the wedding the happy couple went to live with Ernest's parents at 25 Melville Road, leaving 251 Cavendish Street uncharacteristically empty. Emily Jane watched, with tears in her eyes, as the taxi took Gladys and Ernest to the railway station for their weekend honeymoon at a bed and breakfast in Felixstowe.

It was with a touch of sadness that she had seen the gradual emptying of her busy but happy house as the majority of her family and lodgers had embarked on a new chapter in their lives. Albert Charles had emigrated to New Zealand where he married his sweetheart Marjorie, William West was serving in the Royal Marines and living at Chatham in Kent, although his wife Emily was still living in Ipswich with her parents in Bramford Lane. Doris was married to Chip and living in James Street; but the heart of her house, the children, was the part she missed most. Basil and Marjorie were with their parents, of course, and Leslie Bushen was living with an uncle and aunt. Now there were only two family members left, George Henry junior, recently retired from the Royal Navy, and his wife, yet another Emily.

Emily Jane often sat quietly, picturing her home in her mind's eye when it was noisy with children; it provoked in her a feeling of sadness and loss.

******

For a halfpenny in the local grocery shop it was possible to buy a bag of sweets or broken biscuits and a Luka bean. Luka beans, some called them Locust beans, were black/brown in colour and had the appearance of a shrivelled runner bean with a pod that was as hard as a bullet protecting the sweet tasting bean inside. They were a big favourite with the local children who loved to collect and eat them. No surprise that it was a favourite time for all of the kids who lived in the vicinity of the docks and Stoke Bridge in particular when the 'Luka' boat came in. The large steamships carrying the beans moored in Butterman's Bay, off Pin Mill, and transferred their cargo to a small fleet of barges. These barges docked by Stoke bridge, adjacent to Mason's oil mill, and their cargo was manually offloaded. The dockers placed two thick wooden boards from the dockside to the barge enabling them to walk across, pick up a sack of beans and carry it to the warehouse. Inside the warehouse the sacks were placed on a continuous lift. This lift consisted of a vertical belt with small platforms attached to it, the platforms were large enough to hold a sack which would be lifted to the upper floor level where they were emptied, by a couple of labourers, into a large hopper. It took all day for the team of stevedores to unload the barges and it was exceptionally heavy work.

Along the route from the barges to the warehouse there was inevitably a line of spillages and these escaped beans became the object of the school kids' interest. Family income for the majority of households was low and consequently most children were underfed and constantly hungry so they quickly pounced on the liberated beans carpeting the dockside, eating their fill and stuffing their pockets to overflowing for later. Needless to say Basil and Kenny became two of the most ardent collectors.

Although the stevedores didn't mind the kids collecting the spillages, so long as they didn't get in the way and disrupt their rhythm, the mill owners were none too happy because, if they were cleared up at the end of the shift, there would probably be two or three extra sacks full to process. So despite the fact that the kids were doing no harm, the dock authorities, together with the mill owners, decided this practice could not continue. They enlisted the services of a police constable as a deterrent, with the expectation that it would stop the 'stealing' in its tracks, of course they hadn't reckoned on Basil and Kenny. The constable was in his late fifties, portly in stature with big bushy sideburns that poured into a thick moustache, he was in all probability selected for the task because of his imposing presence, and he readily accepted the challenge under the misapprehension that, as he was approaching retirement, patrolling the dockside with only a small group of children to supervise had to be a soft number. He was designated to patrol the dockside at the time the youngsters would be coming out of school.

Of course Basil and Kenny saw this exercising of authority as somewhat of a challenge to their ingenuity, a challenge that they were only too keen to take up. The boys put their heads together and came up with a ploy that was both very simple in its concept whilst capitalising on the relatively sluggish appearance of the mature sentinel. They collected together all of the interested children at school and told them of the plan which would be put into operation that afternoon as they made their way home.

As soon as school was dismissed Basil and Kenny divorced themselves from the rest of the gang and casually strolled onto the dockside, in full view of the constable, and proceeded to pick up the spilt beans. The loitering sentry spied them immediately.

"Hey you boys, stop that now." The constable boomed.

Kenny looked at Basil who returned his gaze, they both shrugged and resumed their collecting.

"I said stop that. You are stealing!" the constable broke into a slow, laboured jog toward them. The boys continued to collect their treasure until he was almost upon them before making off. The constable was encouraged to chase after them because he thought he was close enough to make a collar and therefore an example of them.

"Hey! You boys stop! I'll have your names!" he called after the retreating boys, who ran sufficiently fast to stay out of reach and sufficiently slow to maintain the constable's optimism. Of course he never stood a chance of catching them but their plan relied on him retaining the belief that he could. His overweight frame slowed him compared to the lithe agile boys but for his part he assumed his authority would make them stop.

As soon as the duo disappeared around the corner of the warehouse, eagerly pursued by the puffing constable, the second part of the plan swung into action and the rest of the boys and girls emerged from their hiding places to grab their fill of beans unhindered. The constable, finally returning from his unsuccessful chase out of breath and wiping his sweating brow with a white handkerchief, gaped at the gaggle of youngsters helping themselves to that which he was employed to protect. Agitated with his lack of success he shouted a warning and once more gave chase to the nearest group, somewhat slower than before and sweating profusely. The gaggle of children scattered but ensured that some were just slow enough to maintain his interest in them and as soon as the chase was out of sight Basil and Kenny returned to fill their pockets and ambled home with a satisfied smile on their cherubic faces.

School holidays made it even easier for the school kids to collect their booty, the boys and girls arriving an hour before the time they would be leaving school so that when the constable arrived they had been and gone and the dockside was bean free, much to his disgust. In all the time that Basil collected the beans nobody was ever caught by the constable but there was a period when nobody dared to collect the beans, and it was all Kenny's fault.

It was during a school holiday when the two best friends turned up to collect their haul of beans, only to find that there were none, worse still there was no barge to be unloaded. Undaunted Kenny went to the big sliding wooden door that sealed the entrance to the warehouse and gave it a tug. It slid open a couple of feet.

"C'mon Bass, let's have a butchers around." He poked his head inside and found the warehouse deserted.

They both slipped inside and closed the door. Thin shafts of light speared down toward them from some holes in the roof giving the place an eerie feel. The boys looked around the dark dank interior, the warehouse seemed totally deserted. In front of them was a massive steel hopper that stood about fifteen feet high with a funnel at the bottom which hovered above a rubber conveyor belt that ran through a hole in the wall and disappeared. Level with the top of the hopper was a wooden platform and beside it a rope with a block and tackle was strung over a pulley in the roof. An old wagon stood in one corner and the boys made a beeline for it, climbing into the high seat and pretending it was part of a cowboy wagon train. They aimed their imaginary rifles at attacking Indians making believe they were shooting them to protect the rest of the settlers who were crossing a wide open prairie.

Ten minutes and the interest in the wagon turned to boredom and they looked for something else to amuse themselves. There were a few piles of old sacks and a few rusting tools, mainly rakes and shovels, they failed to spark any interest. Finally their eyes alighted on the rope.

"Fancy a ride to the sky Bass?" Kenny's imagination was working overtime.

"How are we gonna do that?" Basil's brow furrowed.

"Easy."

Kenny ran to the rope and picked up the block.

"They must use this to lift sacks when they load wagons." He explained, "You stand on the hook and I'll hoist you up."

Basil stepped onto the hook and held tight onto the rope as Kenny began to pull and slowly

Basil rose up until he could almost touch the roof before Kenny lowered him to the dusty floor again.

"That was brilliant, your turn" said an excited Basil.

Kenny stepped onto the hook and Basil raised him up. At the top of his ride Kenny was much higher than the mouth of the hopper and he happened to glance into it, he could hardly believe his eyes.

"Hey Bass." He shouted down excitedly.

"Sssshhhh, somebody will hear you." Warned Basil, looking around nervously, half expecting somebody to come bursting through the door at the end of the warehouse.

"There's a load of beans in here, just waitin' for us."

"Yeah!" Basil's eyes opened wide with expectation of a big haul. "I'll come up." In his excitement he let loose the rope and Kenny came crashing down onto the worn wooden floor with a dull thud.

"Agh Jesus what did you do that for?" Exclaimed Kenny as he rolled painfully on the dusty boards, rubbing first his right elbow and then his backside.

"Sorry Kenny, I forgot I was holding the rope." Basil said extending a helping hand to assist his friend to his feet.

"Don't make my arse hurt any less." He said frowning. "Let's get them beans."

They both scooted round to the back of the hopper and ran up a set of steps that lead to the wooden platform at the head of the hopper and peered into the gaping opening. Sure enough the hopper was about quarter full of their favourite beans.

"I'll get in and fetch 'em, see if you can find a small sack or something to put them in. Get ready to fill your pockets." Grinned Kenny as he slipped through the opening into the coffer. He was totally unprepared for what happened next. He had expected that when his feet hit the beans he would have been standing on top of them, but as soon as his weight came to bear on them he began to sink.

"Crikey Bass!" He exclaimed. "I'm sinking, help me!"

Basil was half way down the steps to begin his quest for a small sack, he froze.

"What did you say?" He hissed.

"I said I'm blinking well sinking into the nuts, get me out of here."

Basil ran back up the steps and lay on the floor of the platform stretching his arms as far into the hopper as he could, but to no avail. Try as he might he could not reach Kenny's outstretched hand. Kenny, standing stock still, became more and more anxious as he felt the beans slowly enveloping him. He began to panic and struggled to free himself, but the more he struggled the faster he sank, until, as the beans reached the level of his armpits, he felt his feet touch the bottom. Relieved he expected that he could push himself up but as he strained his right foot slipped through a hole in the bottom of the hopper and he sank deeper, the beans now touching his chin. He stopped struggling and his downward movement stopped but his right foot was firmly wedged in the hole. He did not know it but the hole that ensnared his foot was the inside of the funnel that fed the conveyor belt. He was stuck fast.

"How on earth are you gonna get out of there?" Asked Basil.

"I don't know but we got to do something; think Bass."

Basil looked around the store to see if there was anything that could help him get his best friend out of the predicament he found himself in. His gaze fell on the rope with the hook.

"I know," said Basil, "stay there, don't go away!"

"I can't go away can I." Growled Kenny angrily.

Basil hauled on the rope until the hook reached the platform, excitedly he grabbed it and lowered it through the opening so that it fell on Kenny's head with an audible crack.

"Ouch! That damned well hurt."

"It's only pain," Basil chuckled, beginning to see the funny side of the situation, a funny side that Kenny failed to see. "Grab the hook and I'll pull you out." Kenny grabbed the hook.

"OK, pull Bass!"

191

Basil put all his weight onto the rope and there was a slight movement followed by a searing pain in Kenny's foot.

"Stop, stop, that hurts." Basil stopped.

"Only one thing for it Kenny, I'll have to get someone to help."

He was very concerned at what the mill workers would say but could think of no alternative so leaving Kenny stuck fast he gingerly passed through the door into the remainder of the warehouse and looked around. There were some big machines that ground up the nuts and from round the back of one of them he heard men talking. He rounded the machine. The conversation stopped immediately and three pairs of eyes stared at him inquisitively.

"Excuse me sir but my friend is stuck." Was all he could think to say.

"Stuck? What do you mean stuck?" It was the man with the brown dustcoat who spoke, it was obvious he was the foreman.

"We was getting some Luka beans and he got stuck."

"What? Where?" The foreman was a trifle confused. "Show me."

Basil led the way back to the hopper and pointed to it.

"In there."

"What! How the hell ...." his incredulity hung in the air like an autumn fog.

Climbing onto the platform the foreman peered into the hopper.

"Hello sir; I'm stuck." Kenny gave the most hopeless expression he could find.

The three men tried to pull him out the same way Basil had, without success, and finally the foreman turned to his two companions.

"We can't get in there or we will sink too." He thought for a while. "Nuthin' for it we'll have to dismantle the funnel."

It took them nearly half an hour to remove two side panels, because the bolts were corroded and did not want to turn, but as the second panel came clear a shower of beans flooded out and heaped on the floor. Carefully the foreman freed Kenny's foot and as it finally came loose his colleagues were able to pull Kenny out with the rope. They deposited him roughly onto the floor in front of the foreman, Kenny looked up into the stern face as a rough calloused hand landed heavily on his left ear. It hurt.

"Right you two," the foreman growled angrily, "I'm going to put this chute back together and you are going to watch me. When I'm finished you are going to pick up every one of these beans and put them back in that hopper, do you understand?"

Two morose faces nodded their agreement.

"Then you are never coming back here again: got it?"

Two more sad and embarrassed nods.

It was nearly two hours later that the boys sauntered out of the main door back onto the dockside. Kenny turned to Basil with a sly smile.

"My pockets are stuffed."

"Mine too." Said Basil.

Happily they ran off home.

******

Always looking to generate a bit of excitement, but temporarily deprived of Luka bean collecting, Basil and Kenny hit on another escapade to fill their homeward journey when school was finished. On the town side of Stoke bridge there stood a deserted and derelict mill, which had intrigued the young explorers for some time, and now its appeal became too strong to resist. They looked around casually to make sure nobody was watching them and while Basil acted as lookout Kenny wielded a length of iron they had found behind the mill to force free one of the planks of wood that had been nailed across the entrance door, leaving just sufficient room for them to squeeze through. Once inside they stood and surveyed the stark, gloomy interior. The roof vaulted far above their heads in the vast cathedral like space that had once boasted eight floors, all long since removed save for a small ledge by the wooden staircase. They kicked their way through the debris covered floor to the foot of the staircase that extended to the very top of the building.

"I bet there's a great view from up there." Basil grinned at Kenny as he pointed to the topmost ledge.

The almost imperceptible nod from Kenny was enough to start them both up the stairs but when they reached the point where the first floor would have been they realised that rather than rising in a zig zag form the stairs only went from left to right, each flight beginning immediately above the one below and that in order to ascend to the next level they would need to navigate the narrow ledge.

"Look; when they took the floor out they left that little bit at the end." Basil indicated the ledge which they realised was only about two feet wide.

"Not a lot of room." Uncharacteristically Basil was showing some nervousness.

"It's easy peasy." Said Kenny confidently. "I'll show you."

He edged onto the narrow floor remnant and shuffled along, it was not too difficult and his confidence grew so that by the time he reached the end he was walking quite quickly. Basil watched his companion carefully until he reached safety at the foot of the next flight of steps and realising it was not too difficult he soon joined his best friend. The next few flights were taken in their stride and in no time they stood at the very top of the building and gazed down at the concrete floor some one hundred and twenty feet below them. They smiled at each other totally oblivious to the danger.

After an hour playing in the mill they made their way home, parting in the middle of the Stoke bridge arch. Basil relished their new found play area and had not noticed how the time had sped by until he walked into the scullery.

"Where have you been 'till this time Basil?" Doris called from the living room as she studied the clock sitting on the mantel. "Your dinner is almost ready."

"Sorry mum but I was kept in at school." He lied. Fortunately for him Doris made no further enquiry, after all she knew that he was a bit of a scallywag so readily believed that there had been cause to keep him in after school.

A few days later the boys played in the mill again but they soon recognised it would be much more fun if there were a few more kids with them. That was easily sorted of course and next day the word was passed around standard four and that evening ten boys played inside the mill along with two particularly adventurous girls. Basil and Kenny showed how brave they were by running up the stairs and along the connecting strip of flooring, familiarity had given them confidence. They were cautiously followed by the others, who were a bit more reticent when it came to the ledge but soon the thought of danger disappeared and they were chasing around too.

"Let's make a target on the floor and see who can get a stone nearest to the centre from the top floor." Suggested Basil.

"Good idea." Agreed Kenny, who straight away found a lump of concrete and scratched a rough target on the floor.

"Get your ammunition boys." Kenny said, throwing the lump of concrete away and stuffing his pockets with smaller stones and lumps of solid earth. "The girls can stay down here and judge who is nearest."

All the boys chased up to the top of the staircase and stood on the very edge of the remaining floor. One by one they lobbed a stone over the edge in the direction of the target. The girls watched where each stone landed and marked the results on the wall. It came as no surprise that Basil was the most accurate. Time ran away with them again and once more Basil arrived home late.

"Where have you been 'till this time Basil?" Doris looked at the clock sitting on the mantel with a feeling of déjà vous.

"I was kept back in school." Basil lied once more knowing his excuse had worked last time. Doris said no more but thought it a bit strange that he was being punished so regularly, he must be behaving really badly. This state of affairs continued for two weeks until one day she decided that enough was enough and she would have to do something, either about his behaviour at school or about the school's discipline regime. That evening, when Chip came home from work, she intercepted him in the scullery and raised the subject.

"I'm concerned about Basil; he keeps being kept behind at school."

"Really? What's he been up to?" Chip had been blissfully unaware that his son was the recipient of regular punishment.

"I don't know, I've heard nothing from the school, he has been kept behind almost every day for two weeks now." Chip raised his eyebrows.

"What does Basil say about it?"

"Absolutely nothing, he just says 'I was kept behind'."

"Where is he now?"

"He's over at Nellie's."

They both waited for Basil to come home for tea and as they sat, eating rabbit pie, Chip raised his head, balanced his knife and fork on the edge of his plate and gave Basil a serious look.

"Are you having problems at school son?" Basil slowly raised his eyes from his plate and a piece of pastry slowly slipped from his fork and sploshed in the thick gravy leaving a splatter on the table.

"No dad." He tried to put on his most innocent expression.

"Is it true that you are sometimes being kept in?"

"Yes."

"So you must be doing something wrong." Chip persisted. Basil remained resolute, he had done nothing wrong and he didn't know why he was being kept in.

"Then we will have to find out, won't we."

"No it's alright dad, I'm sure they won't keep me in any more." Basil wanted the subject to go away and he hoped his assurance that it would not happen again would be sufficient to put an end to the subject. It seemed to work, Chip picked up his knife and fork and finished his meal. No more was said, not that evening at any rate.

Unbeknown to Basil, the next morning Chip arranged to be allowed to leave work for half an hour and he made the short journey to Stoke school and the headmaster's office. The headmaster was equally baffled, as far as he was aware no pupil had been kept in for over a week and there was certainly no record of Basil ever having been detained. Chip hurried back to work satisfied with the assurances of the headmaster that he would establish the truth and deal with it.

It was a surprised and worried Basil who answered the headmaster's call to his office the next morning and, immediately realising that he could not talk his way out of the situation, he admitted to having lied to cover up the home time escapades he and his friends had enjoyed in the old mill. The headmaster was horrified, the mill was in such a dangerous condition it was nothing short of a miracle that no pupil had been injured or even killed. He immediately forbade any scholar from entering the old mill on pain of serious repercussions and he presented Basil with a sealed envelope to pass to his father. All the way home Basil worried over just what his father would say but, in true Chip fashion, all he received was a lecture on always telling the truth. Chip was more concerned that Basil had lied to both him and Doris than he was about the adventurous extra curricula activity.

Another avenue of excitement had been closed to the adventurous duo but that didn't deter them from inventing a new caper.

The boys did indeed keep away from the old mill, encouraged no doubt by the headmaster's threat and the prospect of punishment at home, but they still found plenty of places on the docks to explore and have fun. One game they devised was to see who could jump along a line of barges in the fewest bounds. They leapt from sack to sack and barge to barge, landing on the full sacks of seed, flour or cattle feed, and even sometimes on loose cargo in their quest to see who was most agile. It was quite a dangerous sport as Kenny was soon to discover. One day after school Basil and Kenny were leaping along the barges, with Kenny in the lead as usual when, attempting a massive game winning leap, he gave a mighty push off a sack, which unfortunately did not afford him as much grip as he had expected, and his foot slipped. He still managed to get quite a bit of height but the length of the leap was compromised and he fell short with his legs sliding between two sacks. His impetus still carried his upper body forward and he heard the unmistakable crack of breaking bone at the same time as an acute pain shot up both legs. He lay stunned and in great pain as Basil came scrambling over the sacks toward him.

"You OK Kenny?"

"No I 'aint Bass, I'm in agony."

Fortunately some dock workers, who had been observing the boys antics, realised there was a problem and came to the hapless Kenny's aid. Carefully they lifted him from the barge and laid him on the dockside while one of their number jogged to the office and asked a clerk to telephone for an ambulance.

Kenny was hospitalised for two weeks and in plaster for a further six weeks but, perhaps unsurprisingly, once the plaster casts had been removed, it was only two days before he was walking over the arc of Stoke bridge and crab hunting beneath it again with his best mate Basil.

The Double family, Left to Right: Doris (nee Dumble),
Basil, Charles Henry Philip (Chip), Leonard and
Marjorie.

Ellen Beatrice Double (nee Cotton)
Basil's mother

Chip and Doris on their wedding day

Grandfather Charles with Marjorie in his pony and trap
outside 19 James St as Chip looks on

Emily Jane with four of her children at her husband's funeral: 1913.
L to R: Doris, Albert, William and Gladys.
(George Jnr was away serving as a boy in the Navy)

Basil's first 'wedding' aged 5
Sadly the bride remains unidentified

Great grandmother Jane Double (nee Culpitt) on
her 100th birthday 1929.

Ellen Holland (nee Double) - (Aunt Nellie)
with her sons William, Douglas and Cyril

Basil (age 14) with Marjorie (age 11),
wearing his first pair of long trousers.

The Rising Sun public house on the corner of Princes
Street and James Street, granddad Charles' local.

The paddle steam ships that ran between Ipswich and
Felixstowe. The 'Norfolk' in the foreground with one
stack and the 'Suffolk' behind with two stacks.

Gladys Hurricks (nee Dumble)
with husband Ernest.

Basil's best mate Kenny Wilding with his
parents Frank and Ethel

The Social Settlement at the junction Fore Hamlet and
Duke Street

1931

Returning home from school one Friday in March Basil noticed there was a freshly baked fruit cake standing on the table in the scullery; he loved fruit cake, especially Doris's fruit cake. He felt his mouth beginning to water. Doris was in the yard beating the dust out of her parlour mat, Basil poked his head out of the door.

"I 'aint half hungry mum." He tried to put on a pained and longing face.

"There's some bread in the bin." Definitely not the answer he had wished for.

"I think a bit of cake would be better for me."

"You leave that cake alone, it's for great Grandma's birthday. If you're hungry have a bit of bread otherwise wait for your dinner." Basil was crestfallen.

That night Chip worked his magic with a pallet knife and some royal icing before taking a step back to admire the finished article standing on the table.

"All ready for Sunday."

"Perfect." Said Doris.

Basil had been eavesdropping and locked on to the mention of Sunday.

"What's happening Sunday?" he asked.

"We are going on a journey my boy. We are going to see your great Grandma." Chip explained.

Basil went to bed excited and awoke early, he knew that great Grandma lived a long way away and was looking forward to a thrilling journey. He rubbed his hand on the window pane to clear the frosty condensation and peered out. There was a sharp frost covering everything with a crisp white rime.

"Come on Len, we're going on a train today, time to get up." He bubbled.

"Oh go away Bass, it's too early." Leonard turned over and pulled the blankets round his neck. Undaunted Basil hurried downstairs and into the scullery. He turned the single tap above the brown earthenware sink and stuck his head under the freezing jet of water. A quick rub with the towel that hung over a rail beside the sink and he was ready to get dressed.

"What should I put on mum?" He shouted up the staircase.

"Your clothes are hanging on the fireguard." Doris sounded half asleep.

By the time his parents made it downstairs Basil was dressed in his Sunday best, boots polished to a face reflecting shine, sitting on the parlour bench swinging his legs impatiently. Chip toasted a doorstep of bread for each of them and covered it liberally with fresh dripping while Doris dressed Marjorie. Basil sprinkled salt on the dripping, hurriedly demolished his toast and waited, for what to him seemed an age, for everybody else to be ready to leave. Chip picked up the old biscuit tin containing the pristine cake, Doris filled her shopping basket with a freshly baked loaf and a boiled ham and they stepped into James Street. Leonard smiled down at Marjorie and held out his hand to grasp hers; it felt cold as his fingers enveloped it, while Basil, not waiting for anybody else ran merrily in front in his eagerness to get to the station.

The first leg of their train journey took them from Ipswich to Manningtree. They could only get seats in the unheated third class carriage where the cold frosty air whipped through the open window and swirled round the compartment. The window was open because Basil was intent on leaning out to see where they were and as the train rumbled across the wooden bridge that spanned the river Stour he brought his head into the compartment just long enough to tell everybody that they were nearing Manningtree station. There they had to change onto a train bound for Harwich which unfortunately involved a half hour wait. Chip and Doris made their way, with Marjorie swinging on their arms, to the waiting room where they discovered a small coal fire flickering in the grate; perhaps it would take the worst of the chill out of their bones. Leonard and Basil stayed on the platform to watch the train from which they had just alighted as, puffing and belching steam, it began the pull up the gentle gradient in the direction of Colchester.

It was a short ride from Manningtree station to the station at Mistley and the weak spring sun

211

had finally melted the frost from the footpath as they made the one mile walk to Park Cottages and great aunt Elizabeth's cottage. Great Grandma Jane was sitting quietly in the parlour in front of a gently burning coal fire with a warm blanket wrapping her from the waist down. She was looking quite frail, justifiably so as in two days she would celebrate her one hundred and first birthday, she smiled warmly as she saw the family enter. Sitting beside her was her son Charles who had come over on the train during the week and was staying with Elizabeth, her husband James and Jane for a few days.

Chip went straight to his grandmother and kissed her fondly on the cheek, wished her a happy birthday, turned to his father and taking his hand firmly, pumped it in an energetic handshake. Doris crossed the small room to give Jane a kiss while Basil, who couldn't remember ever having seen his great grandmother before, made a beeline for grandfather Charles.

"Granddad!" he exclaimed as he hugged his grandfather's neck tightly. Leonard moved over to kiss Jane tenderly on the cheek and as he did so he placed his hand firmly in Basil's back encouraging him to do likewise. Basil kissed her cheek quickly, turned to Leonard and made a face.

"She's got whiskers." He whispered to Leonard. His whisper was loud enough for his father to hear but thankfully Jane's deteriorating hearing failed to pick up the remark. He received a disapproving look from Chip.

Doris and Elizabeth made for the kitchen to prepare the birthday lunch while Chip and James took a seat near to Jane. The conversation flowed freely with Leonard joining in at odd times. Basil and Marjorie sat on the floor and listened to the adult discussion with total disinterest.

"This is boring isn't it?" he whispered to Marjorie, a bit quieter this time so that nobody else could hear. Marjorie nodded in agreement.

"Why don't you two go into the garden until dinner's ready." Doris's suggestion felt like the answer to a prayer for the youngsters, after all the only reason that Basil was so excited about the day was the two train journeys and that iced fruit cake. They ran around a bit in order to keep warm before moving into the front garden where they leaned on the gate and watched the odd wagon rumble down the road into the village.

Lunch was a simple affair of boiled ham sandwiches, with Elizabeth's homemade chutney, washed down with great mugs of tea and finished off with a slice of the iced fruit cake. Basil finally got his ample slice.

By four o'clock it was time to make their way back to the station for the journey home, and by the time they arrived back in James Street and had something to eat it was bedtime for Basil and Marjorie. Basil huddled down in his bed pulling the covers high around his neck and was asleep almost as soon as his head touched the pillow and was oblivious to Leonard slipping between the sheets an hour later.

******

Two weeks later and Basil had his second chance to sit the examinations that would decide if he could attend either Tower Ramparts Secondary school or the Municipal school at Northgate. He felt rather deflated that he had been held back in standard four for this school year having previously been moved up a year because he was thought to be above average. The reality perhaps proved he wasn't. His fellow scholars gave the 'swot' a bit of ribbing on his return, but deep down he knew it was his own fault, he had not tried hard enough, being told he was more advanced had convinced him that he could freewheel a bit and now the acid test was upon him. Sadly he failed the examinations again.

******

Doris, now thirty one years of age and with staunch socialist views, had become more involved with the political scene in Ipswich over the past couple of years. She had joined the local Labour Party and immediately became an active member, energetically canvassing during the 1929 election, and elated at the resultant hung parliament that had seen Labour's Ramsay McDonald become Prime Minister. Despite holding more seats than any other party, Labour did not have an overall majority and struggled through this era of depression.

Doris had also become very popular with the local residents and built many friendships, one of the strongest being with Phyllis Strong. Of similar age, Phyllis had two children, a son Walter, who was slightly younger than Basil and a daughter, Mary, just a few months younger than Marjorie, and she delighted in the four children sharing time together, often looking after them when Doris attended Labour Party meetings.

The children could never go to her house on a Tuesday or Wednesday, however, because unfortunately Phyllis lived on the wrong side of Portman Street and her small flagged back yard was one of those that backed onto the livestock market. The market was held every Tuesday and the pens were always overflowing with cattle, pigs and sheep. Unfortunately that was not all that overflowed as the animals conspired to make a particularly unsavoury mess in their pens. This aromatic mixture of cattle, pig and sheep droppings diluted with urine and trampled into a runny mush ran from the pens and ended up in the back yards of all the houses backing onto them. The home owners had asked on a number of occasions for the market to use straw to help soak up the offending sludge but nothing had ever been done, so every Wednesday the women were employed shovelling the effluent out of their yard back into the market and sluicing with buckets of water carried from the single standpipe. It was a lengthy and tiring process.

Phyllis's father was a farm labourer who lived with his wife in a quaint little cottage just outside Levington on the banks of the river Orwell. Phyllis suggested that it would be a good idea, and a pleasant break, if they all went to the cottage for the day during the summer holidays. Doris was quick to take up the offer and so it was that on a bright sunny Monday morning she and Phyllis walked to the bus station in the old cattle market with baskets of food and drink and four children in tow.

Basil and Walter were the first to board the Leyland Tiger bus destined for Felixstowe, running to the back seats they knelt and peered out the back window. They waved to motor cars, cyclists and pedestrians alike as the bus made its way out of the town but once they were on the Felixstowe Road there were precious few other road users and they amused themselves looking at the animals and waving crops in the fields. As the bus approached the Levington bridge Phyllis informed them that they had to get off at this stop but not to worry it would only be a short walk from there to the cottage. Not a problem thought Basil, unaware of just how far that short walk would actually be. The group made their way down Bridge lane, across a couple of fields on well trodden footpaths and along the sea wall to the cottage on the shore.

The children had a great day; it was just like being at the seaside only without all the crowds. They swam, built sandcastles on the foreshore and watched as the passenger paddle steamers plied their way downstream to Felixstowe and Harwich or upstream heading back toward Ipswich.

"That one is the 'Suffolk'." Said Basil, pointing as one of the paddle steamers came into view heading back upstream.

"How do you know?" enquired Walter.

"Because it has two funnels," Basil explained, "the other one is the 'Norfolk' and it only has one." They both stared as the boat cruised past them, the big paddle wheels on the sides smacking the smooth river into a white frothy turmoil. They watched it until it was almost out of sight.

"I wish I could ride on that boat." Mused Walter.

"I'm definitely going to ride it, and soon." Basil made himself a promise, little knowing just how soon that journey would be.

******

Shortly before school broke up for the summer holidays one of Marjorie's friends told her about the 'Band of Mercy', the junior branch of the RSPCA, and Marjorie, who loved animals struck up an interest. Her friend said it was very educational and great fun too, Marjorie dearly wanted to join.

"You are too young to be out at night on your own." Doris had told her when she broached the subject.

"But it isn't late mum, I would be home by eight o'clock. Please let me join." But Doris was adamant. 'Nothing else for it' thought Marjorie 'I'll have to persuade Basil to join too then mum will make him come with me, to look after me.'

"I don't want to." Was Basil's reply when she attempted to recruit him.

"But they have stories, lantern slide shows, lectures and lots more."

"Still don't want to.

"You know that you wanted to have a dog." Marjorie had an idea that she was confident would change his mind.

"Yes, but mum said I can't have one." Basil puffed his cheeks as he remembered the conversation he had with Doris. He kept up his pleas, pestering her constantly for over a month, but she would not budge. "She said I didn't know how to look after a dog and she would only end up looking after it for me."

"Exactly!" Marjorie had a glint in her eye, she knew she had him hooked even though he was still unaware that she was even fishing for him. "If you join the 'Band of Mercy' with me, they will teach you how to look after a dog properly."

"Then there will be no reason I can't have one. Marj you're a genius." His eyes were wide open with excitement as, without another thought he ran to the scullery to lobby Doris who was busy preparing the dinner. Marjorie just smiled to herself, satisfied that the fight was now in Basil's hands.

"Mum, mum can I have a dog please mum." He pleaded with Doris, bursting with anticipation.

"No Basil," she reaffirmed, "I told you before, you don't know how to look after one properly and your dad and me would end up looking after it." She didn't see it coming.

"But if I joined the 'Band of Mercy' I could learn all about what you have to do. Then I could have one *and* look after it." Doris looked at his excited face beaming up at her, she knew she was beaten and she also knew that it was Marjorie who had beaten her not Basil.

"Tell you what." She was stalling, trying to think of a way to avoid a dog in her house.

"Yes." Basil was confident he had won and waited eagerly for confirmation.

"If you take Marjorie with you and look after her, and if you learn all about how to look after a dog. Dad and I will think about it." It was a definite maybe but Basil took it as an unequivocal yes.

The 'Band of Mercy' met regularly and it was with a great feeling of excitement that Basil turned up at the next meeting with Marjorie's hand held firmly in his. They were warmly welcomed and told that the first item on the agenda would, as was customary at all meetings, be a recital of the

219

pledge and the evening would commence with a lecture on cats complete with a set of lantern slides. This would be followed by a rendition of the story of 'Black Beauty' also illustrated with slides. The evening would close with a repeat of the pledge.

They were each handed a piece of printed paper containing the objects of the group, what was expected from each member and the pledge, which they would be required to learn by heart for the next meeting. Taking their places they stood and read the pledge aloud as the rest of the members recited it from memory.

I will try to be kind to all living creatures, and try to protect them from cruel usage.

Basil had only offered to attend as a means of getting his own dog but he found that he enjoyed that first meeting, he learned many things about cats that he had been ignorant of before and he enjoyed the company. He was keen to continue attendance and over the next few weeks he listened avidly to stories related by other members and joined enthusiastically in the singing of songs specially written and compiled by the organisers. He listened carefully to illustrated lectures on kindness towards all species and revelled in the annual summer pet show held in the St John Ambulance hall in Samuel Road. Everybody brought their pets along and were quizzed on how they looked after them, what they fed them, how much they exercised them and there were prizes for the owners of the best kept pets. Basil could not wait to get his own dog, especially now that he knew how to look after it, and win some of those prizes.

Doris was still resisting but he knew it would not be long.

******

There had been an air of sadness in the Stoke School as the summer term drew to a close in July because it was to be the end of an era, not just for Basil but for the whole school. It was to be the last time that bustling children would barge their way through the flaking green entrance doors because the decision had been made to close the school for good. When classes resumed in the autumn they would all be transferring to other schools, Basil and Kenny were bound for Argyll Street.

In the meantime they had the summer holidays to enjoy and enjoy them they did. Kenny's legs had healed sufficiently for him to resume his activities in his favourite playground, the docks. His injuries had not deterred him in the slightest and he was soon beside his best friend Basil gathering their Luka beans and when they got bored with that they pretended the barges were in fact brave galleons bristling with cannon, men o' war fighting the Spanish armada. They walked the towpath of the Gipping as far as Needham Market and visited the tram sheds in Constantine Road to give the trolley busses the once over, pretending to be drivers and conductors. One place they gave a wide berth was the warehouse with the bean hopper.

It was whilst on their way to one of their tram shed visits that they came across a gang of men erecting some new electricity pylons beside the river Gipping, adjacent to the Alderman Road recreation ground. One of the men called out to them to come over, Basil and Kenny looked at each other, shrugged and sidled over to the workmen.

"Hey boys, how would you like to run an errand for us?"

"Depends what the errand is." Kenny was non-committal.

"We need some food for our lunch." The lineman explained. "Wondered if you would go to the bakers in Hadleigh Road and get us some bread rolls and cakes."

"What's in it for us?"

"Cheeky devil. There will be something in it for you alright."

"Okay then."

The lineman gave Kenny two shillings and told him what they wanted but as the boys turned to go he decided that he needed some assurance that they would return and not simply run off with the money.

"Boys, give me your school caps, you can have them back when you return."

The boys dutifully handed over their caps and made off toward Hadleigh Road, it had never occurred to them not to return or to pocket the money, that would be dishonest, and, though scallywags, they were both too proud to be anything other than totally honest. They ran all the way there and back and handed over the rolls, cakes and importantly the change and were rewarded for their errand and their honesty with a whole penny each.

The holidays raced by and before they realised it September was about to bring the school summer holidays to an abrupt end, it was time, once more, to resume their studies. The walk from James Street to Argyll Street was quite a hike for two eleven year olds, a journey that took Basil and Kenny up Princes Street into Friars Street and then via Old Cattle Market, Tacket Street, Eagle Street to Grimwade Street and finally Argyll Street. For the sports lessons they had to walk all the way to the Park Road end of Christchurch Park and after a bruising game of football or rounders they had to walk all the way home, a distance probably approaching two miles. No wonder they were tired each night and slept well.

On his first day Basil found himself in standard five and was made a quick count of which of the Stoke pupils had made the move to Argyll Street. Many of his friends who lived over Stoke or in the Duke Street area, he realised, had moved to different schools, thank goodness Kenny was not one of them. The deadly duo soon evaluated who was up for a bit of a lark and who wasn't. There was, however, no lack of excitement in the school as they got to grips with their classmates, resuming friendships with those who had made the move from Stoke school and striking up a few new friendships, but nobody ever came close to severing the close tie between Basil and Kenny.

One pupil who was allowed into the close group of friends was a feisty lad called Thomas Walker. Thomas was a bright lad who had been advanced a standard in a similar way to Basil three years earlier from standard two to standard three. The difference was that unlike Basil who had been held back in standard four when he failed his secondary exams, Thomas had remained one standard higher. Also in standard five was Albert Walker, Thomas's elder brother, who was, unfortunately, rather slow on the uptake. Thomas was extremely protective of his elder brother both in the classroom and in the playground.

Arithmetic was one subject in particular that Albert struggled with, he just could not get his head around numbers and as a consequence he hated and dreaded those lessons coming round. Mr Longstaff, the arithmetic teacher, was an extremely hard man, he was also the headmaster. His face was long, made to appear even longer with the addition of a straggly beard and curly hair that stood proud of his head. It was this appearance that earned him the nickname of 'Dobbin' amongst the pupils, who thought that he reminded them of a horse. He balanced a pair of wire rimmed spectacles as close as possible to the end of his narrow nose so that they seemed to be perpetually in danger of falling off. He also nurtured the conviction that an inability to learn was always as a result of laziness and it could be improved with a sharp dose of pain. Punishment for getting sums wrong was, therefore, three strokes of the cane administered with gusto across the buttocks of the recalcitrant boy or one stroke across the open palm of a girl. Longstaff was definitely not a popular teacher.

One morning he swept into the classroom and with a flourish scrawled ten sums on the blackboard.

"Okay." He boomed, his hooded dark eyes flashing around the class. "Whittaker, come to the board and write the solution to question number one, showing all of your working." He stepped to the side of the raised platform and folded his arms.

Harold Whittaker deliberately struggled to extricate himself from his desk and slowly made his way to the blackboard in order to give himself time to work out the answer to the sum in his head. He scratched his answer on the blackboard with the stick of chalk that Longstaff offered him.

"Correct Whittaker; back to your seat." Taking the chalk from Whittaker as he passed he extended his arm in the direction of Basil. "Double; number two, go!"

Basil slipped from his desk and grasped the proffered stick of chalk as he made his way to the blackboard with a confident smile. As soon as Whittaker had been called to complete question one Basil had worked out question two, just in case he were called upon, he didn't mind, he was good with numbers anyway. Basil chalked the answer with an arrogant flourish.

"Correct Double." Longstaff was never one to offer praise, that would never do. As Basil held out the chalk he turned his gaze toward Albert and smiled. "Walker major, number three."

Albert was visibly petrified and he just stared at the blackboard with a blank look on his face. Thomas stood up to make his way to the blackboard in the hope that he could save his elder brother but he was stopped in his tracks,

"Not you Walker minor, resume your seat." Longstaff's voice cut the air like a whiplash; he was enjoying seeing the boy squirm. Callously he approached the trembling Albert.

"I said Walker major." He spoke the words quietly and slowly as he held the chalk at arms length. It was obvious that he wanted to embarrass and persecute the pupil who always struggled with his arithmetic.

"Well boy?" he hissed.

"I don't know how to do it sir." Albert looked pleadingly at his persecutor.

"Then I shall have to give you some extra tutoring shan't I." A satisfied grin spread across Longstaff's face.

"Out the front boy." With that he grasped Albert's ear roughly, Albert winced, the ear was twisted, Albert cried out with pain as he was dragged to the front of the class.

Basil noticed that Thomas's face was getting redder and redder as he watched his brother being humiliated, his anger rose.

Longstaff pulled the stool out from behind his desk and bent Albert over it. He took his cane from the desk drawer and flexed it menacingly. Thomas's breathing became audible. As the cane swished through the air and landed painfully on his brother's rear Thomas clenched his fists. The strokes continued until the customary three had been delivered but they did not stop, four, five, six, Albert cried pitifully and then the dam burst. Thomas leapt from behind his desk, grabbed a chair, raised it above his head and charged toward the astonished teacher.

"You bloody rotten bugger!" he screamed as he brought the chair down on the unfortunate teacher. The chair broke into several pieces and for a second the classroom held its breath waiting for the eruption. All that could be heard was poor Albert's sobs.

Longstaff rounded on Thomas and, forgetting Albert's learning encouragement, he swept him off his feet and, tucking him under his arm like a parcel, strode off in the direction of his office, a thin trickle of blood snaking its way from his brow toward his starched collar. In the absence of a corridor the journey took him through two other classrooms where the startled pupils and teachers watched silently and open mouthed as he stormed past with his cargo. They heard the crash of wood on wood as the office door slammed shut, followed shortly afterwards by the dull thud of wood on thinly covered buttock as Longstaff meted out his revenge.

For the rest of his school career Thomas was a hero amongst the pupils but it did not escape their notice that Albert was never again caned by Longstaff.

******

Chip heard a rumour at work that the paddle steamers, the Suffolk and the Norfolk, were soon to be withdrawn from service and resolved to take the family on a trip while they still had the opportunity to experience this classic form of transport. He booked tickets for the following Sunday on the 'Suffolk', which was the larger of the two vessels.

Bright and early Sunday morning they had a filling breakfast of porridge before walking to the New Cut where the Orwell steamboats were moored. Basil had always promised himself a trip on the paddle steamers and was pleased he could enjoy the experience with the rest of the family and that he would be able to explore the boat with his elder brother, who would, no doubt, be able to explain how the boat worked. Chip and Doris just wanted to enjoy the ride.

They arrived at the berth to find the 'Suffolk' ready for boarding, her two stacks emitting a steady column of dark grey smoke that drifted listlessly into the morning sky. Basil was pleased and excited that his father had booked tickets for the 'Suffolk' specifically because he had heard it was possible to go below deck and look into the engine room. Originally there had been three paddle steamers operated by Great Eastern Railway Company, the 'Suffolk', the 'Norfolk' distinguishable by the fact that it only sported a single stack, and the 'Essex'. The latter had been sold off in 1913 for war service and was subsequently used as a Thames excursion vessel. The remaining two vessels were retained when Great Eastern Railway was amalgamated into London North Eastern Railway in 1923 but had now reached the end of their economic life.

Basil clambered up the short gangplank onto the deck, encouraging Leonard to keep pace with him. Marjorie wanted to go right to the front of the boat and Doris spotted a couple of vacant seats, although there were a number of passengers who looked ominously as if they could be making for them. Firmly, but carefully, Doris elbowed her way forward with Marjorie desperately hanging onto her hand. They reached the vacant seats seconds before another man and woman and Doris sat Marjorie down triumphantly before taking the seat beside her. The man herumphed and moved towards another pair of seats with obvious displeasure on his face. Chip chuckled as he reached the pair.

There was a sharp blast on the whistle, a stream of boiling steam spurting out, curling as it evaporated in the warm air. The boat slowly moved away from the quay and began its slide downriver leaving the docks behind them and ploughing past Stoke bathing place gathering speed, past the boatyards that extended up to the road bridge on Wherstead road by the Ostrich public house and out into open river. From this point the scenery changed with the Strand to their right and Nacton shores emerging on their left. Pin Mill came and went, the barges with furled sails resting on the shore by the Butt and Oyster public house, whilst on the other shore Levington, where they had spent that eventful day earlier in the year, drifted majestically by.

Basil was keen to see the engine room, as was Leonard. Chip wanted to go too but was unsure whether he should leave Doris and Marjorie, neither of whom was in the slightest bit interested in anything mechanical.

"Can we go and see the engines dad?" Basil asked.

"Of course son, you and Lenny run along." He cast a quick sideways glance at Doris, a glance that achieved its aim.

"Why don't you go with the boys," said Doris, "I'm sure you would find it more interesting than sitting here."

"You don't mind?"

"Of course not, you run along, we will just sit here and enjoy the cruise. We will be fine, won't we Marjorie." But Marjorie was not listening, she was far too engrossed in the scenery slipping by.

The boys strode off in the direction of the staircase in the centre of the boat, Chip cast one last glance at Doris and Marjorie, who was still spellbound with the scenery, before ducking through the door and down the steps. The view that greeted Basil was far better than he had even imagined it would be. Each side of the boat there was a viewing gangway that ran the full length of the engine room, separated from the room itself by only a brass handrail; the three of them leaned on the rail and marvelled at the spectacle that had unfolded on the other side, it was a wonderland of technology.

Two large black steel boilers sat end to end in the centre of the room, one facing forward the other facing backward, each with a large door near to the base. In front of each door was a heap of black shiny coal waiting to be fed into the hungry furnace within. Every few minutes the stoker, his body wet with sweat and veined where the sweat had washed the black coal dust down his body, opened the door and shovelled a dozen or more loads into the greedy fire.

Running from the boilers were big copper pipes with brass joints, all polished to perfection so that you could see your face reflected in them. There were numerous dials attached to the pipe work at different points and an engineer, wiping his oily hands on a grubby rag that was hooked over his belt, checked them all in turn, tapping the glass as he did so. Above the governor was twirling its weights frantically and the beautiful green cylinders with their silver pistons pumping away hissed as the steam was ejected into the stacks. The pistons turned two axles which ran beneath the walkway to the paddle wheels outside, the blades slapped and splashed as they bit into the water dragging the boat behind them before emerging, dripping, as they made another turn.

Basil was captivated. He stood and stared, mesmerised, marvelling at the sheer power of the engine in front of him, until his concentration was broken by the clanging of a bell and a large dial in front of the engineer swung it's pointer from 'full' to 'slow'. The engineer immediately turned some valve wheels and the boat slowed noticeably.

"Felixstowe." Yelled the captain over the loudspeakers.

"That was quick." Said Chip as he lifted his hunter watch. "Goodness we have been down here for nearly an hour, Doris will wonder where we have got to."

Separating themselves from the great engines the three made their way up the stairway and pushed toward the bow of the boat, fighting against the flock of passengers making ready to disembark, until they spied Doris and Marjorie exactly where they had left them. Chip clasped Doris's hand on one side and Marjorie's on the other and followed the boys in the direction of the exit gangplank.

"You were gone an awfully long time, I thought you had left me." Doris chided. "Was it interesting down there?"

"Amazing," replied Chip, "simply amazing." Leonard and Basil answered her question with big broad smiles.

They made their way off the boat and onto the jetty by the 'Three Ships' public house and joined the queue that was waiting for motor bus to take them into town. The bus only made one stop on its journey to the town railway station and that was at the head of the pier which was ideal because that was where they intended to have lunch. Alighting from the bus Chip led the party to the Regal restaurant and they all enjoyed a plate of steak pie with potatoes and peas.

"That was grand." Said Chip as he swallowed the last spoonful of gravy. Chip loved gravy and never left a trace on his plate.

With full stomachs they wandered lazily the full length of the pier, pausing only at the very end to watch the small fishing boats as they bobbed way out at sea.

"I think we ought to go back now." Said Chip sadly, knowing that the return journey would be a long one and they couldn't linger too long. The bus back to the 'Little Ships' arrived just as the 'Norfolk' was being tied up ready to disgorge another hoard of passengers onto the jetty, they joined the queue that was waiting to board.

When everybody was on board, the single stacked paddle steamer pulled away and made for Harwich, on the opposite bank of the Orwell where, once again, passengers were exchanged and the boat finally cut loose heading back to Felixstowe before making the return journey to New Cut in Ipswich, passing the 'Suffolk' just off HMS Ganges at Shotley as she repeated her earlier journey from Ipswich to the coast.

When they arrived home everybody agreed it had been a most enjoyable day. Doris cut a few sandwiches for tea and Chip put the kettle on for a much needed cuppa.

******

October was a very busy month for Doris because another general election had been called and her commitment to the Labour party cause had thrown her headlong into the political campaign. While Basil and Marjorie were at school she spent a considerable amount of time at the Labour party offices in Lower Brook Street, working with the local candidate, Robert Jackson, evaluating the party manifesto and adding the necessary local issues. The final two weeks leading up to the election were spent touring the Ipswich constituency, sometimes with Jackson himself, putting super human effort into the drive to oust sitting Conservative MP John Ganzoni who had held the seat almost continuously since the 1914 election. Another election had been called to be held before the end of 1915 and that was when Robert Jackson emerged to enter the fray as an Independent Labour Candidate, since he was not supported by Labour Party headquarters. The two candidates fought over the constituency from that date on and Robert Jackson had been victorious at the 1923 election only to surrender the seat to John Ganzoni again in 1924. Their combat was to continue until both men retired immediately prior to the candidate selection boards for the 1938 election.

Basil didn't see much of Doris during the daytime and his evenings were commandeered by Doris to be employed in either stuffing campaign leaflets into envelopes or walking round the town pushing the envelopes through letterboxes.

When the day of the election dawned, Tuesday 27th October, Basil rose bright and early. The school was being used as a polling station which meant that he had the day off but sadly he was far from free to find his own amusement. Doris was going to spend the day at the local party headquarters and Basil had been volunteered to work for her. Having left Marjorie in the capable hands of Mrs Strong, Doris and Basil made their way to Lower Brook Street where they found a number of tables had been pushed together and were covered with big paper sheets, each divided into squares, each square containing a voter's name together with their electoral number. There was a separate sheet for each polling station and they would be used to track the voting and predict the probable outcome. When knocking on doors during the campaign lists had been compiled recording whether a voter had pledged their support for Robert or for the conservative candidate. The corresponding squares had been coloured in either red or blue to match the pledge or pencil to denote a 'don't know' or refusal to commit. Doris's objective was to ensure that all of these promised supporters marked in red actually turned out to vote.

Both parties had a campaigner outside each of the polling stations whose job was to collect the electoral numbers from the voters as they left the station. Basil's job, along with half a dozen other boys, some with bicycles, was to visit the Labour campaigner periodically, collect the list of numbers and take them back to party headquarters where Doris was able to check off the names on the big paper sheets giving her a view of those who were yet to vote. Other campaigners visited those yet to vote and those who were uncommitted to try and persuade them to turn out, or in some cases even take them to the polling station in a motor car. It was an extremely tiring day for everybody but Basil enjoyed the hustle and bustle along with the excitement and expectancy.

Once the polling stations were closed, the ballot boxes were sealed and transported one by one to the counting hall, the Corn Exchange behind the Town Hall. Doris accompanied Robert Jackson and the other campaigners to witness the vote counting. Right from the beginning Ganzoni wore a confident smile, he was certain that the decision of the Liberal Party not to put a candidate forward would carry him to victory. In truth Jackson had the same fear, and the coloured sheets painted a less than rosy picture, so it was with a sense of resignation that they waited patiently for the result. Ganzoni's confidence was proven to be well founded when the returning officer declared him the victor.

The previous election, in 1929, had seen Ganzoni hold a slim nine hundred and thirty five vote majority, this time his majority exploded to twelve thousand two hundred and ninety two. Jackson, by comparison only polled one hundred fewer votes than previously but the major factor was the ten thousand Liberal votes in 1929 that swung, almost entirely, in favour of Ganzoni.

Magnanimous in his victory speech Ganzoni left the Town Hall to enjoy his victory celebration in the Conservative offices while Jackson and his team, thoroughly deflated, returned to their homes to lick their wounds.

For the next few days Doris was very depressed, she had held such high hopes of a big swing toward Labour extending across the country, mainly from the working classes, the miners, the textile industries, the shipbuilders, but it had not happened. Nationally there had been a landslide victory for the National Government which had been formed during August following the collapse of the previous Labour government. The bulk of the National Government's support came from the Conservative Party, and on this day they won four hundred and seventy seats and inflicted the heaviest defeat on the Labour Party who lost four out of five seats compared to the 1929 election. It proved to be the last election where one party, the Conservatives, received an absolute majority of the votes cast and was the last general election not to take place on a Thursday.

Basil didn't share Doris's disappointment with the day, he was far too disinterested in politics, it was boring adult stuff, however he really enjoyed all the hype and the excitement of running messages between polling stations and 'headquarters', in fact he had even made a game of it, imagining himself as some kind of spy trafficking important information.

The next morning whist getting ready for school he realised just how tired he was after all that running around and putting his hand into his trouser pocket he discovered a piece of paper with some voter's numbers on it. In all of the excitement he had forgotten to give it in. Thinking that Doris would have no need of it now but also being afraid to tell her he had mislaid it, he disposed of it on the way to school.

******

Weekends and school holidays meant that Basil and his friend Kenny had to amuse themselves, a task they were very competent at. They couldn't spend all their time on the docks or down the tram sheds so there were days when they just ambled round the streets looking for ways to make themselves a penny or two pocket money. Always a good money spinner was going round the local streets with an old handcart collecting newspapers and taking them to Southgate's scrap yard in Long Street, behind the Social Settlement building. Rabbit was a popular meat, it was relatively cheap to buy, Billy Beard the butcher on the corner of Friars Street and Princes Street only charged four pence for a whole one, and some people bred them in their back yard. Basil was always on the lookout for a rabbit skin because they fetched a whole penny each from either Southgate's or the rag and bone man who pushed his handcart, plying his trade, around all the residential streets of the town.

Basil sometimes did some shopping for Doris, a jug of milk from Denny's dairy or taking one of Doris's basins to Stollery the grocer for two penny worth of treacle, or golden syrup. On the way he enjoyed looking in all of the shops along Princes Street, particularly Crickmore's the watch and clock repairer. Mr Crickmore sat in plain view in a cubicle in the window, to maximise the natural light, with his green eyeshade pulled almost down to his eyebrows, his fingers working nimbly beneath a large magnifying glass, and invariably with a mountain of minute springs and cogs strewn across his work desk. Basil always pressed his nose against the glass until Crickmore waved for him to move away because he was blocking the light.

Twait's sweet shop was a firm favourite with Basil and Kenny; it was here they spent some of their hard earned pennies buying lemonade crystals which they ate by licking their finger and plunging it into the bag of yellow sweetness. In no time at all their fingers would be stained bright yellow.

Mr Twait was an extremely likeable man, tall and thin, with sharp chiselled features and a soft voice. He sported a well trimmed droopy, almost Mexican style, moustache and tightly curled hair beneath a shooting hat that he always wore. With the bent pipe that was eternally clenched between his teeth he was a perfect Sherlock Holmes lookalike, apart from the moustache. He was also unique to the area in that he was the owner of a pristine Austin sports motor car which he kept almost permanently garaged in Priory Street. The vehicle only saw the light of day twice a year when he drove, with the roof down, along James Street on his way to a day out with the family in Felixstowe. As he crept along at walking pace, hunched over the wheel, goggles firmly in place, peering intently ahead, he was an object of fun for the local children.

"Out of the way, here comes Malcolm Seagrave." They shouted, and even the kindly Twait saw the funny side and, sporting a broad smile on his face, waved to the children as they jogged beside him.

It was outside his shop that Basil and Kenny had a very unusual experience. They were staring into the window with their noses pressed firmly against the glass, salivating over the goodies on display totally oblivious to everything going on around them. It was no surprise that they did not notice a well dressed young woman who suddenly appeared behind them.

"If you could buy some of those sweets, which would you choose?" Came a very soft and warm voice.

Surprised, the boys turned and looked up into the smiling face of a very attractive young lady. She wore a large blue hat with a big white ostrich feather, that ruffled in the breeze, held firmly in place with an ornate hatpin. Her auburn hair was curled into a bun at the back of her head, giving the hat a rakish look, and a wisp of hair trailed from beneath the hat to gently accentuate her, lightly rouged, high cheekbones. She was very slim and her pale blue embroidered dress hugged her curves. Captivated momentarily the boys stared open mouthed. Her gaze never moved from Basil's eyes and he somehow had a feeling that he knew this young woman, he felt a strange bond.

"Well, which would you choose?" She purred.

"Um! Oh I think toasted coconut squares." Basil replied slowly, unable to draw his gaze from her beautiful blue eyes. There was a softness to her smile.

"Yes, me too." Kenny regained his composure, but the lady kept her eyes locked to Basil's.

"OK. Here you are then." She pressed three pennies into Basil's hand. "go inside and get yourself some."

Her face split with a beautiful smile. Both boys looked up at her in disbelief, Basil quickly closed his hand around the coins in case this captivating woman should change her mind and, tearing himself away, ducked off into the shop. A couple of minutes later they emerged each clutching a small brown paper bag firmly in their hands. The young lady watched them carefully.

"Thank you miss," said Basil, thrusting the open bag toward her, "would you like some?"

"Just a very small piece I think." With that she broke off a crumb of the sweet, popped it into her mouth and turned to leave.

"This is your change miss." Basil held out his other hand, three halfpenny coins lay in the palm,

"That's alright Basil, you keep it for another time." Her voice was soft as velvet.

The boys looked at each other for a brief second.

"How do you know my n ....?" Basil turned to question her but she was nowhere to be seen, she had simply vanished. He looked each way along Princes Street but there was no sign of her.

"Where did she go?" It was a statement rather than a question.

"Blowed if I know." Said Kenny, mystified.

As Basil turned to walk away he spied a small white feather lying on the pavement, and felt an irresistible desire to collect it, he bent and swept it up.

"Must be from her hat." He said giving way to the impulse to pocket it. The boys turned to each other again, then looked down into the bags they held.

"Cor! That's a turn up." Said Kenny.

"Nobody will believe us." Said Basil as they crossed the road, past Latimer's garage and made toward the livestock market.

That evening the white feather went into Basil's cardboard box of treasures.

He never saw the beautiful lady again.

1932

Basil and Marjorie were by now regulars at the 'Band of Mercy' and they were learning how to care for animals properly, although Basil had still to achieve his objective of actually owning a dog of his very own, his prime motive for joining in the first place. He found that he really enjoyed the lectures and the lantern slides although the singing was not to his taste, he was not a singer.

The RSPCA were always in need of additional funds in order to enable them to look after more animals and someone came up with the idea of enlisting the help of the children in their junior branch, but how to make collecting interesting and attractive to youngsters was the problem. The secretary had a brainwave, why not use cardboard collecting boxes made in the shape of animals? This idea really appealed to the children, and to increase the interest still further it was turned it into a competition. Each month the youngsters took a box, one per household, and when they were returned at the end of the month the one that had collected the most money would receive a prize. Almost every month Mable and Grace Hudson, who lived in Beaconsfield Road, managed to collect in excess of five shillings because they had a big family, and they always won the prize.

This did not sit well with Basil, who had an extremely competitive nature, and he resolved that it was high time somebody knocked Mable and Grace off their pedestal, he vowed he and Marjorie would be that somebody. Their next box was coincidentally in the shape of a dog and they enlisted the assistance of all the kids in the neighbourhood to fill it. The box was filled up with coins by the end of the second week so Basil asked for another one, much to the surprise of the organisers; this one was in the shape of a cat.

When Basil had an objective in mind he could be very resourceful and winning that prize was his obsession, he would not be satisfied just winning it, he was determined to decimate the opposition so he devised a sure fire plan. On Saturday afternoon he took the box to Portman Road football ground where Ipswich Town Football Club was playing in the Southern Amateur League. There was a seated area on only one side of the ground and Basil assumed the people sitting in those comparatively expensive seats would be more likely to donate money than those who stood cheaply on the earth banks on the other three sides of the ground. He stood outside for half an hour before the game collecting and then moved to outside Frazer's store in Princes Street to collect from spectators as they made their way home after the game. His box was full to overflowing.

At the end of the month Basil and Marjorie proudly produced their two full collection boxes for the grand count. The Hudson girls smirked as their total was announced as five shillings and seven pence halfpenny, but their jaws dropped when it was disclosed that Basil and Marjorie had beaten them into second place with the amazing total of one pound, ten shillings and four pence.

The organisers couldn't believe how well they had done and the Hudson girls wore an expression like thunder as the prizes were presented. Marjorie was given two rabbits, conveniently one male and one female, which Chip soon housed in a large hutch made from a couple of old packing cases, their offspring were to provide a continuous source of fresh rabbit meat for the family. Doris was a dab hand with a rabbit and potato pie. Basil's prize was a tortoise, that he christened 'Lightning', but it didn't last very long as during the summer it decided to go walkabout never to return. Coincidentally a close neighbour acquired one at the same time as Lightning went absent without leave and despite Basil's protests they defiantly denied that it was in fact Lightning, insisting that they had purchased it from a pet shop, conveniently located on the other side of town. Sadly, as Lightning didn't answer to his name their explanation had to be accepted which made Basil all the more determined to get his dog.

******

Basil was now of an age when he wanted to have a little money in his pocket and the only work that an eleven year old boy could do was either shop deliveries or a paper round. Delivering groceries was difficult to fit in with school so he decided that a paper round would be the best option although there were not many openings available and dozens of young boys were clamouring for each one. Fortunately for Basil his cousin William Holland, who lived opposite them in James Street, worked for Reeve's newsagent in Princes Street and he told the owner that Basil was interested. Walter Reeve agreed to give him an interview. When he arrived at the shop Basil was ushered into the back room for what turned out to be a very formal chat. Walter Reeve was a tall slim man, clean shaven with neatly trimmed sideburns that melted into a rapidly receding hairline. His shirt, with sleeves rolled up and held by silver bands, was stained with printer's ink that had rubbed off the piles of newspapers he handled daily, as were his fingers. Basil was soon to discover that Reeve had a penchant for using a long word when several short ones would suffice, he did this to impress his customers into thinking that he was a very educated man, which sadly he wasn't, often the words were misused or completely inappropriate.

He was obviously impressed with the eager young man who stood before him because he offered Basil a position there and then. Basil felt justifiably proud as there were only three boys employed by the shop and he knew that many of his school friends had aspirations on that position. Legally a boy could not start working before his twelfth birthday so he was given a start date of Monday the first of August at six fifteen in the morning.

When Basil described the paper round to his father it became plain there was no way that he could complete it on foot so Chip decided to buy him a brand new bicycle to use for his deliveries, to be paid for in instalments funded from the wages that Basil would earn. The bicycle, a Rudge, arrived toward the end of July and Basil could hardly believe his eyes. It was a beautiful machine, bright shiny black twenty one inch frame with gold coloured coach lines, sparkling chromium handlebars and wheels, mudguards also jet black with gold coach lines and equipped with oil lamps both front and rear. It had cost Chip two pounds, nineteen shillings and six pence from the Co-operative store in Carr Street.

Equipped with the new bicycle Basil was almost ready to start work, there just remained the matter of a letter of authority from the education office in Tower Street. No school student could legally work without this piece of paper so Chip obtained the necessary form, filled it in with the relevant information on employer, proposed hours of work and level of wages, and submitted it to the authorities. The education office went berserk when they received the application because in his innocence Chip had completed it honestly, stating that Basil would commence work at six fifteen in the morning and finish at eight fifteen. The problem was that a twelve year old was, by law, not permitted to start work before seven o'clock in the morning. Chip had no option but to submit a revised form stating Basil's hours as seven o'clock to eight fifteen, the approval was thus given and he turned up at the shop promptly at six fifteen on Monday the first of August, it being physically impossible to complete the paper round in seventy five minutes. What the authorities didn't know would not hurt them.

Basil's round proved to be a mammoth one. At six fifteen he picked up a canvas bag full of newspapers from the shop and began by cycling up Princes Street to the Sun Insurance building where he would make his first delivery. He then proceeded via Museum Street and Elm Street to make deliveries to the Golden Lion Hotel, Tavern Street as far as the Homely Hotel, the Queens Hotel, the bakers shop on the corner of Friars Street and Queen Street before heading back to the shop.

If a customer in a hotel left their footwear outside their room door it meant that they wanted them to be cleaned and polished overnight and the porter who carried out the polishing was known as the 'boots'. The 'boots' also sold newspapers to the customers on a commission basis, so Basil delivered the papers directly to the 'boots' in the entrance hall of each hotel. Three copies each of the Daily Mirror, Daily Sketch, Daily Mail, Westminster News, Daily Gazette also known as the News Chronicle, Daily Herald, The Times, The Telegraph, The Morning Post and the Guardian. One hundred newspapers in total. The newspapers cost one penny each and were very thick, many of them containing advertisements and comics.

Having completed this delivery Basil returned to the shop to collect bag number two, which would be solely for houses, and he started by delivering to one side of James Street before moving on to Priory Street and Portman Street, about thirty newspapers in total.

Returning to the shop once more for bag number three he delivered to the other side of James Street, Cromwell Street, Friars Bridge Road and Edgar Street. Bag number four was destined for Curriers Lane, complete with its myriad courts, as far as the Black Horse public house before moving on to the 'Mount' and part of Tanners Lane.

Finally bag number five serviced the remainder of Tanners Lane, Lady Lane, Stirling Street, St Matthews Church Lane, St Georges Street, Fitzroy Street and finally the Cornhill.

It was a massive task for a twelve year old and by the time he had finished delivering the five bags his shoulder was sore and aching, as were his legs, but this was only the start of his day. It was eight fifteen by the time he returned home which only gave him forty five minutes to have breakfast and walk to school, he was never allowed to take his bicycle to school, and in truth he never wanted to, he was much happier walking with Kenny and his mates. Sometimes Doris wanted him to go to the butcher in Upper Orwell Street, next door to the Spread Eagle public house, so he had to run all the way there and back before running off to school. By the time his lessons started Basil was feeling very weary and he did drop off to sleep in class on one or two occasions only to be rudely awakened with a sharp slap on the head from the teacher's hand.

That was only half of his working day however, because after school, having walked home, he had his evening round to complete. The route was different from the morning one because the large hotels in the town centre did not require evening papers. He delivered his first full bag of the Ipswich Evening Star covering an area from the shop in Princes Street to the railway station, taking in Edgar Street, James Street, Portman Street, Cecelia Street, Challon Street, Metz Street, Sedan Street and the Princes Hotel on the corner of Commercial Road. Returning with an empty bag he collected bag number two and delivered to Russell Road, Constantine Road, West End Road, London Road, Crane Hill and then onto the Dickens Road estate, recently constructed to re-house the town centre slum clearance. His route included Copperfield Road, Dickens Road and Pickwick Road returning via Hadleigh Road, London Road as far as Barrack Corner, Mill Street, Portman Road and finally back to the shop.

His evening round was also his Sunday morning round and by the end of the day he was totally exhausted. Not surprisingly he usually went to bed immediately following his dinner.

Although there were no newspapers to be delivered on Sunday evenings, Basil and the two other paperboys were required to work in the shop sorting returns, sweeping and cleaning in general and finished by cleaning the shop windows.

For this long week of hard work Basil was paid the princely sum of three shillings and sixpence of which two shillings was handed over to Doris for food and lodging, eight pence went towards paying for the bicycle and eight pence he had in his pocket as spends. This accounted for three shillings and four pence, the remaining two pence was paid in the form of a book allowance. In other words Basil could have any magazine he wanted up to the value of two pence. He chose a weekly magazine cum comic called 'Boy's Cinema' which had all the news and stories from Hollywood and the world of the cinema. Always interested and excited by the movies Basil learned which films were being released, all the gossip on the film stars and behind the scenes secrets of the industry. When he had read it from cover to cover a few times he would exchange it with another paperboy for the latest 'Wizard' comic.

Despite it being hard work Basil enjoyed working through August and September, he liked being a paperboy, but as the weeks marched into October, November and December, the mornings became darker and colder making it rather more of a necessary chore. The days when it was raining or very windy were not only uncomfortable they were dangerous because his oil lamps often blew out and he had to stop and relight them or run the risk of a car or lorry mowing him down. Being a paperboy was a dangerous occupation in 1932.

******

Despite having to get home and collect his bicycle before reporting to the newsagent for his evening round, Basil did not hurry unduly when school was done for the day. Along with Kenny he usually took the same route home which was different from the route they took to school in the mornings, for one very good reason. Having quickly walked from Argyll Street along St Helens Street they walked along Carr Street in the direction of the Cornhill, Princes Street and home. However, half way along Carr Street was the Lyceum, previously the home of movies but now the home of live shows.

The Lyceum had been a centre of entertainment for many years and it looked fairly grand with three large pillars supporting a cantilevered portico. The frontage, set back from the footpath, was of wood painted in dark green gloss and there were three large brass lamps that hung down to light the entrance in the evenings. Most interestingly for Basil and Kenny though was the narrow, dark and damp passageway that ran down the side of the theatre that had, at its furthermost end a pair of big doors that when open revealed the stage. Invariably these doors were partially open, mainly for ventilation, enabling the boys to watch the rehearsals for the live shows.

Every year during the autumn the circus came to town and they no longer used the Hippodrome but used the Lyceum as their venue mainly because it provided easier access for the animals and equipment. The Lyceum stage was around twenty five feet below ground level and a big ramp was constructed so that the horses, elephants, tigers and so forth could enter. It was a special treat when Basil and Kenny discovered the circus rehearsals and practice sessions were under way because they could watch them from the side alley. That week Basil was late for his evening paper round every day.

Being the only one in his circle of friends with a bicycle Basil decided at the end of October to go collecting chestnuts and he wanted Kenny to go with him. He had heard that there was a wood full of chestnut trees near Somersham and decided that would be their destination. Paper round completed he cut himself a dripping sandwich, wrapped it in greaseproof paper and set off, meeting up with Kenny outside the Rising Sun public house.

"Hop on Kenny, I'll give you a crossy." Kenny hopped on to the crossbar, side-saddle and off they rode.

The wood was not difficult to find and, keeping his bicycle close by to avoid any possibility of it being stolen, he opened the shopping bag and they busied themselves breaking the spined husks apart and filling it with the sweet kernels.

Their labour was interrupted by a sound that shocked them both.

"What was that Bass?" Kenny looked around.

"It sounded like an elephant."

"Don't be daft, there aren't any elephants here."

"It must have been the wind then." Explained Basil. Satisfied they had solved the riddle they returned to breaking husks and gathering their chestnuts. The unmistakable sound of a lions roar brought them up short.

Leaving the partially filled bag of nuts they crept off to investigate. As they emerged into a clearing they were astounded at the sight that confronted them, they had stumbled into the winter quarters of the Royal Italian Circus. They stood there spellbound taking in the sight of wagons with cages of lions and tigers, picketed rows of show horses and half a dozen large grey elephants. So they had not been dreaming and it definitely was not the wind in the trees playing tricks.

"'Ello young a boys." Basil turned to find a tall dark haired man with a long curled moustache standing behind him.

"Sorry sir," he exclaimed nervously, "We were just collecting chestnuts and heard these strange noises."

"Don't worry, is no problem." The man went on to explain that the circus was going to spend the winter sheltered here in the woods.

"I am Luigi Carnivale," he said, "and I am the circus master."

"I'm Basil, and I'm a paperboy." Was all that Basil could think to say.

"And I'm Kenny, and I'm not a paperboy." Basil gave his friend a confused look.

"You like animals yes?" asked Carnivale.

"Yes we do, very much." Basil stammered before announcing proudly, "I'm a member of the 'Band of Mercy'."

"I'm not." Cut in Kenny again.

"The bandy what?" evidently he had never heard of the organisation.

"Never mind." Basil's pride crumpled.

"Would you like to see the animals closer, is almost the time for the feeding; you could help the feed if you like."

"Wow, yes please." The boys exclaimed in unison.

Basil and Kenny spent a wonderful afternoon seeing all of the animals up close, not too close in the case of the lions and tigers. They helped feed the horses and the elephants, even did a bit of horse grooming, until they realised with disappointment it was getting late and it was high time they made their way home. Basil pedalled his way through the lanes, with Kenny on the crossbar holding tightly onto the bag, both whistling happily; it had been a fantastic day.

Outside the Rising Sun they halved the haul of chestnuts before heading home.

"Is that all you got?" Doris chided as she looked into the bag at the pitiful collection of chestnuts. Basil just smiled, slung his paper bag over his shoulder and rode off to the paper shop.

******

Christmas was a happy time that year in the Double household, all of the family in James Street got together at number 19 for Christmas dinner, twelve people in total in an extremely small house. Charles supplied a second dining table, which Leonard and Basil carried across the road from number 18, along with a bench and two chairs. Nellie supplied three additional chairs brought over by William and Douglas, and Chip spent the morning setting up and laying the tables, ably assisted by Leonard. The tiny living room was bursting at the seams and there was not much elbow room, but nobody was complaining. Doris and Nellie spent the whole morning in their respective kitchens cooking and the whole meal came together perfectly at lunch time to be eagerly demolished by the hungry clan. After lunch the room was cleared, save for one table, in order to allow room for the party games, singing and drinking with the evening rounded off as Chip carried the Christmas cake from the kitchen. Doris had cooked the cake, rich with brandy, while the icing, smooth as glass, was once again the work of Chip.

Unfortunately Boxing day brought everybody crashing down to earth when the news filtered through that great grandmother Jane had passed away in Mistley, on Christmas Eve, at the grand age of one hundred and three.

1933

Basil's route to Argyll Street school took him through some of the better streets in the town as well as some of the worst. From James Street he walked up to Friars Street, through Old Cattle Market and Dogs Head Street into Tacket Street and then Eagle Street. In Eagle Street there was a shop owned by Edward 'Ted' Weeks who made cough sweets on the premises to his own recipe, he also sold them outside Portman Road football ground on match days, no doubt taking advantage of those who had shouted too energetically. His motto, emblazoned on his shop window, was 'cough no more'. Basil had been given one or two to suck when he had a sore throat but they didn't seem to make any difference to him.

Outside the window was a grating in the footpath allowing light to enter the cellar window. It also collected leaves and other detritus that blew along the street or had been dropped by pedestrians. On his way to school one day Basil happened glance through the grating as he walked over it and to his surprise saw a penny coin laying on top of the rubbish.

"That's handy" he said to Kenny. Basil stood looking into the window until he was sure Ted Weeks was watching him. He then fumbled as if he had dropped something, put on his most surprised expression before making his way into the shop leaving Kenny outside on guard.

The bell on the spring tinkled his presence as he opened the shop door and walked up to the counter.

"Please Mr Weeks," he began, "I was looking at your sweets in the window deciding which ones I would buy when I dropped my penny, it went through the grating."

Weeks dropped his head so that he could look at Basil over the top of his half glasses. Slowly he shook his head.

"Oh yes! Do you know you are the third boy this week to claim that penny." Embarrassed Basil ran out of the shop.

His route from Eagle Street took him through Rope Walk with its many courts consisting of ten houses down each side. All of these houses were simple one up one down dwellings with only one entrance door. Outside in the courtyard there was a communal toilet and a single water standpipe. The toilets very rarely worked properly, they were always overflowing into the courtyard and even by the relatively poor standards of James Street these were no more than disease breeding slums. There were always packs of skinny dogs and hundreds of cats running around scavenging for scraps of food, scraps that barely existed. Basil and Kenny counted the number of cats they spotted between Eagle Street and Grimwade Street and regularly reached a total of fifty or more.

Having made it past the bacteria breeding ground that was the Rope Walk they turned into Grimwade Street and up to Argyll Street.

The homeward journey, in the cold weather, was the reverse, exchanging the possible rehearsals at the Lyceum for a quick warm up half way. Either side of the road outside the Blue Coat Boy public house in the Old Cattle Market stood a row of trolley busses with a traffic island in the middle. On the island there were underground public conveniences with a parcel holding counter where shoppers could leave parcels to be collected later, but best of all was the inspector's office and the shelter. The resident inspector was a short, slim man with a withered arm and his job was to make sure that the busses departed on time but best of all, in the wintertime he had a coke burning brazier that glowed away all day. On cold days Basil and Kenny hurried from the school, which even in the warm weather always seemed to be freezing cold, down to the bus shelter to stand by the brazier warming themselves in its golden glow. The inspector, who was a friendly and amenable old man, would let them warm for a few minutes before moving them on.

"OK boys, you should be warm enough by now. Move along home and let the ladies and gentlemen warm themselves." Reluctantly they would depart but they were warmer than they had been all day.

Once home, of course, it was time for Basil to get his bicycle out and begin his paper round. Things didn't always go smoothly though and he suffered a few setbacks, most notable was when he came hurrying out of the yard beside the Black Horse public house in Black Horse Lane and collided with a man on another bicycle. They both ended in a crumpled heap in the road with a few newspapers strewn beside them, the breeze gently turning the pages one by one. The man got up, dusted himself down and picked up his bicycle, all seemed to be fine so without another word he hopped on his bicycle and pedalled off in the direction of Elm Street. Basil was left sitting on the road nursing a knee that dribbled blood down onto his woollen socks and a sore behind. Blowing out his cheeks he gathered the spilled newspapers, before the breeze could take them down the road, and stuffed them into his canvas sack. Gingerly he rose from the ground and picked up his bicycle; unfortunately his front wheel was slightly buckled and would not turn. He had to carry it home before continuing with his paper round on foot. Naturally it took him considerably longer than usual to complete the round and he was exhausted when he finally got home. Chip had already seen the damaged bicycle and had begun to repair it while Basil was doing his deliveries.

"Don't worry son, I'll have it fixed ready for your morning round." He smiled.

Adding insult to injury, the following evening Reeve, the newsagent, had a stern word with Basil saying he had received a number of complaints from customers because their newspaper had been delivered late and unbelievably he saw fit to give Basil a right telling off. Aggrieved Basil stomped off home that night muttering angrily to himself.

******

The first Saturday in July was the day Ipswich set aside for the poor children's outing. First run in 1927 it was intended that it would give underprivileged children a treat, a day to remember in their otherwise Spartan existence. Entry was by ticket only, tickets that schools distributed carefully only to those children deemed to come from families whose parents struggled to provide the basics in life and to whom treats were an unknown pleasure. Despite every care being taken there were still a number of instances where children from families who were above the relevant criteria sneaked in. Local dignitaries, businessmen and those who felt they wanted to assist in this worthy cause volunteered their vehicles, their money and most important of all, their time.

This year was a landmark year for Basil because he managed, for the first time, to get his hands on a ticket. Unfortunately, although he was desperate to go, he had one significant problem, namely his newspaper round. He could easily complete his round and get home, have his breakfast and run to Alderman Road recreation ground in time for the beginning of the outing but there was no way that he would be back home in time to do his evening round. He could not tell Reeve where he was going because, although the family as a whole struggled to make ends meet, he was earning three shillings and sixpence a week from his paper round and so technically he was not poor and therefore not eligible to go on the outing. It was a bit of a dilemma but one for which Basil had devised a relatively simple solution and so on the Friday he approached Reeve.

"I'm afraid that I can't work the round tomorrow evening Mr Reeve."

"Oh! And exactly what precipitates your decision to deprive me of your services Basil?" said Reeve overusing the English language as usual and giving Basil a quizzical look.

"My uncle is very ill and my father and mother are going to visit him for the day."

"And perforce is it their insistence that you accompany them on this mission of mercy?" Reeve pressed.

"No, but they won't be back until late and I have to stay at home and look after my little sister Marjorie."

"I see; I suppose I can endeavour to engage your colleagues to substitute your round on this occasion," he paused, "but I insist that you report here bright and early on Sunday in order to resume your occupational commitments."

"Oh yes, I'll be here Sunday as normal." Basil walked away with his first bag of the day slung casually over his shoulder, a satisfied smile on his face and a feeling of excited anticipation deep inside.

Saturday the first of July dawned and Basil hurried to the paper shop to get his morning deliveries completed as quickly as possible before running home for his breakfast of bread and jam. Giving Doris a swift kiss goodbye he made for Alderman Road recreation ground and the herd of youngsters gathering excitedly for their special day.

Waiting for them was a plethora of vehicles and Basil stared open mouthed, as he looked along the lines of motor cycles with sidecars, cars large and small, vans, busses and lorries. Each vehicle was brightly decorated with streamers, flags and bunting, some being made to look like railway locomotives and one even disguised as a thatched cottage. It was a truly colourful sight.

The children were split into groups and loaded into the vehicles, Basil climbed onto the back of a lorry bedecked with straw bales for the children to sit on and grabbed what he felt was the best vantage point at the front so that he could lean on the top of the cab and get an excellent view of the journey. It was almost lunchtime before everybody was loaded onto a transport and the procession was ready for the off.

"Remember which vehicle you are on," shouted the chairman of the organising committee as he made his way along the line of vehicles, "because you must be on the same vehicle for the return journey." He then climbed onto his solo motorcycle, pulled his goggles down from his leather flying helmet to cover his eyes, and kicked the engine into life.

Making his way slowly to the head of the line he encouraged all the vehicles to fire up their engines, with an exaggerated flourish of arm movements, which elicited wild shouts and cheers of joy from the children. When he received the thumbs up from one of his colleagues, indicating that the convoy was ready to move off, he waved his arm in a circular motion in the air and pointed forward, reminiscent of a wagon train master in a western movie, put his motorcycle in gear and led the fleet of assorted vehicles toward the Portmans Walk exit. The procession was finally on the move and the young passengers let loose once more with wild, excited whoops and cheers.

As the cortege moved from Friars Bridge Road into Princes Street children not lucky enough to be on the outing, left their dinners and rushed from their houses intent on watching the spectacle, some even had a sausage or a potato in their hand as they lined the street to cheer on the revellers.

"Here they come. Here they come." They shouted animatedly for, despite their disappointment at not being lucky enough to get tickets themselves they were equally swept up in the euphoria of the departure. As his lorry swept past the end of James Street Basil was able to pick out his cousins William and Douglas on the pavement and the three smiled and waved energetically to each other.

The cheering and waving followed the procession as it made its way along Tavern Street and onto Woodbridge Road, heading out of town toward their final destination, Rookery Park in Yoxford. It was a very long drive which took almost an hour and a half to complete, taking them through Woodbridge, Ufford, Wickham Market and Saxmundham.

Arriving at their destination each vehicle was met and welcomed by the owner of the park, Sir Guy Hambling Bart, who shouted his greeting, wished all the children a lovely day enjoying the extensive grounds of his house.

All afternoon the children were entertained with races, games, ponies and donkeys to ride, Punch and Judy shows, exhibitions of sheepdogs at work and farmyard animals such as pigs, sheep and cattle that they could get close to and pet. Some of the children had never seen these animals before, other than perhaps in pieces in a butcher shop, and they were fascinated by them. There were lashings of lemonade and sandwiches served in a big marquee tent on the lawn in front of the house, and even some barrels of beer for the volunteer drivers and organisers.

The afternoon seemed to evaporate and all too soon it was time for the vehicles to make the homeward journey carrying their exhausted but happy cargo. As the motorcade made its way out of the main gate and turned toward Saxmundham the children on Basil's lorry noticed one of the policemen who had accompanied the outing, directing the traffic. One of the boys pointed at him and started to sing.

> "*I wouldn't like to be a bobby*
> *Dressed in other peoples clothes*
> *With a belly full of fat*
> *And a sausage on his hat*
> *I wouldn't like to be a bobby.*"

The children laughed at the song and cheered when the policeman, appreciating the funny rhyme, saluted them with a broad smile on his face. Then all the children on the lorry began to sing and before long it seemed as if the entire line of vehicles was joining in, singing their hearts out.

Basil was in good spirits and happier than he had been for a long time as the convoy slipped into Ipswich via Woodbridge Road and made for Alderman Road. Unfortunately he didn't notice, as his lorry rounded the Cornhill into Princes Street, that a pair of eyes hidden in the watching crowd had picked him out and the envious gaze threatened trouble. The eyes belonged to Billy Sumner, who was the third paperboy at Reeves newsagent along with Basil and his cousin William, but who was, more importantly, Reeve's favourite and could do no wrong.

The following morning, when Basil turned up for work, he was greeted by a grinning Billy. Not knowing the reason for the grin Basil innocently began to sort out his papers for the first delivery bag.

"Mr Reeve sir." Said Billy sardonically.

"What is it boy?"

"I saw Basil on one of the lorries last night." Basil froze.

"On one of the lorries? What is it that you are attempting to elucidate boy?"

"I was standin' on the steps of the town hall when the kids outing came back to town last night. And I saw Basil on one of the lorries, he went on the outing." The smirky grin returned to his face as he looked Basil straight in the eyes.

"Is this accusation correct Basil?" boomed Reeve.

"Yes Mr Reeve sir." Basil had no intention of trying to deny it.

"I am astounded at your behaviour boy; you told me an untruth? You alleged that you had to administer to your sister."

"Yes sir, I'm sorry sir."

"You lied to me boy!" his voice rose until it sounded like thunder as he momentarily lost his command of big words. "I would be within my employer's confines to relieve you of your position in this business immediately." He had by now recovered his composure. "It is also my civic responsibility to notify the organisers of this recreational event that you falsified your domestic circumstances in order to attend." The veins stood out on his temples and his cheeks were beginning to flush.

"Recover your bag and commence your deliveries this instant." He shouted. "Remove yourself from my gaze forthwith, and in your absence I will decide my course of action." As Basil made his way submissively to the door he added. "I shall, as a minimum punishment deduct sixpence from this week's remuneration ... now DEPART!"

As Basil passed Billy he deliberately kicked his ankle.

"Thanks Billy, I owe you." Billy frowned and rubbed his sore ankle.

Every day for the next week Reeve threatened to tell the organisers of the outing but that did not worry Basil unduly because the worst they could do was to ban him from subsequent outings and by next July he would hopefully be embarking on his permanent employment career path having left school and would be too old to qualify for the jaunt in any case. He smiled to himself; the fantastic day he had enjoyed was worth all the aggravation.

******

August saw the invasion of the canvassers. Basil noticed every day that there were two or three pairs of men calling at each house and he wondered what they were up to, he didn't have to wait long to find out.

Shortly after finishing his breakfast, he sat in the living room reading his 'Boys Cinema' magazine when there was a knock on the front door. Wiping her hands on her apron Doris tutted as she made her way from the scullery and swung the door open to reveal two men in suits, one carrying a small briefcase the other holding a wooden clipboard.

"Good morning madam." Said the tallest of the pair as he raised his trilby hat a couple of inches off his head. The second man, the one holding the briefcase, just smiled. "I am representing the national newspaper industry and we have come to Ipswich to find out what newspapers are being read here."

"Oh yes." Doris sounded suitably unimpressed.

"I wonder if I might ask madam which morning newspaper your household reads."

"Why?" They would not get information that easily from Doris. Basil smiled to himself in admiration of her.

"Well we believe that our newspaper may be better for you."

"Better for me than what?" Basil's smile broadened, they had more than met their match with Doris.

"Better than the newspaper you are currently reading."

"If you don't know which one I read what makes you think that yours is better?" Basil began to chuckle audibly behind his magazine, Doris was winning.

"We believe that the Daily Mail would be better for you, assuming that you do not currently read it that is." He smiled a sickly smile and Doris immediately lost interest, there was no competition for her. "If you would like to change we can advise your newsagent and make the change without you having to do anything." He straightened up and fingered his spectacles, pushing them higher on his nose.

Doris had better things to do with her time and simply wanted to get rid of them now that the verbal contest had been won, so she agreed. The sickly smiler made a note of the house number on his clipboard and made some polite parting noises before she closed the door.

"Are you really changing mum?"

"Of course we aren't Basil I just agreed to get rid of them; anyway do you think that I would have that Conservative rubbish in my house? We are staying with the Daily Herald."

The canvassers seemed to have toured most of the town, and had enjoyed considerable success it would seem, judging by the pages of addresses they delivered to Reeve's shop the following week. Reeve, however, was a shrewd man and he gave the lists to the three paperboys and told them to ask the customers if they really wanted to change. It came as little surprise to find that almost every customer had only agreed to change their newspaper in order to get rid of the canvassers and they were perfectly content to continue with their usual one, only a small handful of households actually changed.

Two days later Basil turned up for work, parked his sparkling bicycle at the kerb, he had spent the previous Sunday polishing it until it gleamed, and entered the shop. It took him less than five minutes to prepare his first bag of papers and when he had finished he hoisted the heavy bag over his shoulder and walked out the door. As he emerged his jaw dropped almost to the pavement, there was no sign of his bicycle. Quickly he cast his gaze up and down Princes Street but it was deserted. No sign of his bicycle anywhere.

"Mr Reeve, Mr Reeve," he shouted as he burst back into the shop. "my bicycle; it's gone. It's been stolen."

"Stolen! But you have only been present in this establishment for a mere five minutes. Are you positive of its removal?" Reeve strode out the door and stood on the pavement looking right and left. Three bicycles stood at the kerb, two of them belonging to the other paperboys.

"Is that not your velocipede?" Reeve pointed to a hulk of a bicycle that stood slightly to one side of the others. The rusty wheels were slightly buckled with a number of spokes missing, the chromium on the handlebars was flaking, the frame was an indeterminate colour beneath the dirt and grime, the front mudguard was missing and the seat was split.

"No that's certainly not mine, my bicycle is almost new." Basil was beginning to well up at the thought that he may never see his smart new bicycle again.

"You possess no alternative recourse than to visit the constabulary office and report the crime while I engage the other delivery operatives to undertake your long distance deliveries. On your return you will have to undertake their immediate town deliveries, in addition to yours as a pedestrian."

Basil dragged himself up to the police station beneath the town hall and stood in front of the forbidding desk.

"And what might you be wanting lad?" The desk sergeant leaned forward onto the counter. He was a tough, swarthy looking character with a full moustache and bushy sideburns. The three metal chevrons on his collar, the symbol of his rank, were highly polished and his uniform was crisp and spotless. He tapped his pencil on the desk as Basil related the events that had led up to the discovery of the theft, and then scribbled the odd note in his ledger.

"Can you describe the missing article in detail?" He enquired.

Basil described his bicycle in the minutest detail and the sergeant scribbled a few more notes in his ledger.

"OK lad, the constables will keep an eye out for it on their patrols." With that he dropped his gaze and studied some paperwork on the desk. Basil didn't know for sure what he should do until the sergeant lifted his gaze over his spectacles and nodded his head toward the door. Basil realised he had been dismissed and he grudgingly made his way back to the shop. It was, of course, much later than normal when he got home and he had to skip his breakfast in order not to be late for school.

His day passed very slowly for he was in a sombre mood, how was he going to be able to afford another bicycle, how was he going to be able to complete his paper round without one. Massive problems in the mind of a thirteen year old.

As it often does, fate had a way of solutioning his problems for him. Arriving at the paper shop to start his evening round Reeve told him that a police constable had called in during the afternoon to say that Basil was to present himself at the police station as soon as he could.

It was a different sergeant that greeted him with a firm look as Basil crept toward the desk, wondering if he was in trouble but unable to think of any reason why he should be.

"Ah, you must be Basil Double!" the sergeant made it sound like a crime. "Come with me lad." Leaving the desk in the capable hands of a constable the sergeant led Basil down a couple of corridors before emerging into a small yard. He smiled as he pointed to Basil's gleaming bicycle standing in the corner.

"You found it for me!" Basil exclaimed excitedly as he rushed over to reclaim his pride and joy.

"Not so much found it, it was brought in."

"Somebody found it?"

"Not exactly. It was a gentleman who brought it in, said that he had taken it by mistake. Apparently your bicycle and his were standing together outside the shop and he took your bicycle erroneously, thinking it was his own. Seems he did not realise his mistake until he had cycled all the way to Stowmarket."

"Was that *his* bicycle that was left outside, but it was nothing *like* mine."

"My thoughts exactly, for a start his was a twenty three inch frame, yours was a twenty one inch. His was in a poor state of repair whereas yours is obviously looked after. Apart from that the man in question is around six feet two inches tall so he must have felt like a pimple on an elephants arse on your bicycle." The sergeant smiled warmly. "I don't think he will do that sort of thing again; we

276

had a little talk." He thrust out his whiskery chin in self satisfaction.

Basil signed a register of found property to confirm that his bicycle had been restored to him before emerging onto Princes Street and happily riding down to the shop to begin his paper round. It felt like the happiest paper round he had ever done.

That was not to be the last time he came into contact with that particular police sergeant during the summer, nor would it be the last time that his bicycle went absent without leave.

It was during the summer school holidays, Basil had finished his paper round and had a hearty breakfast of boiled egg with toasted soldiers to dip, and was sitting in the living room wondering what he should do with the rest of his day. Marjorie came in from the yard having just given her rabbits their morning feed and that gave Basil an idea. He would gather a load of dandelion leaves for Marjorie's rabbits. He knew where there were loads of succulent plants not far away so he gathered up his paper delivery bag, grabbed his bicycle and disappeared out the back gate.

Adjacent to the Alderman Road recreation ground, near the river Gipping, there was a Royal Navy wireless station. It had two wooden masts that must have been sixty feet high with various wires and cables attached to them. The cables led down to a wooden shed that housed all of the associated electrical equipment. Basil knew that within the boundary fence grew the most luscious dandelion plants in town and there was a place, near the river, where the security fence was not secured to the ground and he could, with little difficulty, wriggle underneath. He leaned his bicycle against the fence near the entrance gate, thinking anybody who came around would assume it belonged to a wireless operator or someone associated with the shed. In fact Basil had never actually seen anybody at the shed and the grass growing hard against the door was testimony to it not being inhabited for some time.

Once inside, even though he was careful to stay out of sight, it only took him a quarter of an hour to fill the canvas newspaper bag to bursting and making his way to the gap under the fence he stuffed the bag through the hole before wriggling through himself. Hoisting the bag on his shoulder and giving a quick final look round to make sure his visit had been undetected he made for the gate but as he turned the corner his heart sank into his boots, once more his bicycle was nowhere to be seen.

Now he knew he had a really big problem, he should, of course, report the theft to the police, especially if he hoped to ever see his bicycle again but he should not have been trespassing on the Royal Navy land in the first place and that could land him in trouble. He soon worked out what he had to do. Quickly he ran home, gave the dandelions to a grateful Marjorie, and ditching his paper bag he disappeared out of the back gate before anybody had a chance to challenge him.

It was a rather crestfallen and somewhat embarrassed Basil who presented himself at the police station looking up into the eyes of the same sergeant he had faced only a few short weeks before when he collected his bicycle.

"Sergeant, I have to report that my bicycle has been stolen."

"Again?" the sergeant looked stern.

"Again." Said Basil uncomfortably.

"You will have to look after it a bit better won't you m'lad. And where did this offence take place this time?"

"On Alderman Road rec. I only left it for a minute while I talked to some mates and when I turned round it had gone." The sergeant took the details and made another entry into his ledger.

"I will let you know if we find it." He said lightly, returning his pen into his top uniform pocket.

"Could you let the newsagent know when you find it please because I don't want to have to tell my dad unless it's absolutely necessary." Basil smiled weakly, a smile that was returned with a knowing nod by the sergeant.

Later, when Basil turned up to start his tea time paper round, Reeve greeted him with a stony face.

"I am not particularly thrilled to have the local constabulary frequenting my establishment on official business Basil. This is the second instance that you have precipitated a visit." He was obviously unhappy which made Basil wonder if there were things going on within the shop that Reeve would rather the police did not discover. "It would appear that your bicycle has been retrieved once more, you should repossess it forthwith."

Joyously Basil ran up Princes Street to the police station and presented himself, once more, before the duty sergeant who opened his ledger, all the time staring at him until his face split with a friendly smile.

"Seems it's your lucky day lad, you won't have to tell your dad about losing your bicycle now will you?"

"Thanks to you and your constables." Basil was trying to get on the good side of the sergeant.

"Now if you could just sign to say you have your bicycle returned to you."

Basil picked up the pen just as the main doors clattered open and a constable struggled in with the collar of a scruffy young lad held firmly in his grasp, in his other hand was a canvass bag.

"What's this Wilkins?" The sergeant raised his eyebrows.

"This is the urchin who has been causing problems in the town centre all day Sarge."

"Aha! What has he been up to?"

"Well firstly he was seen riding that bicycle we recovered earlier. He has also been stealing from at least three shops in town. Apprehended him outside his home in St Matthews Church Lane with some of the stolen goods on him I did." The constable raised the canvass bag to indicate that it held the stolen property.

"What a coincidence," grinned the sergeant, "this young lad is the owner of said bicycle. Pleased to get it back he is."

"I dint take no bike." Protested the urchin. "You can't say I did."

"He was observed by one of the aggrieved shop owners Sarge," offered constable Wilkins, "riding the said bicycle to make his getaway."

"I dint touch no bike, never clapped eyes on it. That shop man, he's a liar." The young boy protested. The sergeant glowered at him, turned and went into an adjoining room returning with a birch. It made a hard cracking sound as he slammed it on the counter in front of the boy. The boy shrank back, visibly disturbed. The sergeant leant forward menacingly, giving the birch a tap as he did so.

"Start telling me the truth boy or you'll get a taste of this across your backside." He stormed. The boy quivered noticeably.

"Take him into room A constable, I will be there presently."

Even before Basil left the building the boy had confessed to taking the bicycle and a number of other minor crimes including stealing the entire contents of the bag. Whether it saved the skin on his rear end Basil was never to know. All he was concerned about was getting his bicycle back undamaged without the family knowing it had ever gone missing.

1934

1934 was to be another momentous year in Basil's life and many changes awaited him. He was entering the transition phase when he would emerge from the chrysalis of a schoolboy into the grown up world of adult employment, but that would not be the only development.

The first change came early in the year and was a hugely memorable one. Arriving home one evening in March from completing his paper round Basil sat with the rest of the family at the dinner table. It was a surprisingly quiet affair which was rather unusual in the Double household because dinner time was normally when they shared the events of the day or discussed the news. It was not until everybody had finished eating and the plates were taken into the scullery that Chip and Doris broke their silence and finally shared their news.

"We decided some while ago," started Chip, "that this house is just too small for us all. It is not right that Marjorie has to share our bedroom, she is now at an age where she needs some privacy and it will be a welcome change for me and your mother to have some privacy too. So we have been looking into moving to another house."

"Moving to another house?" Leonard exclaimed.

"Yes moving to another house," Chip nodded, "and we have been lucky enough to be able to find one in an area we know well."

"Where's that?" Questioned Leonard.

"Cavendish Street." Chip waited a few seconds for the news to seep in before continuing. "A lady who lived in a house just up the hill from Grandmother Dumble has died and her landlord is looking for new tenants as soon as possible." Chip explained.

"And because it is very difficult to find tenants at short notice at the moment the landlord has set a rent which is just about affordable for us." Cut in Doris.

"It will be a struggle," Chip explained, we will all have to make sacrifices but we can just about afford it. We have my wages from the foundry, the money that your mother earns with her dressmaking and sewing and the board that you pay Leonard."

"I pay board too!" Basil cut in indignantly.

"Yes Basil, your contribution will help too, especially as you will finish school soon, and Marjorie's rabbits will help too providing some meat, as well as being able to sell some to neighbours. It will all help." Doris smiled at Basil's serious expression.

"But the thing is that we are both of the mind that it will be worth the risk and too good an opportunity to miss." Chip looked across to Doris and smiled a satisfied smile.

"I agree." Leonard nodded sagely. "But I suppose I will still have to share a bedroom with Basil." He turned to Basil and smiled. Basil recognised the comment was meant as a joke and smiled back.

So that was how it came to be that in April the household moved out of number 16 James Street and into number 271 Cavendish Street. After they had loaded their meagre belongings onto grandfather Charles' cart Chip and Doris went back into the house for the last time to check that nothing had been left behind.

"Give me a few minutes will you Dolly, I just want to say a proper goodbye to the old place." Chip wore a sad expression, in sharp contrast to the three children waiting eagerly by the cart. Doris nodded knowingly and silently closed the front door behind her.

Chip stood in the centre of the living room, slowly and silently looking around. Twenty years of memories began to flood his mind. He saw himself carrying Beatrice across the threshold on their wedding day, full of excitement at the thought of building a new life together but tinged with apprehension as they knew he would soon be marching off to war. He remembered the joy he felt as Beatrice presented him with Leonard in the summer of 1915 and how they doted on the new bundle that tied them even closer together, if that were possible. He glanced at the wooden staircase and recalled the disturbed sleep as Beatrice fed the tiny infant. He felt again the pain they both experienced when the day finally dawned, in early November 1915, when he had to leave for his posting with the Royal Field Artillery, their kisses and their parting embrace that had seemed over far too soon.

In sharp contrast he recalled the deep joy they shared as he burst through the door in February 1919 to enjoy his demobilisation leave. They had thrown themselves into each other's arms and smothered each other with kisses celebrating the ecstasy of their reunion, vowing that never again would they allow themselves to be parted.

He savoured once more the elation they both shared when Beatrice presented him with his little Basil, but his smile soon faded and tears welled in his eyes as he pictured his beloved Beatrice as she sat hunched in her chair, blood covering her chin and splattering her clawing fingers as she choked her life away. Chip sank to the floor, put his head in his hands and wept, he wept for Beatrice, he wept for himself, and he wept for his boys who had been torn forever from their mother's love.

The door opened and Doris slipped silently into the room. Kneeling beside him she took his head and placed it on her shoulder, held him in her firm embrace and swayed him to and fro.

"I understand my darling," she whispered, "so many good and bad memories for you but you now have to leave them here and make new memories with us in a new home."

Chip nodded slowly, he would always carry those memories with him but he vowed to himself that he would never speak of them again, he would never let anybody near those special treasured memories, they were his and his alone and he would take them to his grave. Wiping his eyes dry he left the house and aimed a forced smile toward the expectant children. The look that Leonard gave him, and the resigned smile, told Chip that he was not the only one to remember.

As Charles led the pony and cart down James Street, with the children walking alongside, Chip cast a final glance over his shoulder before steeling himself and walking toward a different life.

Part Four

The Cavendish

Street Years

(The second time around)

1934 (Continued)

271 Cavendish Street was a reasonably sized terraced house, a mansion in comparison to the house they left in James Street, and it even had a small front garden. The front door opened directly into the front room, a room solely reserved for special occasions, which sported a small fire grate with a tiled surround and mantelpiece. A settee and two chairs were positioned around the fireplace and there was a small table in one corner and a tall standard lamp in the other. A short passage or hallway linked the front room to the living room. There was a door on the left hand side of the passage opening onto some dark stone steps leading down to the coal cellar. The living room was of a slightly larger size to the front room with its own fire grate and doors that led to the scullery in one corner and the staircase to the first floor in another.

The scullery, which Doris soon christened the kitchen, had a gas stove on one side, a sink with its own tap on the other whilst across the rear wall was a tall pantry and a bath, with a wooden cover so that it could be used as a work surface.

The steep staircase leading from the living room and had a sharp turn at the bottom and led up to a small square landing with a bedroom to both the left and to the right. The one to the right, and therefore the front of the house was to be for Chip and Doris while the one to the left, the rear of the house, was for Leonard and Basil. Beside the window of the back bedroom, which overlooked a long sloping garden, there was a door and three steps down to a small third bedroom; this was to be Marjorie's room.

Outside there was a toilet, which was built onto the house but was only accessible from outside, and a wooden storage shed for garden implements and especially for Basil's treasured bicycle. The garden inclined away from the house and the soft sandy soil would soon provide the family with loads of much needed vegetables, something that their cobbled patch of back yard in James Street could never do. Leonard was keen to begin planting seeds and, along with Chip and Basil would soon busy himself tilling and planting the soil.

Not that Basil had much time for gardening. He was due to leave school in July of 1934, in only three months time, so the education committee declared that he would see out his school days at Argyll Street rather than suffer the upheaval of moving to the nearer Derby Road School. He was also determined to continue with his paper round for Reeve until he left school which meant he had to rise even earlier in the morning in order to cycle to Princes Street, deliver his papers, cycle home, have breakfast and then walk the one mile to Argyll Street. Once school was finished for the day he had to walk home, collect his bicycle and return to Princes Street for the evening deliveries. By the time he returned home and ate his dinner he was so exhausted that he read a book for a while or worked on his wooden models of current aircraft before falling into his bed for a deep sleep before repeating the procedure all over again the following day.

His social life changed dramatically too. He had his gang of mates in the James Street area but, of course, he had to leave them behind and despite visiting a few times, mainly over the weekends, he soon found himself to be left out and it was not long before he stopped going back at all. As for the youngsters of Cavendish Street, they had all moved on in the six years he had been away and he discovered the street to be a 'closed shop' with him the unaccepted outsider. The strong bond between Basil and Kenny held firm for the three months until school finished but sadly, as they left Argyll Street for the last time and went their separate ways, they lost touch and the friendship failed to survive, they were destined never to meet again.

One Saturday morning found Basil wandering around the streets of the town after completing his paper round, looking into the various shop windows. One of his favourite shops had always been Martin and Newby, on the corner of Fore Street and Orwell Place, it was a treasure trove of tools and hardware of every size, shape and use and it fuelled within him a desire to create. He bought some basic tools over the course of a few weeks and together with some pieces of wood he came across he fashioned little figures and aeroplanes.

Opposite Martin and Newby was a butchers shop and a cafe that served tea and delicious cakes, Basil was feeling a little peckish after his paper round so he popped in and enjoyed a steaming cup of tea and a big slice of his favourite fruit cake. Nearby was the famous Jacksons pie shop with their unique tasting pork pies and apple pies. The pork filling was cooked to a secret family recipe and although many people tried to emulate the formula, nobody ever came even close to that unique peppery taste.

Strolling past Drury's sweet shop Basil glanced briefly at the thick set, heavily bearded, shopkeeper behind his counter, sweets didn't interest him much now that he was maturing into a handsome thirteen year old. He ambled past Deeks the pork butcher, the Tankard public house, the Unicorn hotel and John Bull the butcher stopping outside Brands. Brands always intrigued him with their special way of taking money. He went inside; he could not resist the temptation.

Standing just inside the doorway his eyes lifted to the ceiling where there was a network of metal tracks, each consisting of two rails about two inches apart, that ran from above each counter position all the way to a cash office situated high in the rear corner of the shop. He didn't have to wait long for somebody to make a purchase, a man standing at a counter near the front of the shop handed some coins to the salesman. What followed always intrigued Basil. The salesman put the coins into a semi-spherical pot, along with a hastily written invoice, and screwed another similar pot on top to form a ball. At the side of the salesman was a continuously turning belt with cups attached to it, and the salesman popped the ball into one of the cups as it came round. The cup continued its journey lifting the ball up to the ceiling until it became level with the track network whereupon it was tipped onto the rails and very slowly the ball began to travel the length of the track until it dropped off the end and into a padded box in the cash office. Basil watched as the cashier opened the ball, retrieved the money and the invoice, placed the change and a receipt into the ball and sent it back to the salesman on a parallel track.

Basil thought this ingenious, only one cashier was needed to service the entire shop, the takings were secure and it was all thanks to the imaginative use of gravity.

******

Now they had a garden Basil thought it was time for him to resurrect the subject of the dog he had so longed for. He was very pleasantly surprised when Chip immediately agreed to his request; in fact he could have one as a present for his upcoming fourteenth birthday. Being a member of the 'Band of Mercy' he asked the RSPCA to help him find a suitable candidate from amongst their collection of strays and, on his birthday, Basil walked to the shelter with Marjorie at his side, to collect Paddy, his very own companion. Proudly he walked him home, on the end of a length of stout string, refusing all offers from Marjorie to hold the string for a while. Arriving back at Cavendish Street the string was removed so that Paddy could run free in the garden whilst Basil went indoors to ask Doris if she had a brush he could use to groom his little partner. Doris had an old hair brush she no longer used, Basil accepted it gratefully and raced into the garden intent on making Paddy's coat smooth and shiny. Paddy was a fairly small wire haired terrier with a beautiful coat that was predominantly white except for a small patch of brown on his rump.

Basil doted on Paddy and brushed him every day after completing his paper round. One Sunday he even decided to bath him which proved to be more problematical than Basil had at first expected. Paddy didn't think much to the initial wetting, and he cared even less for the application of copious amounts of soap, but when it came to rinsing him off in the tin bath outside the back door, Paddy thought it a step too far. He leapt out of the bath and ran indoors, through the kitchen and into the living room where, finding all the doors closed and with Basil rapidly cutting off his retreat into the garden, he decided this would be the perfect time to shake himself dry. The soapy water left his coat in a wide, wet arc and sprayed the furniture and the walls. Doris, frantically running into the room to chase the sopping dog shouted to Basil.

"Get that blasted dog out of my house immediately."

Basil chased him around the dining table, Doris aimed a swipe at him with a dish cloth and Paddy took the hint running past them both and out into the back garden, not stopping until he was as far from Basil, Doris and the frightful tin bath as he could get. From that moment on Paddy was banned from the house, he had to sleep in the outhouse along with the gardening tools and Basil's bicycle, but he did have a soft blanket that Doris found for him in a moment of compassion.

Although Basil took him for walks every day and even tied him to his bicycle so that he could accompany him on his paper rounds, Paddy nurtured a desire to be free. His longed for opportunity appeared when Leonard inadvertently left the garden gate open while he put his bicycle in the outhouse one evening after work. There was a flash of white as the excited canine made his bid for freedom, out the gate, into the road and off down Cavendish Street in the direction of Bishop's Hill. Basil ran after him as fast as he could but by the time he reached the bottom of Cavendish Street the happy hound had disappeared. Basil searched for his errant friend for a couple of hours but could find no trace of him, and finally he slouched home a disconsolate young man. He searched again the following day, once more to no avail, and sadly he resigned himself to the reality that he would probably never see his playmate again. So upset was he that he refused to speak to Leonard and even accused him, unfairly, of deliberately releasing the dog.

Imagine the surprise on Basil's face when he returned from his paper round two days later and found Paddy sitting beside the garden gate. At least he thought it was Paddy but he could not be absolutely certain because the dog that tilted his head at him as he approached was far from white. He was more of a dirty brown colour and what's more he stank something awful. It didn't take a Sherlock Holmes to work out where the errant mutt had spent the past two days, in the pig sties of White Elm Street. His odour was pungent, to say the least, and Basil was charged with giving him a good bath with carbolic soap before he was even allowed anywhere near the outhouse. Paddy fought vigorously against the bath but this time Basil held him firmly by the scruff of the neck until he was clean and acceptably dry.

That might well have been the end of the matter except that two days later Paddy went missing again; it seems that his original foray had only served to increase his desire for freedom. This time the gate had been firmly closed but when Basil scoured the garden looking for the runaway he discovered a hole had been dug, by industrious paws, under the fence and into the neighbour's garden. The hole was filled in and, like clockwork, Paddy returned the following day, once more steeped in smelly, clingy pig muck. Out came the galvanised bath and the carbolic soap and Paddy was once more restored to his sartorial splendour. Unfortunately Paddy had now become an uncontrollable nuisance and the following day he decided to pay another visit to his friends the pigs, having dug another hole under the fence.

"It is obvious that he will continue to escape Basil," Chip advised, "and we just cannot keep having him come back covered in pigs muck every day." He shot a questioning look toward Basil who returned a resigned expression.

"OK dad, I understand. He will have to go back won't he."

"I'm afraid so son. I really am sorry but I know you understand where I'm coming from." Basil nodded knowingly.

Paddy spent the night tied up in the outhouse and the following day Basil reluctantly walked him back to the RSPCA and handed him over. He had wanted a dog for so long and he had waited very patiently for this opportunity, but it had only lasted for three short weeks. Sadly he raised his hand in farewell to the confused dog, turned and trudged sadly home. 'One day,' he said to himself, 'one day'.

******

Time was marching on and Basil still had no idea what he wanted to do for a career. With only five or six weeks left before he would hang up his school cap for the last time he was still undecided although he had one or two embryonic ideas. He was very good at arithmetic and quite fancied a job where he could utilise that skill but careers like accountancy or banking were not open to boys from his level of schooling. The first job application he submitted was to Avery scales, who made weighing machines for shops and warehouses, where he thought his ability with numbers would be ideal. He was given an interview.

On the day he turned up in his Sunday best with his hair brylcreemed and waited nervously outside the door of the manager's office. It was a nerve wracking experience for one so young but on being called he summoned up all his courage, took a deep breath and strode into the office with confidence. The interviewer was a kindly looking man, neatly dressed and with an unmistakable air of importance. He asked Basil a number of questions concerning his hobbies and schooling, and seemed to be suitably impressed with the answers he received.

"Just one final thing," he hesitated, looking down at the pad on which he had been scribbling notes. Basil held his breath. "Basil. I need you to take a short mathematics test before you leave, I will then let you know my decision by letter." Basil was dismissed and taken to an adjoining room where there was a desk with paper and a pencil and a page of arithmetical questions.

He must have performed successfully with the test because two days later a letter landed on the front doormat containing a job offer. There was one difficulty though, the company required him to start work one week before the end of the school term but when he approached the education authorities they flatly refused to release him, saying that he must complete his final week in school. Basil was shocked, he could not understand the logic behind their decision and when he passed the information on to the manager at Avery Scales the job offer was withdrawn, Basil was extremely disappointed.

'What to do now?' Basil thought. It occurred to him that his lifelong love of books could make a move into the printing or bookbinding trade a favourable move. He wrote a letter of application to Cowells printers but was disappointed to receive a reply informing him that there were no vacancies for school leavers at that time, another dead end.

Cousin Douglas Holland had already secured a job as an apprentice bricklayer with Thomas Parkington, the builders who had a yard on Princes Street, and he had heard that there were vacancies for apprentice carpenters. 'How about a career in the building trade' Basil mused, there was always a demand for builders, his woodwork marks at school were very good and he enjoyed making figures and models out of wood, perhaps carpentry was his real calling. Everything happened in a rush after that, he wrote a letter of application which was answered by return of post with an appointment in two days for a formal interview. He was successful at the interview, passed a small practical test and was immediately offered an apprenticeship beginning the second week in September. Basil was overjoyed, he had managed to secure a job he was sure he would enjoy and he would have a few shillings in his pocket each week too.

He was not satisfied though and didn't rest on his laurels. There was a gap of six weeks to be filled between finishing school, on Friday the twenty seventh of July, and starting his carpentry career on the seventh of September, but how to fill it profitably?

Since leaving school, Leonard had been working for the Co-op, in their grocery shop in Fore Hamlet at the bottom of Cavendish Street, and coincidentally he had booked his ten day summer holiday commencing the twenty seventh of July. Leonard approached the shop manager who agreed that Basil could fill in for his brother as a holiday relief for the ten days that he would be absent. The agreement was for him to work from Monday to Saturday evening, with Wednesday afternoon off for early closing, and Monday to Wednesday the following week.

Proudly Basil turned up for his first day of real adult work promptly at seven thirty on Monday thirtieth of July, he had envisaged himself serving customers in the shop and was rather disappointed when he was informed that he would be doing home deliveries. The manager escorted Basil out to the back yard where he found a handcart, with steel rimmed wheels, and a pile of wooden boxes.

"These are the lists for you to deliver. Go through each list in turn and put the items into a wooden box. When you have filled enough boxes take the cart and deliver them and then come back for more." The manager thrust a handful of papers into Basil's hand and disappeared into the shop.

One by one Basil went through the lists and sorted them into an order that would give him the shortest possible route with a minimum of backtracking. He then went through each order in turn, placing the required items into the wooden boxes, a stone of potatoes here, two pounds of carrots there, tinned food too. He stacked the boxes carefully and securely on the handcart and finally began the round pushing into Fore Hamlet. His first route took him up Cavendish Street and it was soon plain to him that he had forgotten one important factor when he planned the routes; inclines. Cavendish Street had a fairly steep hill when walking but it was a hundred times worse when you were pushing a fully laden handcart, missing this factor meant that he had piled too many boxes onto the cart. By the time he reached Alan Road, at the top of the hill, he was exhausted, and it was still only nine o'clock in the morning. He completed the deliveries, all in the Upper Cavendish Street, Alan

Road, Newton Road and Tomline Road area and finally let the empty cart pull him down Cavendish Street to the shop where more lists awaited him. This time the route was up Bishop's Hill and he wisely split the deliveries into two loads, he was too tired to attempt another mammoth uphill push.

Despite the work being exhausting Basil nevertheless enjoyed it. He felt as if he was an adult now, his schooldays slipping far behind him, and he was earning his wage like other men. He was forced to surrender his paper round but that did not bother him unduly, after all delivering newspapers was a schoolboy's job wasn't it.

When his ten days were almost completed the manager approached Basil and informed him that the Foxhall Road shop was looking for a relief the following Monday for ten days and, because he had worked so diligently, he had recommended Basil to fill the position.

The work was almost identical to the Fore Street shop except for two important differences. Firstly the delivery routes did not involve much in the way of hills, so he could load his handcart up fully without any worries, and secondly he was charged with collecting the money from the customers. To him this showed a great element of trust and he relished the responsibility right up to the last Monday when events took a massive turn for the worse.

He returned from his second round of deliveries to be confronted by a stern faced manager.

"Step into my office please Basil." The manager's bushy moustache twitched as he rolled his lips. Basil followed into the office and stood in front of the desk whilst the manager made himself comfortable.

"I have just been tallying your takings from this morning."

"Yes sir." Basil's innocent expression showed he had no idea what was coming.

"It is ten shillings short." Basil's jaw dropped.

"Ten shillings sir? That is not possible, I am always most careful with the money."

"Nevertheless that is the case. Now I know small mistakes can be made when giving change so when the takings show a surplus I put that aside in order to make up for any shortages. But ten shillings is too large a sum."

"I can't understand how it could have happened sir." Basil was visibly upset, although he was not being accused directly of stealing he felt that the suspicion must be there. Turning his pockets inside out he said "Look sir, I haven't taken it, honest."

"Basil, Basil, don't get upset. I know that you have not stolen it. I think what you have done is given somebody change for a one pound note when in fact they gave you a ten shilling note."

"I am so sorry sir; will you be deducting it from my wages?"

"No lad, but please be much more careful in future."

Basil returned to his handcart and began loading up his final round for the day. The whole situation had a very sobering effect on him, so much so that the next day, when the manager approached him to say that the Springfield Road shop needed a relief the following Monday, he declined.

"You don't have to worry Basil; they need you for rural deliveries so you will be working with another man on a horse drawn cart. You will not have any dealings with the money side."

That was a different situation altogether, Basil quickly changed his mind and accepted.

Reporting for work at Springfield Road the following Monday Basil spent all that day in the storehouse behind the shop weighing out bags of flour, rice, sugar, currants, sultanas etcetera as well as forming pats of butter. All the produce had been delivered to the shop in large sacks and before it could be offered for sale it had to be split into smaller quantities, neatly sealed in small brown and blue paper bags. Loads of these small bags were loaded onto a cart and readied for the next day.

Early on the Tuesday morning Basil swept into the yard on his bicycle, keen to start the day's work. He was really looking forward to it because this was something very different from anything he had ever done before. He was immediately set to work loading fresh vegetables onto the cart, Alfred, the driver and salesman, harnessed the freshly groomed chestnut horse between the shafts and Basil climbed up onto the smooth wooden seat, Alfred settled beside him and they were ready for the off. Slowly they trotted out onto Bramford Road, turning into Sproughton Road after the railway bridge, and headed in the direction of Sproughton village itself. The cart was effectively a mobile grocery shop and during the morning they stopped at regular, pre determined locations, to be greeted by a gathering of chatting housewives, waiting to buy their daily supply of groceries. The housewives told Albert what they needed and while he retrieved the pre-bagged items Basil slipped a nosebag over the horse's neck before weighing out the loose vegetables on the big brass scales at the rear of the wagon.

During the course of the week they called at Bramford, Burstall, Flowton, Somersham, Nettlestead, Little Blakenham, Great Blakenham and Claydon. Basil thought it great fun and enjoyed it immensely, talking to Alfred and hearing all of the unusual things that had happened on the round over the years the two became firm friends and for a while Basil nurtured the thought that he might have made a mistake going for a carpentry apprenticeship where he would be tied to one location, maybe this would be a more exciting and interesting job to take on permanently. His daydream was dispelled by Albert when he told him how different the job was in the winter, when the rain and snow changed the landscape and the horse and wagon became caked in mud. Basil could imagine the extreme bitter cold and his clothes soaked through when it rained, perhaps it was not such a good idea after all. Finally saying goodbye to Albert, and pocketing his hard earned wages. Basil cycled home with a satisfied smile on his face.

******

Chip bought tickets for the whole family to go to see Bertram Mills Circus, which was pitched on Alderman Road recreation ground, as an August Bank Holiday treat. The tickets, the cheapest available, had cost one shilling and nine pence each, which was rather expensive, but Chip felt it could possibly be the last family outing, seeing as Leonard was working and Basil had left school and was about to start his apprenticeship, which made it, in his opinion well worth the expenditure.

The show was excellent with plenty of animal acts featuring lions, tigers, elephants, horses and sea lions. Marjorie laughed out loud when the sea lions clapped their flippers to get some herrings. One of the elephants sat in a specially reinforced car and drove around the ring, swinging the steering wheel with his trunk. Basil noticed the car failed to follow the turns the elephant was making and, on closer inspection, realised that it was a scam and there was a man, concealed under the elephant's seat, who was actually driving the car. Nevertheless it was amusing.

Apart from the animals there was the usual death defying trapeze act, although there was a safety net and of course there were the clowns, no circus could ever be complete without them, with their bright red painted smiles and big red noses, throwing water over each other and hitting one another with planks of wood, it really was funny. One clown picked up a bucket and ran around the raised ring edge, chasing his colleague, when he tripped and the contents of the bucket went into the crowd. It was a shower of paper clippings that flew into the surprised audience and not the shower of water that they had feared. The show ended with the human cannonball, the intrepid missile, wearing a white boiler suit and a silver helmet, slipped down the barrel of the cannon which was aimed at a net on the other side of the arena. The fuse was lit, there was a pause before an almighty bang, accompanied by billows of grey smoke and out from the midst of the smoke shot the human projectile, tumbling in mid air to land, back first, in the safety net. Applause rang out as he bounced in the air and swung himself down to the sawdust arena, arms outstretched, milking the admiration of the crowd. It was a very enjoyable evening.

There was yet another treat in store for the family, well all except Leonard that is. Every year that Chip and Doris had been married the family had spent their one week summer holiday in a bed and breakfast in Felixstowe, but this year Chip had managed to book a week in a bed and breakfast in Lowestoft. Marjorie had never heard of Lowestoft so she was very excited to think that they were going so far away, Basil had heard of it but was not exactly sure where it was and Leonard didn't really care where it was as he was not going there in any event.

Early on Saturday morning Basil and Chip picked up their cases and, along with Doris and Marjorie, set off on the relatively short walk to Derby Road railway station. Leonard said goodbye to them on the doorstep before returning to the kitchen to make his favourite breakfast, porridge. Later he grabbed a bag of clothes and walked down the road to spend the week with his grandmother and grandfather Cotton at number 120, déjà vous for Leonard, he had lived with his grandparents for seven and a half years immediately after his mother died.

The happy holidaymakers took the short train ride from Derby Road station to Westerfield Station, just outside Ipswich, where they changed trains for Lowestoft.

Arriving at Lowestoft station they stepped out into beautiful warm sunshine with no idea in which direction they should walk to get to the bed and breakfast on Kirkly Cliff Road.

"Wait here Doris, Basil and I will ask for directions." Chip said as he nodded to Basil and together they made towards a rank of taxis.

"That's quite a step, that is." Said the taxi driver when they asked him which way they needed to go. "You need to take London Road North, take the bridge over the river, keep left on Royal Parade, then Marine Parade and after a quarter of a mile or so that becomes Kirkly Cliff Road."

"How far is that all told?"

"It'll be more than a mile, too far to walk if you have cases."

"Are there any motor busses that go there?"

"There is one that runs down London Road South, but even then it's a bit of a step from the stop." The taxi driver told him. "I can take you and the family to the door for a shilling."

Chip thought for a while, it seemed to be rather expensive at a shilling and the cost of the holiday had left little enough money for extravagances. Chip decided they would walk it, thanked the taxi driver and returned to the family.

"We can walk it easily," said Basil, "we have plenty of time and a mile's not really that far."

They set off, with Basil and Chip carrying the cases, and after about forty five minutes they arrived outside the bed and breakfast. It looked quite grand from the outside and they were not disappointed when they reached their rooms either. They had two very comfortable, well appointed rooms. Basil shared with Marjorie in a cosy room, with bright flowery wallpaper, on the third floor at the back of the house; the ceiling sloped so that Basil had to be careful he didn't hit his head when he looked out the window. Marjorie flopped onto the bed, tired from the journey, while he unpacked their case and put the clothes in the small wooden wardrobe. Chip and Doris had a larger room on the second floor at the front of the house, Doris was very pleased there were no houses on the other side of the road and she could see across the promenade to the sea.

"You put your feet up Chip while I unpack." Doris offered, Chip was relieved, the walk had taken a lot out of him, he was finding that recently he had become less mobile. Unbeknown to him and Doris his health was beginning to decline as a result of the injury he sustained during the Great War.

It was late afternoon by the time they had unpacked and had a short nap but they were all eager to explore. They retraced their steps, until they came to Cliff Road which took them directly onto the upper promenade. Below them, accessed by a number of paths, was another lower promenade which bordered directly onto a beautiful golden sandy beach. They made their way down to the lower promenade, just to the right of the Claremont pier.

"My but this is a big promenade," said Chip, "much longer than Felixstowe I should think."

"I think it goes all the way to the port this way." Said Basil pointing to the north.

"And I can't see the end down here either." Chip pointed to their left. "And look at all those beach huts."

The beach at Felixstowe, up to now the only one they had been used to, was a shingle beach so the soft sand came as a very pleasant surprise. Marjorie wanted an ice cream so they wandered to the pier and found an ice cream booth. As they strolled along Chip was eyeing up the huts.

"You know," he said wistfully, "I have often thought how nice it would be to have a beach hut at Felixstowe, but they are rarely up for sale and so expensive, one in the 'Star' recently was advertised for twelve pounds." He let the muse hang in mid air before it disappeared like a soap bubble. However, it did not disappear completely, it lodged somewhere deep in Basil's head.

They had a great, relaxing week. Chip spent a lot of time sitting on a blanket on the beach with his jacket off and his sleeves rolled up and his trilby hat tilted at a rakish angle, which was the closest he ever came to sunbathing. Doris was continually by his side only slipping off to get some sandwiches for lunch, while he relaxed under the watchful gaze of Marjorie. Basil wandered off northwards on the promenade, over the river bridge and onto the fish dock where he watched as the drifter fleet offload their catch of herring, cod and haddock and the trawler fleet with their plaice and sole. It intrigued him to see the big pots being swung off the boats and their contents poured into wooden boxes along

311

with copious amounts of crushed ice, ready for their transport by train to the London markets.

Unfortunately a week passes very quickly when you are having fun and before they realised it the time came to make the long walk back to the railway station and ultimately home. As they walked into the kitchen in Cavendish Street they were greeted by a delicious smell and Leonard's smiling face. Grandmother Lydia had prepared a stew for their return, knowing they would be ravenous, and Leonard had put it in the gas oven to cook through and had laid the table. The expression of relief on Doris's face was a joy to see.

"A perfect end to a perfect holiday." She said as she gave Leonard a kiss on the cheek.

******

Monday the seventh of September was a very special day for Basil, his first day as a wage earning adult in a permanent job. Excitedly he breakfasted, swung his jacket on, before hopping on his bicycle and freewheeling down Cavendish Street hill toward Fore Hamlet. The workshop and yard of Thomas Parkington, builders, was on Princes Street, just a short distance from his old home in James Street and he joined the short queue of workmen as they filed in for their seven thirty start.

The letter he received confirming his apprenticeship instructed him to report to the workshop foreman, but he didn't know where that was, and was looking anxiously around when a small, kindly looking man about forty years old, with a pipe firmly clenched between his teeth, approached him.

"Are you looking for somebody son?" his voice was soft and gentle and reminded Basil immediately of his father.

"I'm looking for the foreman's office; I'm the new apprentice carpenter."

"Ah! Ok you come with me."

Basil followed up a wooden staircase into a workshop, the kindly man indicated toward a small office at one end. Basil thanked the man and tapped nervously on the open door.

"C'min." Was the brief reply to his knock. Basil stepped inside and waited. Eventually the foreman looked up from the papers on his desk.

"You must be young Basil Double." A statement rather than a question.

"Yes sir."

"OK! Have you got an apron?"

"Yes sir." Basil fingered the pristine apron in his bag. Doris had made it especially for him, knee length with a fairly large pouch in the front for tools.

"Good. Oh and cut out the 'sir' business, I'm Mister Chandler to you."

"Yes sir ... erm ... I mean Mister Chandler." Chandler smiled, a friendly smile, Basil thought 'I think I could like him'.

"Right, follow me."

Basil followed closely as Chandler walked through the workshop, announcing to nobody in particular that this was Basil the new apprentice boy. When they had finished the tour of the upper floor Basil followed Chandler down the staircase and the process was repeated in the lower workshop. Basil wondered what he would be learning on his first day, would it be different kinds of joints, would he actually make something, his mind boggled. As it turned out he need not have concerned himself unduly because for the first couple of weeks he was either painting wood with pink primer in an adjacent workshop or labouriously sandpapering wood smooth and at the end of the working day sweeping the workshop floor, in fact doing all the mundane jobs that were unpopular and boring to the experienced workers. He was feeling rather deflated but it did enable him to get to know some of the other carpenters. When he complained over dinner one evening Chip explained that it was the normal way for an apprentice to begin, you had to start at the very bottom and, with experience, work your way up; it was the same in the foundry. It was essential to realise that the humdrum and monotonous tasks were not beneath you.

"It won't last long son," he said gently, "then you will begin to learn from the bottom up. Mind you, as the junior you will still get most of the uninteresting jobs."

Basil felt reassured if somewhat impatient.

After a couple of weeks Basil was called into the foreman's office and informed that the following Monday he would be moving to the upper workshop to begin his education in earnest. Chandler led him to the far corner of the joinery shop and opened his hand in the direction of the kindly man who had directed Basil to the foreman's office on that first day.

"I'm placing you in the care of Mister Aldous, you will be well advised to pay close attention to everything he tells you, he is one of our best and most experienced carpenters." He paused. "I'll leave him with you Fred." With that he turned and made his way back to his office.

"Mister Aldous, that's a bit formal son isn't it. You call me Fred."

Fred was a very gentle and fatherly man who sucked away at his pipe of St Julien Flake most of the day while guiding Basil's eager hands and mind. It was not long before Basil had learned the basic joints used in carpentry and he assisted Fred making garden gates, doors and windows. He still ended up doing much of the sanding and priming, as Chip had said he would, but only for Fred and one or two of the carpenters on the first floor.

For a week's toil in the joinery shop he received the princely sum of ten shillings, half of which he gave as Doris as housekeeping, two shillings put aside in a tin to enable him to purchase the tools of the trade that he would require. He was left with three shillings to do with as he pleased. He bought his first tools, after his fourth week, for the sum of three pounds and five shillings. They were bought through the firm so he was able to pay them eight shillings outright and pay the remainder off at two shillings a week.

Fred Aldous proved to be a wonderful teacher and their association soon developed into a very close relationship, Basil looked on him as a second father and for his part Fred regarded Basil as a son. A deep friendship developed that would last for a lifetime.

1935

As time moved on Basil became more confident and relaxed in his work, he was quickly accepted by the other workmen who enjoyed his hard working ways and his wicked sense of humour. Under the expert guidance of Fred Aldous he rapidly developed his woodworking skills and progressed to having his very own workbench with a locker underneath, to house his expanding collection of tools, and he was given very small projects of his own to work on. He took them in his stride and worked very hard to become competent and looked forward to being able to work on some larger projects unsupervised.

The workshop building was a two storey affair, the top floor accommodated eight carpenters, seven experienced plus Basil the apprentice, all of whom were fully occupied making doors, windows, kitchen cabinets, gates and all the other wooden fittings necessary for house building. The benches were arranged with five along the rear wall and three on the front, this was to allow access to a pair of opening doors in the middle of the wall. The doors opened outwards and had a beam protruding above them with a block and tackle hoist attached to it. This was where large pieces of timber were hoisted into the workshop and completed items were lowered to ground level using the same method. Basil and Fred had adjoining benches in one corner beside the doors. At one end of the workshop, adjacent to the staircase was the small rectangular, half glazed office, the home of Mr Chandler.

The ground floor was occupied by another six carpenters who were engaged on individual projects unconnected with the house building operation. Their benches were spaced further apart because they often built large items, with four along the back wall and one either side of a pair of doors similar to the ones above. At the end of the ground floor workshop there was an engine room that housed a big gas powered engine. The engine turned a drive shaft with a large flywheel at one end and various sized pulleys along its length. These pulleys powered saws, planes, lathes and drills, on both floors, via a network of leather belts and shafts suspended from the ceiling. It also supplied power to the main sawmill adjacent to the workshops where larger pieces of timber were cut to size. At one time the main shaft was connected to a steam engine, fired by a combination of coal and waste timber off cuts, but this had been replaced a few years earlier.

When he was given slightly more complex work Basil found it extremely interesting and under Fred's expert tutorage mastering the different types of joints proved to be no problem, all except one that was. He struggled a bit with the dovetail joint which required extreme accuracy with a tennon saw and a chisel if it was to be tight and strong.

It wasn't all hard work though. Chandler was a betting man and mid morning, regular as clockwork, he would leave his office and disappear down the staircase and into the engine room where he would study the racing pages of his newspaper, working out which bets he would place during his lunchtime break. He was usually absent from his post for at least half an hour. One day, as soon as Chandler had disappeared down the staircase, Albert Humphries put down the chisel and mallet he had been using to make a mortise and tennon joint.

"Fancy a bit of fun chaps?" Albert had a big grin on his face.

"What kind of fun?" George Wallace was interested.

Albert reached under his bench and removed a rectangle of wood which he passed to George.

"Stand that up against the wall, it's the wickets."

"Cricket!" exclaimed George. "Good idea."

Albert retrieved another piece of wood, one that he had previously fashioned into the shape of a cricket bat, and a sorbo ball. The eight of them had a very enjoyable interlude playing half an hour of cricket. A close watch was kept on the stairs and as soon as Chandler appeared through the power room door the sports gear was hastily stowed so that as his head emerged everybody was busy working. It became a regular occurrence, they would have half an hour of cricket while their foreman was absent and they were never discovered, although Basil always felt that the friendly foreman knew exactly what was going on but elected to retain harmony in the workshop by turning a blind eye to their antics.

During the lunch break, weather permitting, all of the carpenters from both floors congregated in the yard to devour their sandwiches and when they had finished they enjoyed a brisk kick about. The big stable doors of the timber store were used as the goal and, being the youngest, it usually fell to Basil to be the goalkeeper. More and more Basil enjoyed being at work, the other carpenters were a happy and friendly bunch who rarely had reason to argue amongst themselves, and they all liked the cheerful fourteen year old.

******

Basil enjoyed having his extended family living in such close proximity to him and, since his return to Cavendish Street he had seen much more of his aunt Gertrude from the Cotton side of the family. He still nurtured a soft spot for his mother's sister and his feelings were returned tenfold by the mature spinster aunt, they had immediately revived their cinema going and visited one cinema or other almost every week.

On the Dumble side of the family there was the warm hearted Emily Jane, who had always enjoyed a full house but who now lived alone.

When she wasn't engaged in activities for the Labour Party or busy making clothes, Doris spent many hours with her mother, and Basil liked to visit her whenever he could because there was still a strong bond between him and Emily Jane, a bond that had been forged when he lived with her following the death of his mother.

When Gladys married Ernest Hurricks they initially moved in with Ernest's parents but following the arrival of their daughter Joyce in 1931 the house in Woodville Road had become too crowded and they had moved to number 3 Wilsons Dwellings in Bramford Road.

Ernest worked as a journeyman painter obtaining work wherever he could and on the seventeenth of May he had been scouting for work in the Nacton Road area of town. His brother, Percy, lived in Avondale Road, which was quite close, and as it was only six thirty in the evening he called in on him to see if he would like to go for a beer or two. Percy agreed, he was really pleased to see his brother, and they walked to a public house where they played darts and sank three pints of mild beer. Ernest looked at his watch and was astonished to find that it was already ten fifteen.

"I must go; Gladys will be worrying where I am." He got up to leave.

The two walked to Percy's house to collect Ernest's bicycle and as he was about to leave Percy noticed that there was no front light.

"You can't ride home at this time without a light," he said, "it's dangerous and if the constables see you, you could be in trouble."

Percy knew he had a spare light in his shed so he rummaged around until he found it, fixed it on Ernest's bicycle and lit it.

"There you go, that's much better."

"Thanks Perce," Ernest vaulted into the saddle and started his ride home.

"Cheerio: see you next Friday." He called over his shoulder as he pedalled down toward Powling Road, Nacton Road and home.

He enjoyed the sensation of cool fresh air flowing gently through his tussled hair as he pushed on the pedals. Five minutes later he reached the junction with Felixstowe Road and pushed on to the top of Bishops Hill before sighing and beginning his freewheeling descent.

Bishops Hill was slightly unusual in that it was very wide for most of its length, wide enough for three cars abreast of each other. Lower down, however, the road narrowed forming a bottleneck with the width of the downhill carriageway being reduced by half.

At the bottom of the hill two motor cars were driving uphill in the opposite direction to Ernest, the second vehicle being driven by Mr Noel Creasey, who was a flying instructor at Ipswich Municipal Airport. He was anxious to get home, he had endured a long day and was quite exhausted, his car was only using side lights, the headlights being switched off.

Daniel Watt, a chemist who lived on Nacton Road was returning home and pushing his bicycle up the steep hill when, as he came level with the White Elm Inn, he was passed by the two cars travelling at around twenty five miles per hour. It looked to him as if the second vehicle was intending to overtake as he was driving in the middle of the road.

Creasey looked at the clock set into the walnut dashboard of his Riley coupe and cursed, he wanted to get home to bed and the car in front seemed to be going so slowly. He turned to his passenger Harry McClane.

"Why is this idiot going so slow, can't he see there is nothing about?"

Irritated he down shifted the gears and pressed his foot harder on the accelerator and moved toward the centre of the road.

"The road widens here, I should be able to overtake him." He could see no cars coming down the hill toward him, relieved he pressed the accelerator as far as it would go and pulled the steering wheel to the right. He saw the flash of a light and pulled the steering wheel hard to the left.

There was a loud bang and the windscreen in front of him shattered.

Ernest whistled as he freewheeled down the hill, gaining momentum. He anticipated the bottleneck and moved toward the centre of the road.

Suddenly there was a car directly in front of him and his blood instantly turned to ice. He slammed into the front off side of the car and was catapulted into the windscreen, before being thrown into the air and landing in a bone crunching heap on the tarmac.

Creasey sat transfixed, what had happened? He heard shouting.

Watt watched as the car appeared to attempt an overtake, he heard several crashes, the car appeared to bump towards the nearside pavement and he saw a man lying by the off side of the car.

McClane was level with the rear wheels of the leading car when he saw the light of a bicycle coming toward them, it crashed into the off side headlamp and the windscreen shattered.

Being a chemist Watt had knowledge of first aid and dropping his bicycle he rushed to the stricken cyclist. Bending over Ernest he felt for his carotid artery but could detect no pulse.

Five minutes later, at eleven o'clock, two policemen arrived, PC Harding and PC Tomline followed shortly afterwards by an ambulance. Ernest was immediately stretchered into the ambulance where he was examined by Percival Willett, a St John Ambulance attendant, who could detect no signs of life. The ambulance conveyed him to the Anglesea Road hospital where Doctor Harold Kelson confirmed that Ernest was dead, his skull had been smashed like a fragile eggshell and his brain was extensively lacerated.

Recovering his composure, Creasey was adamant the collision was not his fault, he had only moved toward the centre of the road in order to see past the car in front, the cyclist, he asserted, was in the middle of the road. He insisted he had not attempted to overtake the leading car. PC Harding measured the positions of where Ernest and the motor car had come to rest, entering the details in his notebook. Returning to the car PC Harding studied the damage and noted the front offside headlight was bent back and the sidelight was broken off completely. Ernest's crumpled bicycle lay forlornly beside the car. PC Harding knew it was time for him to undertake the job he disliked the most; he had to inform the family.

He looked down at the wallet he had retrieved from Ernest's jacket and found a letter inside, it bore the name Ernest Hurricks, and his address. Puffing out his cheeks he climbed onto his bicycle and headed for Ernest's home.

It was eleven forty five, Gladys was asleep in bed, little Joyce was in a cot at the bottom of her bed. They were both awakened by a banging on the front door.

"Oh no! Your father has forgotten his key yet again." Exclaimed Gladys, dragging on her dressing gown she plodded barefoot down the wooden stairs.

She opened the door expecting to see the embarrassed face of her husband but instead there stood the solemn looking PC Harding with an open notebook in his hand.

"Mrs Hurricks?"

Gladys nodded slowly and a mask of dread closed over her face. Instinctively she knew there was only one reason the police would call at this time of night, the constable was the bearer of dreadful news. Her hands went to cover her mouth and she began to wail.

"Not my Ernest. Please god no, not my Ernest."

"I'm dreadfully sorry ma'am." The constable said softly.

Gladys collapsed onto the floor, sobbing uncontrollably and repeating over and over, "Not my Ernest, not my Ernest."

Three days later, Monday the twentieth of May a coroner's inquest was held at Ipswich Town Hall. All of the witnesses were in attendance and one by one they presented their evidence to the coroner, Mr C T Dawson, and a jury of twelve.

Answering a question put by Mr Cutting, from the solicitors Gotelee and Goldsmith, representing Creasey, PC Harding said cyclists proceeding down the hill were inclined to go to the middle of the road on approaching the bottleneck.

"A great number of cyclists," he continued, "went down the hill too fast. At the distance he was from the bottleneck there was no need for the deceased to be other than on the correct side."

Ernest had been thirty five yards above the bottleneck.

In his summing up the coroner said.

"It cannot be suggested that it was reasonable for a cyclist to come down a hill twenty feet from his near side. That was where the deceased was found and the evidence, on the whole, did suggest that he was not carried far following the collision. The evidence also seems to show that the car could not have been going fast at the time, and it seems to me that the violence of the impact must have been due to the speed of the cyclist himself."

The jury retired and upon their return the foreman, Mr A Cooper, delivered a verdict of accidental death, and exonerated the driver of the car from all blame.

Gladys broke down in tears. She was supported by her sister Doris and cousin Gertrude as she was helped from the room. The coroner gathered his papers and tapped them into neatness on his bench.

"My condolences Mrs Hurricks." He said gently, and then in a firmer voice. "Court dismissed." Before retreating through the door into his chambers.

Gladys found it difficult to come to terms with her loss and, together with her daughter Joyce, moved back to Cavendish Street to live with her mother.

******

327

The first week in September Basil and the other first floor carpenters were having a bit of fun while Chandler occupied his usual position in the engine room studying the equine form. This time it was not cricket they were playing, they were having a putty fight. Rolling pellets of the smooth soft putty they flicked them at each other using their steel rulers as catapults.

Chandler exited the engine room door, Albert spotted him and whistled the warning sound, rulers clattered on benches and putty pellets were once more amalgamated into a ball.

Chandler's head emerged and he turned to look across the workshop.

"Basil, my office if you please." It was a summons and Basil quickly ran through all that he had been doing searching for something he could be admonished for.

"Close the door Basil." He did as he was instructed, "How much do we pay you each week Basil?"

"Ten shillings Mr Chandler."

"No we do not." Basil was apprehensive.

"From today we pay you twelve shillings and sixpence a week." Chandler could hardly contain his amusement. He knew he had worried Basil and he rather enjoyed doing it.

Basil returned to the shop floor wearing a sullen expression and was greeted by worried looks from his workmates. Returning to his bench he continued with the work he had been doing before the putty fight without a word. Eventually George could stand the tension no longer.

"Well? Spill the beans, what did he say?"

"Oh just that I have got a two shillings and sixpence a week pay rise because I have been here one whole year."

The workshop descended into peals of laughter.

"You really had us going there lad." George laughed.

That afternoon they had to replenish their stock of wood so they sent Basil down to the wood store to prepare bundles in the sizes they wanted. Opening the barn doors, that also served as a football goal, he eyed the racks of timber all sorted by size. There was one rack of rough, unplaned wood that had a two inch by four inch cross section, known obviously as two by four. Another rack above it had the same size wood but it had been planed smooth and was called two by four planed. There were other racks with two by two, two by one, three by three, six by two and so on.

Basil looked at his list and decided to get all the two by two first and, having put it in a bundle on the ground beneath the workshop doors, grabbed the lower end of the block and tackle and secured the bundle. When it was firmly attached he hauled on the other end of the rope to raise the bundle to the waiting hands of his comrades on the first floor. He performed the same exercise with the other sizes of timber until there was only the six by four left to lift. This timber bundle was very heavy, too heavy in fact for him to haul up on his own, so a couple of the carpenters grabbed the rope ready to pull it up for him. Then George came up with an idea.

"Hey Basil, seeing as you are coming up in the world now, why don't we celebrate by hauling you up with the timber?"

"That's a good idea," said Basil, "that will save me climbing up the stairs too."

Without another thought Basil balanced on the timber, one foot either side of the rope, and held on. George called another couple of carpenters over, it would take four of them to haul up the weight of wood plus Basil.

Slowly, and in jerks, Basil was raised toward the gaping opening that was the access to the workshop. He was approaching the doorway when the owner of the company paid an unannounced visit to the joinery shop. Thomas Parkington was a short stout man with a thick beard and bushy sideburns. His red bulbous nose provided a perch for a pair of wire rimmed spectacles hooked over large ears that also supported his bowler hat. He was a deeply religious man who believed in hard work and had little or no tolerance for amusement or frivolity and the carpenters knew that he would become very angry if he saw that they were playing the fool. Being totally engrossed with giving Basil his lift in life, the four on the rope didn't see him enter.

"Good afternoon Mr Parkington sir." Fred Aldous said in a loud warning voice, he was not engaged on the rope.

"Gentlemen." Greeted Mr Parkington.

The four on the rope looked to each other wide eyed and then, as one, let go the rope just as Basil's head was beginning to appear over the floor level. The weight of timber and Basil, were now unsupported and the whole combination plummeted to the ground accompanied by a loud clatter of crashing timber and a youthful scream of pain.

Parkington paced to the open doorway and looked down at the tangled heap of timber and Basil.

"What on earth is going on?" he boomed. Basil recognising him instantly decided an excuse was needed rather than an explanation of what had really been going on, and he quickly replied.

"The rope broke Mister Parkington sir."

Parkington herumphed and made for the foreman's office, closing the door noisily behind him. Basil reattached the timber and while George and his companions hoisted it, with big smiles on their faces, he made his way through the lower workshop and up the staircase.

"You buggers," he said as he emerged into the workshop massaging a sore rear, "that damned well hurt."

"It would have hurt much more if old Parkington had seen you riding the rope." George explained. "Still, nothing broken hey."

1936

Basil still hadn't given up on his desire to have a dog of his own, despite the debacle with the pig loving Paddy, and his second chance arrived suddenly one Saturday morning in the spring. He had to walk to a haberdashery shop in Felixstowe Road, near Alan Road, to collect some material Doris had ordered, and he thought, as it was a pleasant morning, he would take Marjorie along for company. When they reached the top of Bishops Hill Marjorie stopped. Basil thought she was catching her breath but when he looked down into her face he found she was wearing a smile as big as a barn door.

"There is a pet shop along here," she said pointing along Rosehill Road, "I would much rather go there to look at the animals than go into a boring old drapers shop." Basil thought for a while. 'No harm can come to her there' he thought.

"Ok," said Basil, "but make sure you stay outside and only look in the window so I can find you when I've done."

"Of course I will," Marjorie grinned.

He watched as she skipped happily away toward the shop, chuckled and made off to collect Doris's material. The bell above the door clanged as he entered and Mrs Allinson, the proprietor, acknowledged him from behind the counter with a nod. She was busy serving another customer so he amused himself looking at all the different materials, buttons etcetera, on the over stacked shelves. Eventually the other customer left and he smiled as she passed him.

"Good morning Basil, have you come to collect Mrs Double's dress material?"

"Yes please."

In no time at all he was out of the shop and, with a big roll of material wrapped in brown paper slung over his shoulder, he made his way back to Rosehill Road. Arriving outside the pet shop he found Marjorie as expected, only she was holding a length of rope on the other end of which was a small dog. It looked quite scrawny and as if it could do with a good meal but when it turned its big brown pleading eyes to greet Basil his heart melted.

"What's all this?"

"Isn't he just adorable Basil?" Marjorie cooed.

"Yes but what are you doing with him?"

"The man in the shop said I could have him."

"What, he just gave him to you?" Basil was a bit suspicious.

"Yes. Mind you if mum and dad say we can keep him we will have to come back and pay him a shilling. Do you think we will be allowed to keep him? I do so hope so." Marjorie was obviously in love with the gaunt little pup.

"I don't know, but don't get too attached yet and don't be upset if they say no."

Side by side they walked home, Basil toting the roll of material and Marjorie trying to prevent herself being pulled along by the deceptively strong dog.

"He doesn't half pull," Marjorie complained, "he makes my arm ache, it don't half give me gyp."

"That sounds like a good name for him," said Basil, "we can call him Gyp."

Doris thanked Basil as he struggled through the back door sideways with the material.

"Now I can get on and make that dress Mrs Middleditch has ordered." Doris' expression changed from pleasure to confusion as she watched Marjorie follow behind with the energetic bundle of bones.

"What's this?" she frowned at Marjorie.

"It's Basil's new dog mum." She smiled at the expression of surprise flooding over Basil's face. "Please say that Basil can keep him."

Basil took a breath ready to deny ownership but was surprised into silence when Doris said that it was alright to keep the dog.

"His name is Gyp, and he is ever so good." Continued Marjorie oblivious to Basil's consternation.

"He's your responsibility now Basil," Chip uttered from behind his newspaper, "just be sure he behaves."

Over the next few weeks Gyp did behave himself and he was quite a little character but Basil began to get a rather concerned because despite being well fed and exercised Gyp did not seem to grow, he did not put on any weight and stayed rather scraggy with ribs clearly visible and suffering the odd bout of sickness.

It was in the early hours of one summer morning that Gyp, who always slept on a blanket in the kitchen, began barking, waking everybody up.

"Basil, shut your dog up will you." Chip called out tiredly from the front bedroom, Basil was reluctant to get out of bed.

"Gyp, Gyp, stop that barking." He shouted in a firm voice. It worked for about thirty seconds before the agitated barking resumed. Basil shouted down to him again and this time he stopped for about a minute, just long enough for everybody to be almost asleep again, before he resumed his barking, this time more aggressivly.

"Basil, please get him to shut up so we can all get some sleep will you." Doris was equally annoyed at having her sleep interrupted. Gyp refused to stop.

"Basil," Chip was getting annoyed, something that rarely happened, "go and sort out that damned dog .... now."

Basil climbed out of bed wearily, shrugged his feet into his slippers, and trudged, complaining, down the stairs. Walking across to the kitchen door he swung it open all prepared to have a go at Gyp for disturbing everybody and being so disobedient, but his annoyance disappeared in an instant as a cloud of smoke wafted from the kitchen. He ran back to the bottom of the stairs.

"House is on fire, quick, house is on fire." He shouted up the stairs as loud as he could.

His alarm generated rapid movement upstairs and all four joined him in the living room almost before he had a chance to move. Chip was the first one to reach the kitchen, and having looked around could find no fire but as the smoke gradually cleared it exposed the problem that had caused the panic.

The front gas ring on the cooker was still alight and beside it were the remains of a cardboard box that had contained the weights for the kitchen scales. Being near the flame the box had gradually smouldered through, fortunately without actually catching fire, and all that was left was a pile of ash with a set of weights sitting in the middle. Straight away Leonard realised it was his fault and he explained to Chip and Doris that when he had come in that evening, after taking his girlfriend to the pictures, he had made himself a cup of cocoa and must have forgotten to turn the gas ring off.

Chip just chuckled.

"Oh well Lenny, no lasting harm done, and accidents will happen." Then turning to Gyp, who was sitting bolt upright on the floor panting, head tilted to one side looking wistfully at Basil, "And as for you young Gyp, it seems as if you could have saved all our lives had the box caught fire." He ruffled the dog's ears. "Come on everybody; back to bed."

"Did you turn the gas off Lenny?" Chip called over his shoulder as they all climbed wearily up the stairs.

Everybody burst out laughing.

Gyp was certainly the saviour of the family on that occasion but unfortunately he still failed to thrive and, despite visits to the vet, he became weaker and weaker and sadly died three weeks after his lifesaving actions. Basil buried him in the garden and made a simple wooden cross to place at his head. He really loved Gyp.

******

The summer was a hot one, ideal for being on the water in Basil's view, so one Sunday he decided to take a trip on the paddle steamer the 'City of Rochester'. Built in 1904 it was originally operated by the Medway Steam Packet Company, plying its way along the Kent coast, up into East Anglia and across to France. Requisitioned by the admiralty it served as a transport during the Great War before being returned, in 1919, to the newly formed New Medway Steam Packet Company Limited where, in 1931, it had replaced the old 'Suffolk' and 'Norfolk' paddle steamers previously operated by the Great Eastern Railway Company and then London North Eastern Railway Company. The current route ran from New Cut Ipswich to

Harwich, Dovercourt, Felixstowe pier, Walton on the Naze and Clacton on Sea and back by the same route.

His journey was taken alone this time, unlike his earlier trip on the 'Suffolk'. Catching the early sailing from New Cut he stayed on deck for the whole of the journey to admire the scenery along the banks of the Orwell, alighting in Felixstowe, at the end of the half mile long pier. He bought a cup of tea from the small cafe and sat on one of the many benches, to watch the world go by. Two other steamers arrived and departed as he watched, one from Great Yarmouth and one from London.

Making his way toward dry land for lunch he paid his two pence and climbed into the electric tram for the ten minute ride from the head of the pier to the landward end. Taking his seat he looked around, he could see the whole extent of the Felixstowe peninsular, stretching from the Landguard Fort in the south to Bawdsey on the north shore of the river Deben. As the tram rattled and clattered toward the shore the view became narrower and focussed mainly on the seafront with its bed and breakfast houses, Butlin's amusement arcade, Spa Pavilion and dozens of multicoloured beach huts.

Exiting the tram Basil sauntered westward, towards Butlin's amusement park and lunch. Whenever he visited Felixstowe he felt irresistibly drawn towards Butlins or more accurately, to the boating lake with the monkey island in the middle. Today was no exception and munching his way through a bag of chips, soggy with vinegar, he sat and watched the antics of the monkeys. Whenever anybody in a row boat went too close to the island the monkeys screeched and jumped up and down, making a dreadful din which made Basil chuckle to himself. He remembered the time when he had sat watching the monkeys and one had managed to escape across the water and ran amok in the grounds until it was cornered and caught by a pair of keepers.

As the sun began to lose its power Basil made his way back to the pier but this time he paid the penny fee to walk to the paddle steamer berth and arrived in time to catch the four thirty sailing for Ipswich and the New Cut. He arrived home in time for dinner, contented, relaxed and rejuvenated.

******

Work for Basil was going better and better. He proved to be a quick learner enjoying every day and when September rolled around it surprised him to realise that he had been there for two years. The stout and strong sixteen year old was a far cry from the timid fourteen year old who had sheepishly entered the gates back in 1934.

He received his annual pay rise and now earning the vast sum of fifteen shillings a week which he proudly announced to his co workers. The discussion that lunchtime over cheese sandwiches turned naturally to wages and he was initially surprised to find that the other carpenters were earning thirty five shillings a week. He thought perhaps that was a bit unfair especially as he was undertaking similar work to them now, that was until Fred explained to him they were all qualified carpenters and he was still an apprentice. They all had families to support and quite a few of them actually lived in houses owned by the company so their rent was deducted directly from their wages. The rent for houses was between eight and ten shillings per week, depending upon the size of the house.

Basil had now mastered the vast majority of the necessary woodworking skills and had been set to work on his own special projects, albeit small ones initially gradually progressing to more complex ones. One of his early projects was a large dog kennel and run, incorporating steel bars, to house a security dog.

Fred had a project that necessitated a particularly complicated joint so he called Basil over to see how it was made. The two of them bent over the wood, in deep discussion, fully engrossed in their joint and were completely oblivious to anything happening around them. The bench nearest to Fred's was occupied by Alexander, a pleasant man in his fifties who kept himself to himself mainly because he was profoundly deaf, consequently he always worked in a kind of vacuum, unable to join in conversations and banter unless he downed tools and concentrated on others hand movements. This particular day Alexander was studiously constructing a staircase, busy cutting the long grooves, to accept the treads, using a long wooden handled chisel and mallet. The blade of the chisel was a good eighteen inches long and it could fit flat for the entire length of the groove.

Tapping the chisel firmly Alexander encountered a knot in the pine, a knot that he could not cut through. He gave the chisel a harder hit, still no joy so he gave it an almighty whack. He watched in frightened disbelief as the chisel blade came free of the handle and shot, like a crossbow bolt, across the shop, passing between the startled figures of Basil and Fred and embedding itself into the wall, quivering. Fred and Basil gaped open mouthed at the blade trembling in the wall, then at each other, then at the astounded and apologetic Alexander. They had both come so close to serious injury.

Basil's term in the joinery shop was about to come to an ignominious end, mostly of his own making, and definitely as a direct result of his pride.

At the foreman's end of the workshop were two buckets, one under a cold water tap which caught the water when the carpenters washed their hands, or tea mug. The other was used by the older men to spit into, often as a result of chewing tobacco. It was normally the task of the apprentices to thoroughly clean the workshops at the end of the week and Basil being the only apprentice in the joinery shop, the task naturally fell to him. One week Basil was asked to empty both buckets, he had successfully managed for two years to only empty the one containing water and had avoided the spittoon. This week was different, he was instructed by the foreman and was unable to avoid it, or was he.

He emptied the water bucket but flatly refused to touch the foul smelling, thick brown spit filled bucket. Chandler urged him again to empty the spit bucket and once again Basil refused.

"OK." Said Chandler turning his back and walking away. "See you Monday."

Monday arrived and the bucket still festered in the corner, nothing more was said. Basil thought he had got away with it, and he had, until he finished the project he had been working on, a garden gate. With no other project allocated to him he presented himself in Chandler's office.

"I have finished that gate Mr Chandler, can I have my next job please?"

"Certainly Basil; your next job is to empty the spit bucket!" Chandler stared unblinking at Basil.

"I'm not touching that filthy bucket, sorry." Basil looked him square in the eyes, his defiance was obvious.

"Empty the bloody bucket Basil." Chandler was beginning to colour up.

"Sorry Mr Chandler, that bucket is disgusting; I'm not touching it."

"In that case I have no more work for you."

"So; what do I do?" Basil was a bit worried but remained adamant.

"You had better go and see Mr Parkington." He paused, obviously expecting this move to finally break Basil's resolve. "Off you go."

Basil presented himself outside the door of Parkington's office and was soon ushered inside. He explained that Chandler had no more work for him and Parkington's brow furrowed; he knew that there would be a reason for Chandler's refusal because there was plenty of work outstanding. He asked Basil to explain why there was no work for him. Basil was completely honest and explained his refusal to empty the revolting bucket. Parkington understood and probably sympathised although he didn't dare let it show, he had to back his foreman. He made it clear to Basil that a foreman should be respected and his instructions should be followed without question.

"Now," he asked, "are you going to go back and empty that infernal bucket?"

"I'm sorry sir, but no I am not."

That gave Parkington a dilemma, on the one hand he had to support his foreman but on the other he did not want to lose the investment he had made in Basil both financially and morally.

He rubbed his chin, thinking deeply.

"Well I suppose you could do with a change; I am moving you to the portable building shop, there is no foreman there, you will be on your own cognisance. But," he made the silence hang in the air, "I shall be watching you carefully Double, don't let me down. Now go and move your things."

Basil left the office relieved and rather excited at the prospect of acting on his own initiative.

Once ensconced in the portable buildings workshop he embarked on his first project, building a ten foot by eight foot shed for a customer. Ahead of him lay other projects, greenhouses, summerhouses, garages and the like.

He never did empty that infernal bucket.

1937

It was while he was building a garden shed for a customer that the germ of an idea that had hidden itself in the recesses of Basil's brain, during the family holiday in Lowestoft three years earlier, emerged from the darkness. He had noticed with deep concern that his father's health was slowly deteriorating and he remembered overhearing the conversation his father had with Doris where he described the injury he had suffered in Palestine in 1917. At the time he was a driver wheeler in the Royal Field Artillery and also one of the company farriers. It appeared that an explosion had spooked a horse that he was shoeing and it kicked him in the back causing serious nerve damage. It always rankled Chip that when he had applied for a war disability the returned report bore simply four words 'Albuminuria, disability nil, rejected', he wondered if Brigadier Doctor J F Setterfield, who signed the rejection, would say the same were he to be in his shoes suffering the pain. As time progressed Chip was becoming less mobile and suffering numbness in his muscles from time to time, he knew that things were only going to get worse.

Basil remembered his father saying, on their holiday, that he would love to have a beach hut, and now Basil resolved to build one for him. In the evenings he drew out the plans and worked out the dimensions that would be within Felixstowe council regulations. He made a cutting list, a list of the timber he would need and their sizes, and ordered the timber from a local supplier. When it was delivered he told all the family that it was a garden shed he was building for somebody as a private venture and, of course, everybody accepted that explanation. He worked in the outhouse evenings and weekends until it was completed, he even assembled it in the back yard to ensure it all went together correctly, of course it did.

With the construction completed he contacted Felixstowe Council to rent a plot on the beach hut site adjacent to Orford Road. Now the only problem for him to solve was transport, how to get the hut to Felixstowe. He put the word out at work and was very surprised, if not a little worried, when Parkington summoned him to his office.

"What is this I hear about you needing to transport a shed Basil?" he enquired. "I hope you haven't been using my time to do private work."

Basil explained why he had built the beach hut, including the fact that his father's health was declining slowly as a result of injuries sustained in the Great War. It was at this point that Parkington's demeanour changed totally.

"You mean to tell me that you have done this for your father, a war veteran who is still suffering from the conflict?"

"Yes sir."

"And he doesn't know about it?"

"No sir, I was hoping to have it ready for dad's birthday as a surprise."

"Well Basil, I think that is a very admirable thing that you do." He patted Basil on the shoulder. "And do you know what I am going to do?"

Basil looked at him blankly.

"I am going to transport your hut on one of our motor lorries at no charge; what do you say to that lad?"

What could Basil say? He was completely dumbfounded.

"Thank you sir, that is so generous of you."

"Nonsense lad, when do you want to move it?"

"On July third sir, that way I can complete and paint it ready for dad's birthday on the thirteenth, although I will take him to it on the Sunday before, the eleventh."

So, thanks to the generosity of Mr Parkington, everything was set. It raised no eyebrows when a firm's lorry drew up outside 271 Cavendish Street early on Saturday, nor when the driver helped Basil load the building onto the back, and even less when the two of them drove off.

The driver not only helped Basil unload the sections of the hut and carry them to the plot, he stayed to help erect the hut too. Before the driver stowed the stepladder and disappeared, Basil managed to put the rubberised felt on the roof to keep out any moisture. Stepping back and admiring his handiwork he felt justifiably proud. He looked at his watch and realised it was much later than he had surmised; he also felt a pang of hunger. Briskly he walked down the road to the fish and chip shop and managed to buy himself some dinner before they closed. The rest of the day was spent busying himself putting all the fittings inside. He had made a fold down table and a bench as well as some cupboards to store such things as teapot, cups, saucers, plates and cutlery. It was almost dark by the time he finished so he made himself a pot of tea, using a primus stove he had borrowed from a friend at work, and lay on the floor to sleep the night away.

Next day was spent painting the whole hut, inside and out before walking to Beach Station to catch the train back to Derby Road and home. Chip was sitting in his chair reading the newspaper when Basil walked in.

"How did it go son?" he asked, crumpling the newspaper to one side. "Did they like their shed?"

"I don't know, they weren't there so they haven't seen it yet dad." Basil smiled inwardly. "By the way, Parkington is going to give me a little bonus this week for working over the weekend. I thought next Sunday, being your birthday; I would treat you all to a day out at Felixstowe."

"That would be wonderful son, thank you ever so much." Chip turned toward the kitchen. "Did you hear that Dolly? Basil is taking us to Felixstowe next Sunday for my birthday."

During the building of the hut Basil had only confided in one person, his favourite aunt Gertrude. She had given him a few ideas during the planning stage and had managed to amass a large box of crockery and cutlery which she had hidden in her bedroom away from prying eyes. On the Friday she bought some basic provisions, tea, sugar and biscuits, packed them into the box, along with a primus stove and a bottle of metholated spirit she had found in her father's shed. The Saturday morning before his father's birthday, Basil told Chip and Doris he was taking Gertrude out for the day and walked quickly down to number 120 to collect both her and the box. They carried the box between them, hoping against hope as they hurried up Cavendish Street hill that nobody would see them and ask what they were carrying. Fortunately they did not see a soul they knew all the way to Derby Road railway station and were soon sitting like happy conspirators on the train bound for Beach station Felixstowe.

Gertrude looked all around the hut and judged that Basil had done a magnificent job, she unpacked all the provisions and stowed them in the cupboard and all was set. He had done it; he felt so proud of himself. Just one last look to make sure all was as it should be, it looked just as he had envisioned it would, before locking the door and floating on air as he took Gertrude to the cafe near the pier, and as a thank you for all her help, he treated her to a lunch of steak and kidney pie with mashed potatoes and peas, following it up with a long walk along the promenade, arm in arm, and a sit in the sun on the beach near the pier with a Peter's ice cream cone.

They both whistled as they walked back to Beach Station, smiling to one another, each with a warm satisfied feeling inside.

The following day, as promised, Basil took Chip, Doris and Marjorie on the train to Beach Station. Leonard and his girl friend Marjorie were going to meet up with them later. As they walked off the platform Basil took Marjorie's hand in his.

"Shall we go and sit for a while in the shelter at the end of Orford Road?" Basil said to nobody in particular and strode off, with Marjorie trying hard to keep up with him, he wanted to get them as close to the hut as possible without arousing any undue interest.

"That would be nice," said Chip, "I am feeling a bit tired after the journey, I could do with a sit down perhaps with an ice cream in my hand and watch the world go by."

Basil led the way but when he reached the crossroads with Langer Road he turned right whereas everybody had expected him to head straight up Beach Station Road.

"Where are you going Basil?" Chip called out but Basil kept walking.

"It's quicker this way dad, trust me." He called over his shoulder without breaking step.

"I don't think it is." Grumbled Chip under his breath to Doris as they trooped after the rapidly disappearing Basil.

He led the group into Orford Street, only stopping when he reached the entrance to the hut site, and told them that he was very thirsty and wanted a drink from the standpipe. Chip frowned, this was very erratic behaviour by his youngest boy, but nevertheless they all trudged behind him across the soft sandy ground in the direction of the tap until he stopped abruptly in front of a lovely new, cream painted hut.

"What do you think of this dad?" Basil smiled at his tired father.

"It looks very nice son." He replied; a light was suddenly switched on in his eyes. "Ah, now I understand this is a hut you built at work and you wanted to show it off. Why didn't you say lad?"

"Not quite dad." Basil fished into his pocket retrieving a key; he held it out to his confused father. "I built it at home, it's my birthday present to you."

There was a deadly silence, Chip just stared at Basil, a lump rising visibly in his throat, he was lost for words. Then slowly from the corner of his eye a tear rolled down his cheek.

"I ... I ... I don't know what to say."

"Then don't say anything dad, here's your key, open it up and take a look."

Chip took the key with trembling hands and aimed it at the lock. He had to hold the key with both hands to steady it, slowly he turned it, everybody was completely silent and could clearly hear the click as the tumblers turned. Chip opened the door and revealed the spacious interior.

"You two have a look around, I'll put up the deck chairs I made for you and mum and Marjorie will make us a nice pot of tea.

The tears flowed, not only from Chip but from Doris too. They hugged each other.

"Thank you so much son, it's bloody wonderful." He said with the tears running freely down his face.

"Oh look Chip," Doris exclaimed with joy pointing to a name painted above the door, "he has called it 'Dunedin', that's where my brother Albert is living in New Zealand." She rummaged in her handbag for a handkerchief and piped her eyes, Marjorie cried because her parents were crying and Basil's eyes were wet with pride.

"You're worth it Dad." He said softly.

Chip embraced Basil and smiled through his tears.

"I'm the luckiest, happiest man alive."

******

Back at work Basil was beginning to get a little restless, he had been working in portable buildings for almost nine months on his own cognisance, he felt he was learning nothing new which was not what an apprenticeship was all about. Taking a deep breath he, once more, brought himself to Mr Parkington's office.

He explained his position and made the point that he was apprentice in a building company but had not, as yet, had any site experience. Agreeing with him Parkington told him to complete his current project and then report to the general foreman at the Thompson Road site.

This was more like it, he was put to work immediately on the flats that were being built on Thompson Road and Nandsen Road, just off Bramford Lane, and soon found himself being instructed in the correct methods to lay floors and to fit the doors that he had learned to make in the joinery shop. He also mastered skirting, roofing and fitting kitchens which made him feel much more of a craftsman and he was confident he could turn his hand to anything.

He felt even more like a proper carpenter when he was told that, as he had completed three years of his apprenticeship and was beginning his final year, his pay had been increased to seventeen shillings and sixpence a week.

Fridays the men working on the site liked to have a fish and chip lunch and, being the junior on site, it fell to Basil to take the orders and go to the shop. It occurred to him he could make a shilling or two out of this weekly errand so he bought some salt and a bottle of vinegar, which he kept in his saddlebag, and then on his way to work on a Friday he called in to a baker's shop to buy a loaf of bread and a grocers for a pat of butter. When lunchtime came around he supplied salt, vinegar, bread and butter with the fish and chips for a small charge making around a shilling a week profit which went straight into his savings pot.

Unfortunately things did not always go to plan and one Friday he went round the site taking the orders as usual. He removed his tools from his flail and hid them in a kitchen cupboard so he could use the flail to hold all the wraps of fish and chips, which made carrying them easier, before retrieving his bicycle and pedalling off to the fish and chip shop.

Returning along Bramford Lane the full flail, swinging on his handlebars, caught in his front wheel stopping it dead and inertia took charge, propelling him over the handlebars and depositing him in a crumpled heap on the road. Slowly he sat up and surveyed the scene. His wrists were skinned; he had a graze on his head and had torn a hole in the knee of his trousers. Worse still his bicycle had bent forks and a buckled front wheel and he was sitting amid a selection of lunches scattered all over the road around him. Some of the packets were intact but a number of them had burst open and cast the contents over the tarmac. Undaunted he picked up the scattered lunches, rewrapped them and stacked them back in the flail and knocked on the door of a nearby house to ask if he could leave his stricken bicycle in the front garden until later. He then ran all the way back to the site with his flail held close to his chest.

One by one he handed out the lunches. Some of the men remarked that the fish was a bit gritty this week and the chips were unusually cold but nobody cottoned on to what had happened and nobody complained directly to Basil. On his way home he retrieved his bicycle and carried it across town to his home. The weekend was mostly spent repairing the bicycle ready for use again on Monday.

Sadly for Basil the site was nearing completion and after about three months his work came to an end, all of the flats were ready for occupation and there was only work for a couple of 'snaggers'. A 'snagger' is a workman who corrects any faults or problems that are identified by the purchasers when a completed property is handed over. Basil was destined to return to the portable buildings shop, grateful for what he had learned but disappointed that it was over so soon, he really loved working on a building site.

******

In the autumn Basil thought he would try, once more, to get himself that longed for pet dog and so he returned to the RSPCA who were able to partner him with a two year old spaniel called Toby. Toby had a black head with a white blaze that started just behind his nose and spread out as it went along his neck so that his body was all white; he had a cute black spot on the end of his tail too. Unlike Paddy and Gyp before him, Toby was well behaved, strong and very healthy. He had bundles of energy, loved walks to the park and was most obedient, to the extent that he could be let off the lead without fear of him running off. A strong bond was quickly forged between master and pet, so much so that Toby was very reluctant to leave Basil's side. On more than one occasion, when Basil was cycling to work, he would suddenly realise that Toby was running along behind him. Not having sufficient time to take him home Basil made a bed up for him beside his bench and covered it with a blanket but, although he would happily lay there all day without bothering anybody and without being in the way, Basil was told that a carpentry shop was no place for a dog and so Toby was banned from the workplace.

1938

On reaching his eighteenth birthday in June, Basil was elevated to adult status at work, although technically still an apprentice, and his pay was increased to one pound per week. With it came a change of attitude amongst his co-workers. He had always been a popular employee but the relationship always retained a modicum of adult to adolescent attitude. Now he found the relationship to be more that of equals, an impression that was reinforced where the distribution of work was concerned.

Almost immediately after his birthday he was given a project to build a large greenhouse for a country house near Debenham. Two other carpenters working at an adjacent bench were building a sports pavilion; both projects had to be completed at the same time to allow for joint delivery. When both units had been completed and assembled to ensure everything was correct, they were dismantled and loaded onto a lorry, with the pavilion on the bottom and Basil's greenhouse on top.

The next day was an early start and Basil had to be at the yard by six in the morning and, together with the other two carpenters, load their respective tools onto the lorry and set off to deliver the units. The cab of the lorry was only just big enough for the two carpenters to squeeze in beside the driver, who also acted as a labourer, and Basil had to climb on the back and sit on top of the greenhouse. The load was quite tall and Basil felt a little obvious perched up so high, and not a little worried lest he fall off.

They set off through the town, up Bolton Lane and out onto the Westerfield Road heading for their first port of call, Debenham, where Basil's greenhouse was unloaded and stacked in the customer's garden.

"You put up your greenhouse Basil and us three will go and put up our pavilion." Said Hugh Jeffries, who was in charge of the pavilion project. "When we've done we'll pick you up on the way back, should be with you about five o'clock."

"OK." Replied Basil, and he watched as the lorry drove off in a cloud of exhaust smoke and dust.

Basil knew their destination, Stradbroke, was less than ten miles away and the three of them should be able to complete their work in good time so he thought he ought to get cracking in order to ensure he was ready for their return. The customer showed him where the greenhouse was to be erected and Basil was relieved to see that the ground had already been prepared and levelled in preparation. He measured out the footprint of the structure, marked the ground and proceeded to set a row of bricks to keep the wooden structure away from the soil and protect it from damp to a limited degree. If it had been his greenhouse he would have laid a few courses of brickwork to lift the wood even higher, which would have extended the life of the greenhouse even more.

Using some lengths of wood he had brought for the purpose he stood one side upright, nailed a support to hold it erect before raising one of the ends to marry up with the side. The rest of the construction was easy after that and he quickly puttied in the glass panes which the customer had delivered separately. Four thirty and everything was completed, ideal, now he had half an hour to rest so he sat on a stone wall waiting for his lift home.

Five o'clock came and went with no sign of the lorry.

Six o'clock came and went, still no sign.

He looked at his watch for the umpteenth time, it was seven o'clock. 'OK' he thought, 'better start walking'. He grabbed his flail, thankful that he had not brought too many tools with him, and walked off in the direction of Ipswich hoping all the time that he would hear the sound of the lorry behind him, perhaps they had hit a snag and were still erecting the pavilion. Eventually he came to a telephone box and he remembered the slip of paper he had been presented with before leaving the depot, bearing the work telephone number for Mr Parkington and a home number for use in the event of an emergency,.

"This seems like an emergency to me." He said aloud as he rummaged around in his pocket and retrieved the scribbled note. He pulled open the door to the kiosk and stepped inside. It was then he realised he had never used a public telephone before and was not sure what he had to do. Cautiously he lifted the receiver pressed it to his ear and waited.

"Number please." Came the cheerful voice of a young lady in the earpiece.

"Um! I'm in a telephone box near Debenham and I want to speak to my boss please." Basil found this rather exciting although he hoped that Parkington would not be annoyed with him for calling his home number.

"And what is the number you need please caller?"

He gave her the number and told the operator he had no money to pay for the call.

"Would you like to reverse the charges caller?"

"Yes please."

"Can you give me your name and I will ask them if they will accept the charges."

"It's Basil Double." He told her

"Hold the line caller."

There was a click and the line went dead. He waited.

After about a minute there was another click and Mr Parkington was on the other end of the line.

"Basil, is that you?"

"Yes sir."

"Where are you boy?" The line was crackly and Basil had a little bit of difficulty hearing what Parkington was saying.

"I'm near Debenham sir."

"What's that you say?" Obviously Basil's voice was no clearer at the other end. Basil repeated himself.

"What are you doing there? I thought you would have been back ages ago."

Basil explained that he had finished his work with the greenhouse but the lorry had not returned for him. He thought perhaps they had forgotten him and gone straight back to Ipswich.

"OK you start walking toward Ipswich and I will come and pick you up." Before Basil could answer the line went dead. He replaced the receiver, pushed his way out of the kiosk, picked up his flail which somehow seemed much heavier than it had before, and set off once more in the direction of Ipswich.

It was almost an hour before the big black Humber came into view, its dim headlights picking out Basil's sad and tired figure. He got into the passenger seat and Parkington dropped the clutch and moved off. Basil had expected him to turn the car round but to his surprise they retraced Basil's steps, over three miles worth, and then took the road to Stradbroke. Not a word passed between the two, Parkington was concentrating on the road ahead, leaning forward with his eyes squinting and his nose wrinkled as the dim headlights followed the grassy verge.

As they entered Stradbroke Basil noticed the lorry at the side of the road, directly outside the White Hart public house. Parkington saw it too and pulled the car into the side behind the lorry.

"Wait here." He said as he struggled out of the car door and strode into the public house. Inside he found all three of his employees with full beer glasses in their hands, laughing in the manner of the inebriated. When they caught sight of him standing there with his hands on his hips their collective jaws dropped open.

"I dare say you are aware that you have left a colleague waiting down the road for well over four hours while you intoxicate yourselves." His manner was stern and severe. "Finish your drinks, get that vehicle back to the yard and I will see you all in my office at seven thirty in the morning." With that he turned on his heel and left the bar accompanied by the stares of amazed locals, beer tankards frozen in their journey toward their collective mouths. Hugh Jeffries swallowed nervously.

"Oh shit!" was all he could think to say.

Basil, who had been sworn to secrecy by Parkington, heard that the trio had rather a rough start to the next morning, partly because of their sore heads and partly because of the stiff dressing down they received from their boss, who informed them that Basil had to beg a lift back to Ipswich from a passing motorist, he never revealed that he was the motorist in question, nor how he came to be out in his car in Stradbroke at that time of night.

******

Leonard had developed an interest in electricity and radio, not that he had a use for either in his job at the local Co-op store, and he replied to an advertisement in the 'Evening Star' newspaper for a self build radio set known as a 'cat-whisker' radio. He invested in a soldering iron, some solder and flux and waited for the kit to arrive.

For the four nights following its delivery he sat at the kitchen table, conveniently pulled close to the gas stove, the soldering iron glowing red sitting on the lit burner, and built the unit. Although not particularly interested in the construction of the wireless Basil sat and watched as Leonard studied the instructions and applied them, sometimes, when the instructions were unclear the two young men would discuss what they meant until finally the set was completed.

Leonard connected a battery to supply the power and placed the headphones on his head at a jaunty angle. Switching on, he wound the volume control until he heard a crackling sound in the earpieces and tweaked the 'cats-whickers', which were the only way to 'tune in' to a broadcasting station, until he heard a signal. Eventually it worked and he heard feint music from the BBC.

Each night before they went to sleep Leonard and Basil lay on the bed, one earpiece each, listening to broadcasts from the BBC until the battery ran down. It was quite fun although the reception was nowhere near as good as Chip's Pye wireless in the parlour.

******

The beginning of September saw Basil complete his four year apprenticeship and become recognised as a qualified carpenter, as a result his weekly pay was increased to twenty five shillings.

The world was changing, events across Europe were moving things in the direction of unrest and a feeling of possible conflict was being roused in the newspapers. The family followed events in the newspapers and on the Pye electric wireless. Earlier in the year, Neville Chamberlain had attempted to sway fascist Italy away from German influence by recognising Italian supremacy in Ethiopia, he kept Britain divorced from the Spanish civil war, in which Italy was deeply involved, and he even abandoned British naval bases in Ireland.

Chip was very critical of the moves made by Chamberlain.

"It won't do any good," Chip opined, "I just hope he doesn't drag us into another war like the last one."

Chamberlain went to Germany three times in September in an effort to avert war, and to Leonard and Basil, and indeed most of the country, it seemed as if he might have succeeded when he, along with Edouard Daladier, the French premier, turned their back on Czechoslovakia and allowed Germany to subjugate the Sudetenland.

Listening to the wireless in the parlour with their father, the boys heard Chamberlain echo the words of former prime minister Benjamin Disraeli, boasting of 'peace with honour' and 'peace for our time' but they could not escape the look of worry and despair on their father's face.

From the time that he heard Chamberlain speak Chip became much more broody and silent; he could sit for a couple of hours without speaking, just staring into the fire spluttering in the grate. All the newspapers carried stories of concern for the fate of Europe and it seemed that, even if it were not spoken aloud, everybody was preparing themselves for the prospect of war. It was when the Sunday newspapers released the news that the British rearmament programme had been accelerated that Chip broke his silence.

"If those buggers had been in the last lot, instead of in their warm offices they would not be so keen for war." Basil and Leonard looked at each other.

"War is no game, it's horrible, it's hell." Chip continued. "I think things have been allowed to go too far now." He paused. "It will all start up again soon, mark my words." He rose and threw his newspaper into his chair, giving his boys a look of resignation he walked into the garden and pulled the odd weed from the vegetable patch, deep in thought.

"What do you think?" Basil turned to Leonard.

"I think dad's right, I think you and I will be going to war before long."

Next morning Basil turned up for work to find that even Parkington's was changing to the tune of probable war. He was taken off his project and, together with a team of joiners; he built sectional wooden huts to be used in the training camps that were being constructed across the country to cater for the expected increase in recruits for the services.

Since Basil had moved back into Cavendish Street in 1934 he had spent a considerable amount of time with his favourite maiden aunt, Gertrude. By now all of her brothers and sisters had left home, some to be married and some to go into service, so Gertrude lived alone with her parents George and Lydia Cotton at 120 Cavendish Street, just down the road a bit from Basil. Gertrude had spent a substantial amount of time with her cousin Gladys and, after the birth of little Joyce in 1931, had often taken on the role of babysitter. Since the tragic death of Ernest in June 1935 she had expanded those duties and looked after little Joyce when she came home from school or during school holidays, while her mother was at work. Gertrude had no friends outside of her tight family circle and so her life was built around this tiny enclave of Gladys, Joyce, Basil and her parents.

All the talk of war she found extremely depressing and she was becoming more ponderous by the day. Basil recognised this creeping depression in two of the people he loved most in the world and tried, as much as possible, to lift their spirits. If the weather was dry and not too cold he would take Chip and Doris to their beach hut at Felixstowe, sometimes they would sleep over on a Saturday night which was, of course, totally illegal. As often as he could Basil would include Gertrude in the party.

Gertrude's fragile mental state suffered another debilitating hit just before Christmas, when her father George unexpectedly collapsed and died from a heart attack. Another of her small enclave had left her.

1939

The construction of the sectional huts continued into the new year, such was the demand that they could not turn them out quickly enough and there was no restriction on overtime. Added to that one or two of the joiners had left the company putting more and more work onto those who remained. One Saturday morning Eric Spears announced that he had been offered a job erecting the new camps and that he had been asked to bring with him as many carpenters as he could muster.

"How about it Basil?" He raised his eyebrows. "There is a never ending amount of work and the pay is half as much again as we get here."

Basil thought for a while before turning down the offer.

"If you change your mind, you know where I am." He smiled. "Just let me know."

Two of the younger carpenters left with Eric for greener pastures but the older employees were less keen to spend time away from home in the current political climate.

One morning Basil was busily planking the side section of a hut when he looked around and realised he was the only person under thirty five still working there. That night when he mentioned the fact to brother Leonard he was very surprised at the response.

"Why on earth don't you join them?" Leonard said. "It is an opportunity to earn good money and you will be helping the war effort."

"I'm helping the war effort now."

"Yes, but look to the future brother, you can save some money for when you want to think about settling down."

"That's a long way off."

That night in bed Basil mulled over the wise words his brother had given him. It made sense, Leonard was right. By the end of January Basil was working with Eric once more, erecting huts to form a camp at Berechurch in Colchester and later in Chelmsford. It was impractical and undesirable for the carpenters to travel daily so they stayed in the huts they had already completed. It was very cold, especially at night, but they managed to commandeer some blankets, pillows and even a couple of paraffin stoves to keep themselves warm. Basil didn't return home to Ipswich for two months and was therefore oblivious to the effect his absence had on Gertrude, she felt she had lost him to the war and even if he came back, she told herself, he would soon be off with the forces. He finally found time to visit home at the beginning of March and walked into a bit of a turmoil. Gladys Dumble's health had been deteriorating but she had kept it well concealed so nobody had really noticed, except Emily Jane who tried to raise the subject discreetly with Gladys without success. Being a person who never complained and kept herself to herself, it came as a shock to everybody when she finally disclosed just how ill she was. She had been to see the doctor who had diagnosed advanced breast cancer, there was no cure and no effective treatment, in his opinion she had only weeks to live. She immediately gave up her job in the corset factory and calmly accepted the inevitable, finally passing away, cradled in her mother's arms, a couple of days before Basil's return. It was another massive loss for Gertrude, who partially consoled herself by helping Emily Jane with looking after the young orphan Joyce.

The newspapers and the BBC were full of foreboding as the political situation in Europe worsened daily, causing a dark cloud of depression and resignation to descend on the family home. Chip sat silently in his fireside chair listening to each news broadcast with mounting concern. At night Leonard and Basil, if he was home, would sit together on Leonard's bed listening to the news on Leonard's cats-whisker set, wondering how the situation would affect them.

When Hitler's Germany seized the remainder of Czechoslovakia during the second week of March Chamberlain finally repudiated appeasement and published Anglo-French guarantees of armed support for Poland, Romania, and Greece in the event of similar attacks by Germany. April witnessed the institution of peacetime military conscription for the first time in British history.

"Well Bass," said Leonard solemnly, "that's our future settled. We are for the forces." Basil eyed him with a serious frown.

On the morning of twentieth of June Gertrude rose from her bed, pulled her black dress on, padded down the stairs of 120 Cavendish Street and into the kitchen. She expected to see her mother, Lydia, but there was no sign of her. 'She must be having a bit of a lay in' she thought 'she has been looking rather tired lately'. She began to prepare her breakfast, cut a thick slice of bread and took a jar of homemade strawberry preserve out of the pantry. Lydia made delicious preserve. Gertrude made her way to the bottom of the stairs and called up.

"Mother, are you nearly ready for your breakfast?" There was no reply.

"Mother, are you awake?" Still no reply. Gertrude plodded up the stairs. "Mother, it is almost eight o'clock." She reached the top stair and listened. Silence.

Cautiously she pushed open the door to her mother's bedroom and poked her head inside; the room was dark, the heavy brocade curtains preventing any light from entering. She made her way to the bed and, as her eyes became accustomed to the darkness, she made out the bulk of her mother under the blankets. A feeling of dread swept over her and she sped to the bedside and pulled the covers down slightly to reveal her mother's cold ashen face. Lydia had passed away during the night.

Gertrude burst into uncontrollable tears and lifting her head to the ceiling she shouted.

"Are you taking everybody from me? Are you going to leave me without anybody?" Her head dropped onto her mother's cold chest and she wept copiously.

******

The news reports on the radio and in the cinemas were never ending. In August the Germans and the Soviets signed a non-aggression treaty which frustrated Chamberlain's plan for a mutual assistance agreement between Great Britain, France and the USSR, so instead he signed an Anglo-Polish pact guaranteeing Poland the support of Great Britain should they be attacked.

When the Germans subsequently attacked Poland, on the first of September, Chamberlain issued them with an ultimatum. As in many households throughout the country the Double family huddled round the wireless that dull grey Sunday morning to listen sombrely to Chamberlain as he spoke, in his sad monotonic voice, those immortal words.

"This morning the British Ambassador in Berlin handed the German Government a final Note stating that, unless we heard from them by 11 o'clock that they were prepared at once to withdraw their troops

from Poland, a state of war would exist between us.

I have to tell you now that no such undertaking has been received, and that consequently this country is at war with Germany."

Chip stood, walked over to the wireless and slowly rotated the knob to turn it off. As the volume died down so the mood of the whole family sank.

"Please God," he said quietly, "protect my boys."

Epilogue

Basil spent the first part of the war years in a reserved occupation building aircraft, notably Short Sterlings and De Havilland Mosquitos, and was finally called up to serve in the army in North Africa. Returning to civilian life he once again entered into the building trade for most of his remaining working life. He had two sons, Keith and David and retired early through ill health in 1982. He died in February 2014 at the age of 93 after a brave fight against cancer and Alzheimer's.

Charles Henry Philip (Chip) his health continued to slowly deteriorate and shortly after the war he became wheelchair bound. This did not stop him enjoying his beach hut and he was often to be seen sitting outside enjoying the fresh sea air or sitting in the shelter, on the promenade near the Herman de Stern convalescent home, amid his friends all reminiscing about the Great War and the part they played in it. It was while talking to his friends in the shelter in late April 1949 that he lost track of time and stayed much longer than was good for him. Sadly he developed Pneumonia and passed away on Leonard's birthday, June nineteenth 1949.

Leonard Double Joined royal signals during the war as a radio operator and served in the Far East Cocoa Islands until the end of the war. Following demobilisation he worked for thirty years at Ipswich power station and died, it is believed from effects of working with asbestos, in 1994 aged 79. He had two daughters, Sheila and Linda.

Doris Double (Dumble) a lifelong Labour Party activist she was a close friend of Dingle Foot in the 1950's and 60's. In 1964 she travelled to New Zealand where she had a tearful reunion with her brother Albert (Sonny). Doris died in Sept 1986 in Ipswich aged 85.

Marjorie Dumble served in the WRAF during the war and narrowly escaped death when a shell from a strafing aircraft hit her shoe. She married George Pearce and moved to Nottingham where she had two daughters, Gillian and Mary. She died in 2001 in Beeston aged 77.

Charles Double continued his carting business until he retired at the age of seventy five. He then became bit of a local celebrity walking around the Princes Street area of Ipswich, often with a sunflower in his buttonhole, and visiting his favourite hostelry the 'Rising Sun'. He continued to live at number 18 James Street until he died in Dec 1961 at the grand age of one hundred 100. Shortly after his death James Street and the surrounding streets were demolished to make way for the Greyfriars development.

Emily Jane Dumble continued to live at 251 Cavendish Street and raised Joyce Hurricks. When Joyce married Ernest Pryke they lived with Emily Jane until her death on 2nd December 1954, aged 92.

Albert 'Sonny' Dumble lived in Mornington, Lyttelton Canterbury New Zealand, working as a boilermaker. Upon retirement he moved to Dunedin New Zealand where he died in 1998 aged 101

Gertrude Cotton never recovered from the loss of her parents and her cousin Gladys and fell into a deep depression from which she was unable to recover. The onset of war and the prospect that she might lose her dear Basil was the final straw that pushed her over the edge. On Thursday November twenty third Basil called round to visit her, and tell her that he would be working away for the war effort. As he entered the rear door he walked into a wall of gas and discovered the inert body of his dear aunt on the kitchen floor with her head close to the cooking stove, all of the taps were wide open. She had taken the only route she could see to get away from her depression and join her departed family. She was 51 years old.

Fred Aldous. Following the death of his father Basil became extremely close to Fred who in effect became his surrogate father. A very gentle man, he became an integral part of Basil's family. Fred regularly went on continental holidays with the family. Always to be seen with his pipe of St Julien clenched between his teeth. A legacy from the Great War, where Fred served in the Dardanelles debacle as well as Ypres, left him with only one lung and half a stomach but he carried on in his jovial way until his sad passing in 1969 aged 76.

Mr Belsey, 'Big Bellham' as Basil called him lived in various places as a lodger and never married. In 1940, when Basil returned to Ipswich on leave, he chanced to hear that his dear friend from his childhood days was very ill. He visited him in the Borough General Hospital, the old Ipswich East workhouse, on Woodbridge Road. It was a tear jerking meeting, they had not seen each other for thirteen years, and Basil was upset to see that the big man he remembered had become a thin wizened old man riddled with cancer. 'Big Bellham' passed away ten days after their reunion.

Leslie Bushen had a long and successful career in journalism working for the East Anglian Daily Times in their Ipswich office until he retired in 1978. Basil stayed in touch with his fellow 'orphan' and they often met up socially. Sadly following Leslie's retirement they lost touch with each other.

Sadly unable to locate a photograph

Walter Double worked in an office on Ipswich docks and after the war he joined GPO Telephones where he worked until he retired in 1967. He died in 1987 aged 84.

Kenny Wilding served in the army in Egypt where he contracted TB and was invalided out to become the youngest Chelsea Pensioner! The discovery of Streptomycin saved him from radical surgery and saved his life. He tried to join first the Police Force then the Fire Service but his medical history prevented him from being accepted. Eventually he became a driver for Eastern Counties busses. Sadly he died at the age of 66 from a brain tumour. He never did see his schooldays buddy again.

William West Dumble served in the Marines at Chatham until March 1940 when he was discharged from Navy aged 41. After his discharge he lived with his mistress, Caroline Quinnell, and worked on barges. His wife, Elsie, lived at 329 Bramford Lane Ipswich until her death in April 1946. In June of that year William married Caroline in Chatham. Caroline died in 1974 aged 80, William died 1985 aged 86.

Douglas Holland, who accompanied Basil on many exploits served in the army during the war and was taken prisoner by the Germans in Italy. Always a bit of a terror and a rebel Doug escaped from the transport vehicle that was taking him from one camp to another and was subsequently shot for his attempt at freedom. He was 22 years old.

Sadly unable to locate a photograph

Ernest Cotton went on to become manager of Fisk's grocers on the corner of Gladstone Road and Foxhall Road. Later he ran a pet shop on the corner of Bond Street and Rope Walk and would often pass the time of day with Basil's youngest son David as he made his way, in a school crocodile, to the Fore Street swimming baths for swimming lessons. Unfortunately, although David knew him at the time as Uncle Ernest, he never realised the family connection. He died in 1980 aged 86.

Previously by David Charles

*All titles available exclusively on Amazon in both
paperback and e-book format.*

Black Eyes and Shattered Glass

Chapter 1

Down and out

"Shall I tell you the truth or shall I sit and lie?

You can't understand why I want to die.

What's here inside me, what's here within

I want my life to end, you want it to begin."

Carol Glass

I felt something cold and wet on my cheek. Instinctively I knew it was Candy telling me it was time to wake up. I pulled the duvet aside just enough to squint at the clock on the bedside table, the big red numbers said six-thirty five. Yes it was time to get up. I didn't want to get up, in fact I never wanted to get up again, ever, I just wanted to slip into permanent hibernation and stick two fingers up to a world that was dangerous, cruel and very painful.

I closed my eyes again but Candy was not to be ignored. Her cold wet nose tunnelled into my ear.

"Ok you, I can take a hint." I giggled as I pulled the duvet back and swung my feet into my slippers. "I suppose you're hungry again."

I shuffled into the kitchen and yawned as I pulled the cupboard door open.

"Oh, shite!" There was no dog food. I remembered now, I had meant to get some yesterday but could not bring myself to go out to the shops. I leaned over the sink and rubbed the condensation on the window, making rivulets of water slide down the glass, and peered outside. It was still raining, just as it had been when I'd gone to bed only now it was dark out there too. I love the night, I love the darkness that hides me away from the world. I hate daylight, that's why I sleep in the daytime. Yes, I love the dark, I crave the dark, but not if I have to go outside in it.

This time I had no option, I couldn't let Candy go hungry. I could go hungry, that was not a problem, but Candy relied on me to look after her. I must go to the late night shop. I shuffled back into the bedroom feeling the nervousness building inside me. I pulled my nightdress over my head and threw it onto the bed. My jeans and 'T' shirt were lying on the floor where I had left them, well they were hardly going to pick themselves up I thought as I bent down slowly and grabbed them. The room was cold and I dressed as quickly as I could to retain as much of my body heat as possible. Twice I tripped over Candy, but all I could do was smile at her. I could never be angry with my Candy.

I pulled my coat on and wound a scarf round my neck to keep out the cold January night, lifted my purse from the kitchen worktop and opened it. Four pounds eighty six pence, all I had in the world until my social payment next week. It would be enough. I shoved the purse deep into my pocket, grabbed the dog lead from the kitchen worktop and nervously made my way to the front door. I opened it a crack and peered out; nothing. I clipped Candy's lead on and slipped the security chain, stepped through the door and closed it gently behind me. I stood for a while; all I could hear was next door's television playing the Emmerdale theme.

"C'mon Candy pet, let's see about getting some food for yous, shall we?" I bent to ruffle her ear affectionately, she loved that, and we moved off.

The dim streetlights cast pools of light in a sea of darkness all the way down the road and I found myself hurrying along the uneven paving. The shop was only half a mile away so I would not be gone long. After a short while I saw somebody coming toward me and instinctively felt myself tense, I don't like people, they hurt me as often as not. As the distance between us shortened the figure seemed to grow, it was a man, a man in a hoody top. I cast my eyes to the ground, if I could not see him perhaps I could convince myself he wasn't really there.

Candy pulled on her lead as we passed, trying to sniff the scent of the passer by. I gave the lead a little tug. We had passed; my steps sped up slightly. I listened to see if he was walking away from me but he must have been wearing trainers because I could hear nothing.

"That's a nice arse you've got, darlin'," I heard from close behind me. "I wouldn't mind givin' that a squeeze."

I turned my head anxiously and found myself staring straight into a pair of dark eyes. Embarrassed and frightened I dropped my gaze. I started to walk again, then felt him grab my arm. His grip was like a vice and I was wracked with a searing pain as he squeezed my wasted muscles against my bone, crushing delicate blood vessels. He pulled me round and his other hand roughly grabbed and rubbed my right buttock momentarily before squeezing it hard.

"Not so fast, darlin'," he growled, "You've got a real nice arse, small and firm. Are your tits firm, darlin'?"

Desperately I tried to pull away from him but his grip tightened still more.

"Oh, *Please*, leave me alone." I whimpered as I struggled to break his hold.

"Aw c'mon, darlin' ya know ya like it. How about you an' me havin' a little bit o' fun eh?"

"*Fuck* OFF, and leave me alone," I screamed, my voice trembling with fear and I lashed out at him with my free arm catching him on the side of his head.

"You bitch." He spat the words into my face. "You fuckin' bitch."

He slapped me hard across the face.

With all my might I aimed a kick at his crotch, just as Candy snarled and sunk her teeth into his shin.

"You fuckin' bitch," he roared again as he hammered his fist into the side of my face. I reeled and momentarily our eyes met just before his huge balled fist slammed into my right eye. I felt my skin tear and a warm trickle flowed into my eye. I received another hammer blow to my temple and as I sank to the ground his foot slammed into my face. A kaleidoscope of colours flashed inside my head and a metallic taste filled my mouth. The taste of blood, my blood; I had experienced that taste so many times in the past. I closed my eyes and everything went black.

I don't know how long I was unconscious but I think it could only have been a few seconds. As the darkness slowly cleared from my eyes I found myself staring at the rough concrete paving splattered with my blood slowly mingling with the dirty rainwater. I rolled over onto my back and stared up into the black cloud laden sky. My face was numb and my right eye almost closed from the swelling around it that I could scarcely feel the raindrops. I turned toward the road and lifted myself onto my elbow as a searing pain shot through my torso.

"The bastard." I croaked as I realised he must have landed a kick in my ribs as I lay there unconscious.

Candy was sitting on the pavement by my side and she inclined her head before giving me a lick on the face. My senses were beginning to return and I looked around anxiously, in case my vile attacker was still there, but the road was deserted. My panic began to rise and I vomited on the path. Now I had only one objective, to return home as quickly as I could, sod the dog food, Candy would understand. I stood up, grabbed Candy's lead, and began a painful shuffle home. As I walked I felt the warm sensation of fresh blood as it trickled down my neck and once again I began to see coloured flashing lights in front of my eyes, just a few to begin with but gradually they multiplied until I could see nothing. I was walking from memory, my head began to swim and I felt increasingly dizzy. Gradually everything went black again and I felt myself falling – falling - falling.

Slowly I opened my left eye; my right eye wouldn't open; and I found myself on my back staring at a white-tiled ceiling with bright fluorescent lights. Painfully I looked around me and saw the well known arrangement of electrical equipment, I felt the familiar firmness of the hospital couch, and knew I was in the accident and emergency department of the local hospital.

Again!

My whole body was a mass of pain and my wasted flesh was a mass of bruises.

I was desolate.

Would I never escape this cycle of pain and hurt? I turned my head to the wall and began to cry silently. I remember thinking that this was it; this was the last time; I could not take any more. I decided at that moment that I would end my life at the first opportunity. I would extinguish this life that had been so cruel to me and find peace at long last. What had I done to deserve a life like this? A life that had seen me beaten and abused right from that first doctor's smack as I left my mother's womb.........

A Podenco's Tale

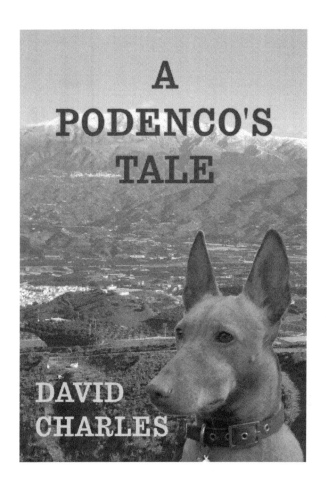

Prologue

Let me introduce myself, my name is Poppy and I am a Podenco. How I acquired my name is of no consequence at this stage, all will be revealed on that subject in due course. What we need to concentrate on at this point is the Podenco bit.

So what is a Podenco I hear you ask? A Podenco is a Spanish hunting dog used mainly in the hunting of rabbits and small mammals. I, however, am no ordinary Podenco. I am a Podenco Andaluz, which means that my strain is mainly to be found in the Andalucia region of Spain.

As an Andaluz I am one of the most intelligent and swiftest dogs around, and may I say, one of the most beautiful you will ever encounter. I have ears that stand proud like those of the Pharaoh hound, from whom I am directly descended. I have long slender legs that any model would be proud of, a barrel chest and a slim waist. I have a beautiful temperament and am faithful to a fault. In my opinion I am the queen of dogs.

I have had a very unusual life up until now and I thought you might like to read about it, so I persuaded David, my pet human, to put it in print for me. I very much hope that you get as much enjoyment from reading my unique story as I have had dictating it.

Before you start reading, however, I just want to let you into an extremely well kept secret. We animals can talk to each other without humans detecting a sound. We can have complex conversations and are capable of intricate thought without you being aware at all. We have emotions too, we love, we hate, we smile, we frown, we feel fear, we feel happiness, we laugh and we cry. We don't have tear ducts so we cannot shed tears, but believe me we cry inside.

So you see we are not dumb animals, in fact in my experience no animal is dumb. Apart from the odd human that is.

I was born on April the first but as you will discover I was no April fool. The year was 2009 and the place, an old outhouse, that had definitely seen better days, and which formed part of a finca, or farmhouse, in the Axarquia region of Andalusia in southern Spain. Many decades previously some poor dirt farmer had scavenged rocks from the mountainside and crudely cemented them together with a primitive form of mortar to form the rough stone walls. Only now the cool wind would whistle through gaps that had been left as the ancient mortar crumbled and fell away. The roof beams had, long ago, been spindly olive trees and now provided food for the woodworm. They sagged under the weight of the chipped and cracked rustic tiles that channelled the winter rainwater into the yard beyond. Here and there were spaces where tiles were missing or broken and, during a downpour, if you were not careful where you lie, you could get a thorough soaking. The door was too short for the opening, because the bottom had rotted away, leaving a gap that scuttling rats would hurry through in order to steal some scraps of our food. The floor consisted of dirt mixed with generations of detritus and chicken droppings crushed into a firm warm tilth by thousands of footsteps.

This then was the sight that greeted me when I first opened my eyes to the world; this was to be my world. The dogs called it 'the shed'.

I shared the shed with my mother, three siblings, and five adult dogs. All of the adults had a hefty slice of Podenco in them, mixed over the generations with other various breeds which gave them a diverse ancestry. I, on the other hand, was pure Podenco Andaluz, as of course was my mother. I never discovered who my father was and I don't think my mother had much idea either. Whoever he was one thing was for sure, he was definitely pure Podenco too. He was probably a member of another hunter's pack who took a few minutes out from hunting one day, when the hunters were not looking, to have himself a little fun. The Podenco in us made everyone in the pack a natural hunter.

For now, along with my siblings, I lie snuggled to my mother's soft teat, drinking the milk that would one day make me big and strong. I looked up at mother, she was a small dog compared to most of the others, sable and white in colour with the gathering grey of age. She had the sagging teats that only half filled with milk which bore testament to the fact that we were the most recent of many litters. Her eyes looked rheumy as she gazed lovingly on us. She was thin, painfully thin, underfed and tired. Dispirited she just lay there and nuzzled us to her warm belly.

96891469R00213

Made in the USA
Columbia, SC
05 June 2018